Reinventing
American Protestantism

Reinventing American Protestantism

Christianity in the
New Millennium

Donald E. Miller

UNIVERSITY OF CALIFORNIA PRESS

Berkeley / Los Angeles / London

University of California Press
Berkeley and Los Angeles, California

University of California Press, Ltd.
London, England

Library of Congress Cataloging-in-Publication Data

Miller, Donald E. (Donald Earl), 1946–
    Reinventing American Protestantism : Christianity in the new millennium /
Donald E. Miller.
      p.   cm.
    Includes bibliographic references and index
    ISBN 0–520–20938–9 (cloth : alk. paper)
    1. Protestant churches—United States—forecasting.   2. Protes-
tant churches—California, Southern—Case studies.   3. Pentecostal churches—
California, Southern—Case studies.   4. California, Southern—religious life and
customs.   5. United States—church
history—20th century.   6. Calvary Chapel (Costa Mesa, Calif.).
7. Calvary Chapel movement.   8. Hope Chapel (Hermosa Beach, Calif.).
9. Vineyard Christian Fellowship   I. Title.
   BR526.M554   1997
   280′.4′097301—dc 20   96–35140

Printed in the United States of America
9 8 7 6 5 4 3 2 1

To Lorna,
a great source of strength
and inspiration

Contents

CONTENTS

Acknowledgments

Although I remain responsible for the interpretation of the three movements described in this book, I want to acknowledge the creative work of my two principal research assistants on this project, Brenda Brasher and Paul Kennedy, who spent two years interviewing pastors and congregations as well as writing detailed field notes. Michael McKenzie also worked with me for two summers as a research assistant.

I am also deeply indebted to the hundreds of people who graciously consented to be interviewed, including senior leaders in these movements such as Chuck Smith, Oden Fong, Greg Laurie, Bil Gollatin, John Wimber, Carl Tuttle, Kevin Springer, Kenn Gulliksen, Ralph Moore, and Zac Nazarian. I could not have expected fuller cooperation, and I will always remain grateful for the education that I received in my interaction with the members and pastors of Calvary Chapel, Vineyard Christian Fellowship, and Hope Chapel.

I received extraordinarily valuable criticism on an earlier draft of this manuscript, and I wish to acknowledge the insights and criticisms of Dean Hoge, Roger Finke, and James Wind. The person most responsible for shaping this manuscript, however, has been my ever-cheerful editor at the University of California Press, Doug Abrams Arava.

Finally, this research would not have been possible without a grant from the Lilly Endowment. I appreciate the ongoing encouragement that I have received from both Craig Dykstra and James Lewis.

Winners and Losers

Restructuring the Religious Economy

A revolution is transforming American Protestantism. While many of the mainline churches are losing membership, overall church attendance is not declining. Instead, a new style of Christianity is being born in the United States, one that responds to fundamental cultural changes that began in the mid-1960s. These new paradigm churches, as I call them in this book, are changing the way Christianity looks and is experienced.[1] Like upstart religious groups of the past, they have discarded many of the attributes of establishment religion. Appropriating contemporary cultural forms, these churches are creating a new genre of worship music; they are restructuring the organizational character of institutional religion; and they are democratizing access to the sacred by radicalizing the Protestant principle of the priesthood of all believers.

The new paradigm can be found in many places. One of its most typical sites is within the numerous independent churches that have proliferated in recent years. These churches are contributing to what has been called a new era of postdenominational Christianity in America, reflecting a general disillusionment with bureaucratic hierarchies and organizational oversight.[2] Other new paradigm churches remain within existing denominations, but their worship and organizational style differ decidedly from those of the more *institutionalized* churches in their denominations. Indeed, some of these new paradigm churches disguise the fact that they even have a denominational affiliation.

Included in my definition of new paradigm churches are "seeker-sensitive" churches, such as Willow Creek Community Church in

1

Chicago or Saddleback Community Church in southern California. These churches are attempting to design worship services that appeal to those who do not usually attend church. I also want to include in the ranks of the new paradigm a growing movement of churches that identify themselves as part of "apostolic networks."[3] These churches model their organizational structure after the religious leadership described in the New Testament book of the Acts of the Apostles.

It is not particularly helpful, in my view, to use such theological terms as *evangelical* or *fundamentalist* to describe these changes in American Protestantism. Even categories such as *charismatic* and *Pentecostal* are too broad to capture the distinctive character of the revolution described in this book, although many new paradigm churches do embrace the "gifts of the spirit." Nor do I find the terminology of religious "culture wars" very useful,[4] since many of the new paradigm churches cut across political and social issues in innovative ways.

To clarify the character of this revolution—which might even be viewed as the initial phase of a "Second Reformation"—I focus on three movements that I believe fit the definition of new paradigm churches: Calvary Chapel, Vineyard Christian Fellowship, and Hope Chapel. While there are differences among these groups, there are also many parallels (examined in chapter 2). All three movements originated in southern California, so I had convenient access to the "mother" church of each as well as to the founding leaders. But each of these movements has spread across the country—and increasingly the world—so I was not in danger of describing something that was only a West Coast phenomenon. (See appendix 1 for a listing of the geographic distribution of churches.)

Winners and Losers in American Religion

The story of American religion is one of change. In 1776, for example, Congregationalism dominated New England, with more than two-thirds of the region's religious adherents; by 1850 its share had plummeted to 28 percent.[5] Groups like the Baptists and Methodists emerged with a new style of religion that was more experientially based—speaking to the personal needs of people—and they rapidly won converts, attracting people who might not have attended an establishment church.[6] A similar shift is occurring today. Groups like Calvary Chapel, the Vineyard Christian Fellowship, and Hope Chapel are appealing to people who otherwise would probably be only marginally involved in institutional religion.

One way of understanding this shift is to look at religion in economic terms, subject to market forces and market analysis. As Roger Finke and Rodney Stark state, "Religious economies are like commercial economies in that they consist of a market made up of a set of current and potential customers and a set of firms seeking to serve that market. The fate of these firms will depend upon (1) aspects of their organizational structure, (2) their sales representatives, (3) their product, and (4) their marketing techniques. Translated into more churchly language, the relative success of religious bodies (especially when confronted with an unregulated economy) will depend upon their polity, their clergy, their religious doctrines, and their evangelization techniques."[7] This marketplace perspective is useful for describing the growth of movements such as Calvary, Vineyard, and Hope, although one must never minimize the *religious experience* of participants and their stories of encounters with the sacred.

I argue that not only are new paradigm churches doing a better job of responding to the needs of their clientele than are many mainline churches, but—more important—they are successfully mediating the sacred, bringing God to people and conveying the self-transcending and life-changing core of all true religion. They offer worship in a musical idiom that connects with the experience of broad sectors of the middle class; they have jettisoned aspects of organized religion that alienate many teenagers and young adults; and they provide programming that emphasizes well-defined moral values and is not otherwise available in the culture. In short, they offer people hope and meaning that is grounded in a transcendent experience of the sacred.

The very fact that these groups exist, and that many of them were born in the last two decades, confounds traditional sociological wisdom. A number of social theorists writing at the turn of the century in Germany and France thought that religion would disappear by the end of the twentieth century.[8] Mistakenly associating religion with cognitive beliefs, they contended that the "irrationalities" of religion could not survive in an age of reason. If religion continued to exist at all, they thought it would survive only in the private sphere of life or among socially marginal people.[9]

In recent years, however, many sociologists have concluded that this secularization thesis was simply wrong.[10] Religion is robust in many places in the world, especially in the United States.[11] At the same time, religion is constantly changing its shape and form; indeed, the mistake some people make is to interpret a decline in particular institutions (such as mainline Protestantism or the Roman Catholic Church) as implying the demise of religion more generally. Instead, there seems to be something deep within the human spirit that seeks self-transcending experiences and an ultimate grounding for the meaning of life. When established religions do not serve these needs, religious innovation occurs.

Gallup polls from the last quarter century make it obvious that Americans are a highly religious people. About 40 percent of adults claim to have attended religious services within the last week; 69 percent say they belong to a church or synagogue; and 95 percent profess a belief in God.[12] There are 300,000 congregations in the United States, and religion is a $100 billion dollar industry annually, when contributions and religion-related sales are taken into account. But these statistics do not tell the full story. When one examines the details of this thriving religious economy, one finds definite winners and losers as individuals make consumer choices about which group to join.

The so-called mainline denominations are clearly losing their market share.[13] In the past several decades denominations such as the Methodists, Presbyterians, and Episcopalians have lost between 20 and 40 percent of their members. These churches are filled with gray heads, having failed to maintain the loyalty of those who grew up in these churches in the 1960s and 1970s.[14] And without this new generation of leadership, it is uncertain whether they can transform their worship and organizational style to attract a youthful and ongoing following. This uncertainty is the focus of the final chapter of this book.

Research indicates, however, that many conservative churches have been doing quite well during the same period.[15] The Southern Baptists, for example, have grown steadily, forming numerous new congregations in the last several decades. A host of smaller "evangelical" and "high-demand" denominations are also growing. The pastors of these conservative churches present unambiguous answers to the moral and philosophical quandaries of postmodern society. They also offer a constantly evolving menu of programs that respond creatively to people's needs. In addition, they have been enterprising in building gymnasiums and hiring youth directors to engage the children of their congregations.

And then there are some surprises. Groups once marginal to the religious landscape, such as the Mormons, have exploded with growth.[16] They have high birthrates, which also help to explain the growth of conservative evangelicals,[17] but more important, they seem to understand the importance of nurturing family life. Furthermore, their marketing plan makes even the Jehovah's Witnesses look anemic, as the Mormons send self-financed volunteers on two-year missionary stints throughout the world.

The Pentecostalists, traditionally associated with the lower classes, are another group no longer at the margins. Drawing on theories of social deprivation, sociologists have typically portrayed Pentecostalists as people who need a little ecstasy in their lives to compensate for the daily struggle for survival.[18] These sociologists were therefore unprepared when the Assemblies of God and other Pentecostal groups started to attract middle-class adherents. And I believe everyone was surprised when large numbers of Roman Catholics in both the United States and South America decided to abandon their ritualistic churches for the spontaneous worship of the Pentecostalists.[19] Who would have predicted that Pentecostalism would grow faster than, say, Islamic fundamentalism, with more than 400 million adherents worldwide, including expansion in Africa as well as South America?[20]

Amid this proliferation on the religious right, another movement was occurring. A number of well-educated younger Americans chose to drop out of organized religion altogether or turned to Eastern religions, such as Hinduism or Zen Buddhism, which were antithetical to the capitalist values embodied in American Christianity. Their consciousness had been shaped by the anti-establishment sixties and seventies, and they viewed institutional, "man-made" religion as simply serving the self-interest of the clergy, who needed an institution to pay their salaries. "Why not access the sacred directly?" they asked. "Who needs paid mediators—especially ones who parade around in archaic clerical clothes?" These baby boomers have not lost interest in a spiritual quest, and neither have their children; their disillusionment is with "religion," which they identify with hierarchical authority and sterile ritual.[21] In their view, God and ultimate reality are to be found in a personal quest for wholeness, which may draw on the great religious traditions, but is not limited by their claims of exclusivism.

This social context has affected the place of Catholicism within the American religious economy. Initially, Catholicism took a substantial cultural "hit" and weekly church attendance plummeted more than 20 percent between the mid-sixties and the early eighties. Thousands of priests and nuns left their vocations and entered secular jobs.[22] For those who remained, life changed dramatically after the reforms of the Second Vatican Council in 1965. The habits of many nuns came off. Laypeople's roles in the church expanded. Dialogue with other faiths began. But just as the church was becoming more "relevant," recruitment to the priesthood fell off dramatically, and polls showed a widening gap between the views of people in the pews and the doctrines preached by the hierarchy. Declines in attendance have now leveled off; Catholics attend church at about the same rate as Protestants, and in surveys of moral views and practices they increasingly resemble Protestants.[23] But if mainline Protestants are worried about their survival, the anxiety level of the leaders of the Catholic Church is presumably even higher, in spite of their frequent reassertions of traditional dogma and even though Catholics are by far the largest denomination in America, constituting a quarter of the population. The disjuncture between what lay members believe and practice and what the clergy preaches cannot be maintained forever.

Left out of this sketch so far is any attention to Jews, who make up about 2 percent of the U.S. population (incidentally, the same as the Mormons). Many of the tensions I have described are mirrored in Judaism; in particular, orthodoxy has a surprisingly strong appeal and the liberal Reform branch is struggling with some of the same issues as mainline Protestantism is.[24] Moreover, it is time to revise the notion of a "Protestant-Catholic-Jewish America." There is some speculation, for example, that Muslims will equal the number of Jews in the United States within a few years. Indeed, if we count the growing percentage of religious "nones" (those without any religious affiliation)—now about 8 percent, up from 2 percent only thirty years ago—the religious mosaic becomes even more complex.

A Personal Pilgrimage

Before launching into the fascinating story of the people who have joined new paradigm churches, I want to identify my personal relationship to these groups as well as to say a few words about the research for this book. In the early 1980s I wrote a book entitled *The Case for Liberal Christianity,* which in many ways represented the age-old quest to make sense out of one's faith during a period of substantial social change. [25] The book was the product of a young mind trying to pick up the pieces from a graduate education in religious studies. Most of my "true believer" understandings of God and the Bible had been destroyed. I had joined a large liberal Episcopal church where the congregation worried more about social justice than about purity of doctrine. And I was relieved to have found a religious community where I did not need to check my mind at the door when I entered to worship.

In fact, I counted myself lucky to still consider myself a Christian. Many of my fellow students viewed religion as a cosmic projection by which people cope with the anxieties of life. While I agreed that religion (as an institution) was a social construction, I believed that something transcendent empowers man-made religious symbols and potentially gives meaning to the lives of individuals. Nevertheless, I knew that something was missing in my attempt at a cognitive justification for religion, so I vowed shortly after the publication of *Liberal Christianity* to shelve all attempts at writing theology until I was retired and had earned the right to engage in speculative reasoning. Instead, I turned my attention to several highly tangible issues—first genocide and then homelessness—to escape the intellectual challenges of the Christian faith.[26]

After a decade of retreat I found myself asking the Lilly Endowment to fund a project analyzing a phenomenon observed by some of my undergraduate students in the sociology of religion. For several years I had read in my students' term papers about churches that were teeming with teenagers like themselves, played rock music that people could dance to, and met in unconventional places. After visiting a few of these churches, I realized that something worth researching was brewing in southern California. The Jesus movement of the 1960s was long over. Although some of these churches had their roots in that movement, they were decidedly part of the 1990s. Gone were the religious hippies, and in their place were young parents trying to make sense out of the urban environment in which they were rearing their children. These churches preached an old-fashioned gospel, but their music and form of worship were radically contemporary, and their mood was quite different from that of the typical evangelical and fundamentalist churches I had visited.

On receiving a grant I felt some ambivalence. I had vowed to ignore theology for at least another thirty years; yet how could I do so given the biblical literalism of the churches I proposed to study? By this time I had been to enough meetings to know that these worshipers believed not only in the Holy Spirit, but also that Jesus was still in the business of healing people. Furthermore, they believed in demons—and were even casting them out! Yet I had demythologized for myself most of the supernatural elements of Christianity and settled into the Social Gospel emphasis of my own Episcopal church. Would I be willing to spend the next several years attending worship services where people raised their hands in praise, spoke in tongues, and consulted God on the most minute details of daily living?

The Research Agenda

In the five years since this project was launched, many of my initial assumptions have been radically altered. After a few dozen visits to these churches, I no longer found it strange that they involved the body as well as the mind in worship. When I asked permission to study the three groups that became the focus of this project, I was disarmed by the leaders' lack of defensiveness. They gave me and my research assistants total access to meetings we wanted to attend (something that would give pause to many of my liberal coreligionists). Although I never accepted the biblical literalism of these churches, I did discover the power of contemporary music to communicate the sacred, and I found myself genuinely moved by the members' stories of personal transformation and healing.

After being involved in the project a few months I realized what was missing in *The Case for Liberal Christianity:* it was devoid of any real understanding of the emotional and bodily dimension of religion. I had wrongly assumed that the mainline Protestant denominations were losing members because of the dissonance between their faith and the culture. Now I realized that part of the problem was the focus on rationalized beliefs. During graduate school, reading theology, I had assumed that truth was something that could be captured in a doctrinal or philosophical statement. My exposure to these rapidly growing churches taught me that religion is more than assent to well-formulated beliefs. Indeed, I started to wonder if I had the cart before the horse: if, instead, beliefs emerge out of experience. Perhaps I had not made the transition into our postmodern world: I was still dichotomizing mind and body, identifying religion more with the head than with the broader range of senses that are incorporated in worship.

My goal in writing this book, however, is not to put forward my own theology, but instead to describe the pastors and churchgoers in the three movements. Although I do not accept all the teachings of these groups, I believe they have connected with the "spirit" of Christianity in ways that my liberal colleagues sometimes miss—or perhaps fear. Their growth can be attributed to their ability to communicate the sacred in profound and life-changing ways and to embody this experience in postmodern organizational structures.

Throughout this book I have attempted to avoid cynicism, which is the stock in trade of many sociologists of religions. Furthermore, I decided not to make this book a critique of the three movements I studied, believing rather firmly that the declining mainline churches have something to learn from Calvary, Vineyard, and Hope. While it would be easy to criticize certain aspects of these groups from my liberal political perspective, I have instead attempted to understand them— especially the ways in which they are responding to the major cultural crises of our time—leaving the critique to the reader.

In January 1991 I received my grant to study what I called "rapidly growing non-mainline churches." I hired two primary research assistants: Paul Kennedy, who focused much of his attention on the Vineyard Christian Fellowship, and Brenda Brasher, who studied Calvary Chapel.[27] For two years we interviewed members of these groups and their leaders: Chuck Smith from Calvary, Kenn Gulliksen and John Wimber from the Vineyard, and Ralph Moore, the founder of Hope Chapel. We also attended numerous worship services, Bible studies, healing conferences, baptisms, and other meetings. In all, we tape-recorded and transcribed 200 interviews, and we also wrote detailed field notes on more than 200 events. We distributed lengthy questionnaires to people attending four large congregations, mailed questionnaires to all the senior pastors in the three movements, and distributed "testimony" forms at several Vineyard healing conferences.[28] In the chapters that follow I draw on all these sources.

In spite of the differences among Calvary Chapel, Vineyard Fellowship, and Hope Chapel, in most chapters I have emphasized their points of commonality. Separate books could be written on each of these movements, and perhaps in time they will be, but to highlight individual movements would have meant focusing on specific personalities much more than on the religious and cultural significance of these groups, which is my intent in this book.

CHAPTER 1

The New Face
of American Protestantism

A Second Reformation?

I believe we are witnessing a second reformation that is transforming the way Christianity will be experienced in the new millennium. The style of Christianity dominated by eighteenth-century hymns, routinized liturgy, and bureaucratized layers of social organization is gradually dying. In its place are emerging hundreds of new paradigm churches, which are appropriating stylistic and organizational elements from our postmodern culture. This reformation, unlike the one led by Martin Luther, is challenging not doctrine but the medium through which the message of Christianity is articulated. But what makes this reformation radical is that the hope of reforming existing denominational churches has largely been abandoned. Instead, the leaders of these new paradigm churches are starting new movements, unbounded by denominational bureaucracy and the restraint of tradition—except the model of first-century Christianity.

The earliest harbingers of this change emerged during the Jesus movement of the 1960s, when many of the clergy currently leading new paradigm churches, especially the mega-churches with several thousand members, had dramatic conversion experiences. In rebellion against intolerant establishment religion, "Jesus freaks," as they were sometimes called, began Bible studies in parks and started churches in homes, which soon pushed their way into recreation centers and rented school auditoriums as hundreds and then thousands of people responded. Religious experience reinvigorated church doctrine with people getting high on Jesus rather than drugs and embracing gifts of the spirit, such as speaking in tongues, that were normal in the early Christian church. Many of the principles of the Reformation were reborn as ordinary people discovered the priesthood of all believers, without ever reading Martin Luther. Fervent Bible study had a remarkable democratizing effect on these Jesus people, who felt no need for an official seminary-trained clergy to interpret this sacred text.[1]

The roots of many new paradigm churches may lie in the sixties, but it is a mistake to think that today's churches represent socially marginal countercultural values, or that they have not evolved in the last three decades. As cultural norms have shifted to reflect the revolutions of the sixties—and as the movements of that period have moderated some of their ecstatic enthusiasms—these groups resonate with baby boomer and "baby buster" values. Exemplifying the popularity of new paradigm churches in southern California are five Calvary Chapels, each with a weekly attendance of more than 7,500. Every Monday night at Calvary Chapel (Costa Mesa), over 2,000 teenagers pack the auditorium for Bible study. For the last several years, Anaheim Stadium has been filled to near capacity as upwards of 50,000 young people and families have gathered to listen to concerts of Christian rock music followed by a message from evangelist Greg Laurie, a Calvary Chapel pastor and a potential successor to the aging Billy Graham. And this is not simply a southern California phenomenon. Across the United States Calvary Chapels, Vineyard Christian Fellowships, and various independent churches are exploding in size.[2]

Many clergy and members of the declining mainline congregations would like to ignore this revolution in American Protestantism. The typical defense is to label these groups as "fundamentalist" reactionaries. But such dismissals ignore the complexity of these movements. They are not socially marginal. Quite the contrary, these are middle-class churches that represent the mainstream of American society. While conservative theologically, they are relatively avant-garde culturally—much more so than the typical mainline congregation—and they are far from being socially regressive.

In addition to their implications for the future of Protestantism, new paradigm movements warrant our attention for another reason. Changes in religious practice and beliefs mirror contemporary cultural transformations. It is not mere coincidence that large numbers of teenagers, parents of young families, and baby boomer adults believe that the Bible is a guidebook to moral absolutes. Nor is it inconsequential that substantial numbers of middle-class Americans believe in the supernatural, physical healings, as well as spiritual warfare. A careful study of these vanguard religious movements provides a window onto changes in American cultural values.

New Paradigm Churches

The typical new paradigm church meets in a converted warehouse, a rented school auditorium, or a leased space in a shopping mall. These meeting places boast no religious symbols, no stained glass, and no religious statuary. Folding chairs are more common than pews. At the front is a stage, often portable, which is bare except for sound equipment, a simple podium, and sometimes a few plants. People come to worship in casual clothes that they might wear to the mall or a movie. On a warm day, they might wear shorts and a polo shirt. The clergy are indistinguishable from the audience by dress.

Outsiders to these gatherings are often struck by the amount of physical warmth: men as well as women greet each other with embraces.[3] Everyone carries a Bible, and many also have notebooks.[4] The atmosphere is friendly, relaxed, and family-oriented. The building is filled with young couples and their children and single adults, with relatively few people over fifty.[5] The pastors, mostly men in their mid-thirties to mid-forties, are perhaps slightly older than the average age of their congregations.[6]

Worship is typically led by someone playing guitar, who may be joined by several vocalists and individuals on keyboard, drums, and bass guitar.[7] Depending on local talent, there may also be sax, trumpet, or bass accompaniment. The first song is often an upbeat song of praise. The words are projected onto a screen or the bare wall of the auditorium. The term *worship* means singing, and twenty-five to thirty minutes are always devoted to praising God and expressing love for him. During worship interrupting commentary or announcements are kept to a minimum. Many people close their eyes while singing and seem to move into deep interior spaces of reflection and experience; some even wipe tears from their eyes. As the rhythm of worship develops, people may stand and lift their hands in a statement of surrender to God. Others may extend their hands, palms upward, as if to receive a gift. At the end of the worship period—typically without comment—an offering basket may be passed, although sometimes there is simply a collection box at the back of the church.

After the half-hour of worship, the pastor steps forward and greets the people. The mood changes. Somewhat informally, he invites people to direct their attention to a passage of scripture.[8] The teaching is expository, friendly, as he shares the meaning that this passage has for him, frequently adding personal examples. Many of these pastors have charisma, but it is quite different from that of the televangelists. These pastors tend to be understated, conversational, and humble, rather than dramatic and ego-centered. Nevertheless, they clearly believe God speaks to them and that they have a vision for their church and the world. It is also evident that they believe God is in the business of radically changing people's lives. Indeed, the period of teaching frequently ends after about forty-five minutes with an invitation for individuals to commit their lives to Jesus. In the mega-size churches, several dozen or even more people may come forward for prayer and a brief period of counseling with someone who can help guide them on their new journey of faith. The audience often applauds and sometimes even whistles approval of those making such commitments.

After the invitation is extended, the band frequently plays an upbeat melody. At evening services people may linger as the band continues to play. Young churchgoers may even dance in the aisles. The mood is warm and accepting as parents interact with their children and friends. In the more charismatic churches—believing in such gifts of the Holy Spirit as healing and speaking in tongues—the final portion of the service may include a time of "ministry," when people are invited to come forward for healing prayer. Lay members of a ministry team join them in front. Often putting a comforting hand on the other person's shoulder, the lay minister asks about the individual's needs or problems, and the two pray together for healing. The interaction is casual and caring, prayer being a way that members of the community share their concerns.[9]

On leaving the auditorium one typically encounters numerous tables and displays for various interest group meetings. Perhaps a third of the people participate in weekly Bible studies that meet in members' homes. According to participants, this—and not the Sunday morning service— is the real core of the church. There are also groups for parents raising teenage children, those battling drug or alcohol addictions, couples seeking advice on financial management, people recovering from divorce, sports teams, parents investigating home schooling, and more. There is also a full range of men-only and women-only meetings, marriage renewal weekends, family camping outings, movie nights for teenagers, and activities for preteens. What is surprising is how quickly these churches develop a broad range of ministries in response to the spiritual as well as personal and recreational needs of converts.

The typical church originates as a Bible study group in someone's home. Often the leader has been apprenticed in a larger church after having a significant conversion experience there. After several years of being mentored in his new faith, and sometimes after a brief stint in a pastor training program, he responds to a call from the Holy Spirit to start a church. Sometimes he receives this direction in a vision or a dream, but he may simply feel a strong conviction that he should go to a particular city and "plant" a church. Rarely is this individual given much financial support. Consequently, he begins by finding a job in the new community and then invites neighbors and coworkers to a Bible study in his home. If he is truly called by God to be a pastor, it is believed that a growing group of people will gather for study. Some pastors indicate that their first attempts at starting a church were not successful, so they moved from one location to another until they found a responsive audience. And there is often a one- or two-year period when the pastor seriously questions his calling as this small Bible study struggles for survival.

Across the United States, hundreds of these church "plants" have taken root. In a typical scenario, the Bible study outgrows the pastor's apartment, and a search begins for larger meeting space—frequently a community hall, movie theater, or school auditorium. By the time the group reaches 100 or more members, the demands on the pastor's time are such that he is asked by the congregation to quit his secular job and minister full time. If a newly planted church "takes off," the congregation typically moves to progressively larger meeting facilities in the next few years. Often, to the surprise of the pastor, each of these moves results in a rapid expansion in the number of people attending. In retrospect, it appears that limitations in parking and meeting space have controlled the size of the congregation, much as the size of a store may limit the number of customers who can enter.

As the congregation expands, the size of the staff slowly increases: first with an assistant, then a minister of worship, then with someone to coordinate the multiple children's programs. What distinguishes these new paradigm churches, however, is the level of lay involvement in leadership and program development. Mirroring democratic values, clergy encourage members to initiate new programs and projects, which thus reflect the members' own needs and interests. Indeed, so long as these programs fit the values of the congregation, enormous latitude is granted in what ministries are started and how they evolve. The pastor sees his role as facilitating and mentoring members who are doing the work of ministry, rather than attempting to staff these ministries with professional clergy. While having obvious budgetary benefits, the more direct advantage of lay-directed ministries is that hundreds of people become involved in leadership roles, cementing their commitment to the church.

Reflecting member interests, new paradigm churches tend to be filled with programs that deal with the specific needs of those attending them. It is not surprising, then, that small group meetings in homes are at the core of all these movements.[10] Intimacy is in short supply in American society. Members repeatedly say that home fellowship groups constitute the family they never had as children and teenagers.[11] In line with this, various conferences and meetings focus on what it means to be a responsible father and a nurturing husband. The "men's movement," addressing questions related to male identity, is flourishing in these groups. Similarly, extensive programs for women are often led by the pastor's wife or lay women leaders.

Without question, these churches are growing because they address deeply felt anxieties about how the sexes should relate to each other, how to raise children in a violent society, and how to find love in a world that seems to value possessions over relationships. These churches are a counterpoint to secular society: they are safe havens where children can be raised and where individuals can express their personal fears in an unthreatening environment, while feeling that someone is genuinely concerned about their welfare. But the real staying power of new paradigm churches is that they are mediating deeply felt religious experiences, and doing this much more effectively than many mainline churches.[12]

The Decline of the Mainline Denominations

Historians and sociologists of religion widely acknowledge a substantial restructuring among American religious institutions.[13] Religion is not going out of business, as was declared several decades ago, when alarmists announced the "Death of God" on the covers of national magazines.[14] Rather, the religious economy (as measured by church attendance) is remarkably healthy. But the market share of religious "firms"—to continue the economic analogy—is changing substantially. The so-called mainline denominations have fallen on hard times, and although their decline is not as precipitous now as it was in the late sixties and throughout the seventies and eighties, they are still losing members. A casual look at the typical Episcopal, Presbyterian, Congregational, or Methodist congregation reveals a decided absence of young families and a mere handful of teenagers. It does not require a degree from the Harvard Business School to conclude that these churches may resemble the American textile or steel industry in a few years. Huge edifices will remain on many of the major street corners of America, but their endowments will barely support their physical maintenance.

Church attendance peaked in the 1950s, when 49 percent of the U.S. population indicated that they had attended religious services in the last seven days. Beginning in the early 1960s, attendance slowly declined until it bottomed out at about 40 percent in the 1970s, and it has remained at approximately this level to the present. The biggest losers in this decline were the liberal denominations, with some losing 10 percent of their membership in a decade. Many conservative denominations made startling gains during this period, especially Pentecostal and charismatic denominations. For observers, this trend defied common sense. Why would churches characterized by tolerance, rationality, and scientific sophistication be declining while those that were morally strict, theologically intolerant, and emotionally expressive in their worship be growing?[15]

To answer this question, consider the values of baby boomers. They don't like bureaucratic structure, and the mainline churches are monuments of rites and organizational rules. There are at least four reasons they are unlikely to be attracted back into the historic denominations. First, "brand" loyalty has very little meaning to most boomers; the fact that they were raised Methodist or Episcopalian does not determine where they choose to go to church. Second, tradition is more often a negative than a positive word; thus, while a few boomers may like Bach and Mozart, most grew up on bands and singers, not orchestras and choirs, and it is not surprising that they seek out churches with contemporary music. Third, boomers want to be involved in running and managing their own organizations rather than entrusting decisions to someone at the top, such as a pastor or priest. Fourth, boomers tend to be local in their interests and fail to see the value of remote denominational organizations that are spending millions of dollars on issues outside their own community (especially if much of this money is dispensed in bureaucrats' salaries).[16]

These boomer values augur poorly for the survival of the mainline denominations. Obviously, some individual churches have adapted well to the needs and interests of baby boomers. However, recent studies demonstrate that many mainline denominations have effectively lost an entire generation,[17] and there is little reason to speculate that they will be any more successful in recovering market share than many of the industries in the rust belt.

But I do not want to be too pessimistic. To consider an analogy to another sector of business, IBM has been remarkably resilient in continuing to control market share in the computer industry. Nevertheless, the real vitality there lies in the hundreds of "upstart" companies that are close to consumer interests, extremely quick in responding to market niches, and led by young entrepreneurs acting on instinct rather than relying on formulas learned in MBA programs. In the American religious economy, the analogy to IBM and its upstart rivals is instructive. The pastors of the new paradigm churches tend to be extremely bright, close to the age and experience of their boomer congregations, and unfettered by seminary educations that instruct them on how to run a church. There are obvious parallels to a number of software and computer company founders, who dropped out of college and began their careers in garages or dorm rooms. Much like the computer upstarts, churches started by new paradigm pastors are more likely to be on the vanguard of change than are the older, more bureaucratically burdened, mainline "firms."[18]

If Christianity is going to survive, it must continually reinvent itself, adapting its message to the members of each generation, along with their culture and the geographical setting. Making Christianity—or any religion—culturally appropriate need not compromise the integrity of its primary message. After all, truth, however one conceives of it, is always expressed in rooted, culturally specific symbols. The question is whether these symbols communicate their message in the current marketplace of needs and ideas. Churches, temples, and mosques that do not constantly "resymbolize" their message eventually die; in contrast, groups that have the foresight to encapsulate their message in contemporary symbols and forms not only have the potential to survive, but sometimes grow at remarkable rates, as did the three groups that are the focus of this book.

Three Examples of Change

Calvary Chapel, Vineyard Christian Fellowship, and Hope Chapel all originated during the period when the mainline denominations were beginning to experience a decline in market share. All three have grown exponentially since they were founded, and all three are filled with baby boomers and baby busters. In addition, these three movements all began in southern California, the home of many cultural trends that eventually wend their way around the world. By now these movements have expanded well beyond the western states; hundreds of their churches have been "planted" across North America, and recently a number have been started in Europe and the former Soviet Union. Within the last several decades, or even less, these movements have built up many mega-size congregations, numbering in the thousands.

Calvary Chapel was founded in 1965 by Chuck Smith as a ministry for hippies and surfers. It has long since outgrown the tent that in its early years hosted numerous concerts and Jesus movement happenings. Within its fold Calvary Chapel now counts over 600 churches in the United States and another 100 abroad. The first Vineyard church was started by Kenn Gulliksen in 1974, and in 1982 this fledgling movement was passed to John Wimber to shepherd. The Vineyard now has 400 churches in the United States and is approaching 200 abroad. The smallest of the three movements is Hope Chapel, started in 1971 by Ralph Moore, a young pastor affiliated with the Foursquare Gospel church. The mother church in Hermosa Beach, California, has more than 2,000 congregants on Friday night through Sunday evening, and it has spawned another 50 churches, all under the authority of the Foursquare Gospel denomination.

Combined, these movements represent over 1,000 churches, and the "ripple effect" that they are having on American Christianity is profound. Their music and style of worship are influencing hundreds of other churches in the United States, including many mainline and some Roman Catholic churches. But in some ways these three movements are just the lead story. The untold story of American Protestantism is the growth and proliferation of independent churches. Little attention has been paid to such groups, primarily because they are not part of any particular denomination and are therefore hard to document. However, there are thousands of these churches, some of which are loosely associated in "apostolic networks."[19] In addition, there is a new generation of "seeker-sensitive" churches, whose worship style and organizational structure resemble those of Calvary, Vineyard, and Hope.[20] Because of their growth, some observers have speculated that we are entering a postdenominational era.

Given the variety of these new churches, including some differences among the three movements focused on here, it is important to identify the trademark qualities of what I am labeling new paradigm churches. The following twelve characteristics, all of which must be present to some degree, distinguish new paradigm churches:

1. they were started after the mid-1960s
2. the majority of congregation members were born after 1945
3. seminary training of clergy is optional
4. worship is contemporary
5. lay leadership is highly valued
6. they have extensive small group ministries
7. clergy and congregants usually dress informally
8. tolerance of different personal styles is prized
9. pastors tend to be understated, humble, and self-revealing
10. bodily, rather than mere cognitive, participation in worship is the norm
11. the "gifts of the Holy Spirit" are affirmed
12. Bible-centered teaching predominates over topical sermonizing

Overarching all of these characteristics is a spirit of joy and celebration that contrasts strongly with the sterner Protestant (especially Puritan) tradition.

At first, new paradigm groups may seem to fit into such established categories as fundamentalist, evangelical, Pentecostal, charismatic, and orthodox. Yet none of these terms alone captures the essence of new paradigm groups; they all miss the emphasis on cultural currency. The new paradigm groups must be seen as part of a larger, cultural paradigm shift that has substantial implications for the future of Christianity in the twenty-first century.

The New Cultural Paradigm

The 1960s launched a cultural revolution whose implications we are still seeking to understand. Much of the rhetoric surrounding "countercultural" values is currently pejorative and politically condemnatory. Nevertheless, however tired and frayed some of the concepts may be, they are still important reference points in understanding the cultural restructuring being done by new paradigm churches. In particular, new paradigm churches and their members have responded to the *therapeutic, individualistic,* and *anti-establishment* themes of the counterculture.[21] In each instance they have incorporated an element of these values into their religious life, while rejecting other implications of these stances.

Therapeutic: In our interviews with participants in new paradigm churches, they frequently remarked that what attracted them was the openness and honesty of the people they encountered in these churches. As our interviewees groped for words to explain what they meant, they often simply said that people seemed "real"—there were no pretensions, no attempts to be something they were not. Consequently, it was possible to relax, to be vulnerable, to admit one's own hurts and problems, knowing that one would be accepted rather than judged. These are the same values that blossomed in the encounter groups of the sixties and proliferated in various schools of psychotherapy, becoming infused into mainstream culture in the form of pop psychology, self-help books, and talk show gurus.[22] On the other hand, new paradigm churches, while embracing the ethic of openness and tolerance, are hostile to the narcissism they see in contemporary therapeutic values.[23] Indeed, new paradigm churches oppose many of the values of modern psychology, precisely because self-fulfillment is deified by many contemporary therapists and pop commentators. They substitute "biblical advice" for "counseling" and deal with psychological issues in sensitive but often direct, and even confrontational, ways—focusing on moral choices in the present rather than childhood conditioning of past attitudes.

Individualistic: New paradigm churches place an emphasis on individualism: interpreting scripture for oneself, directly interacting with God through prayer and visions, and affirming personal salvation. Individual authority is not relinquished to the rules of an external institution or leader. Rather, each person has the right to question and interpret the meaning of religious truth. Yet these groups reject what Robert Bellah has labeled "utilitarian individualism," for they place an enormous emphasis on personal accountability.[24] Typically this accountability occurs in small group Bible study settings where mentored friendships are valued. As a Christian, one does not live for oneself. Within the community, each member has particular gifts to offer. While considerable emphasis is placed on individual choice and personal interpretation, the committed Christian is held to a purpose beyond self-actualization.

Anti-establishment: Members of new paradigm churches tend to be hostile to institutions, bureaucracies, and routinized aspects of organizational life. For that reason, they reject most of the external symbols of "organized" religion as being false, oppressive, and of human origin. Their churches are unadorned by religious symbolism, and the professional staff is lean and easily accessible to members. On the other hand, new paradigm members place an extremely high value on community, and for many individuals the church is the center of their lives. In other words, institutions are valued so long as they are loving and caring places. It is pyramid-style bureaucracies that these individuals reject, so they tend to be extremely hostile to most forms of denominationalism.

The distinctiveness of new paradigm churches, then, is that they have incorporated aspects of therapeutic, individualistic, and anti-establishment values into congregational life, but they have simultaneously rejected the narcissism of these countercultural orientations. They are in the business of rebuilding marriages; caring for children, not ignoring them to pursue personal goals; and providing viable alternatives to the perceived violence of contemporary culture. To outsiders, they often look conservative as they affirm traditional roles for women, demonstrate against abortion, and bash contemporary psychology. But this is not fundamentalism resurrected. Gone is the authoritarianism associated with that tradition, and absent is fundamentalism's vehement opposition to modernity, its romanticization of the moral innocence of the past and its belief that a return to a bygone era will solve the perceived chaos of the present. New paradigm churches are doing significant "cultural repair" that defies standard religious or political labels.

Primitive or Postmodern?

Since the eighteenth century Western philosophy of religion has been dominated by Enlightenment thought, which prescribed rationality and scientific empiricism as the basis for all explorations of truth. One result is that religious debates have been relegated to discussing the truth or falsity of *beliefs*, making religion a "disembodied," cerebral matter. However, in the last decade or so, many assumptions of

Enlightenment thought have been challenged. The clay feet of rationality have been revealed, and postmodern philosophy is questioning the authoritarian character of any claim to a universal epistemology, or theory of knowledge.[25]

Given this philosophical context, new paradigm churches can be viewed as cultural pioneers of sorts. They are attempting to reintegrate bodily experience into religious life. Worship is not simply a matter of the head, affirming various creeds or acknowledging normative beliefs. Indeed, along with postmodern philosophers, the pastors and members of new paradigm churches are suspicious of the motives underlying doctrinal formulations. Beliefs are important, especially when anchored in the retelling of biblical stories; but beliefs in themselves are sterile. Religion is a full-bodied experience that includes all the receptors—all the senses—with the rational mind being only one locus of information about reality. Right-brain activities (typically associated with nonlinear thought, and in this case with the Holy Spirit) are acknowledged as legitimate.

Whatever the actual reality of the Holy Spirit, new paradigm Christians describe experiences that simply do not conform to the norms of logic and rational discourse. They detail visions, dreams, and other nonrational encounters with the holy. These Christians talk about "feeling" the presence of God during worship and of having a "relationship" with Christ. A relatively high percentage have spoken in tongues, a nonrational form of communication with God that they attribute to the Holy Spirit. Ecstatic joy and profound peace are also experiences that they attribute to a divine presence. In exceptional cases, supernatural healing occurs, demons are expelled, and prophecies are uttered. This is the "stuff" of worship and prayer, not rational discourse.

From an Enlightenment perspective, these experiences are echoes from the primitive side of our nature. Sigmund Freud reduced them to infantile wish fulfillment.[26] For Freud and other scientific theorists, it was time to grow up and live according to the cold logic of rationality and empiricism.[27] In contrast, new paradigm Christians see no reason why they should exclude visions and ecstatic experiences from the realm of religious knowledge. In fact, they see themselves as radical empiricists, while those captive to the Enlightenment worldview are "scientific fundamentalists," excluding a priori those realities they cannot measure and test.

So one can view these groups as primitivists who are rejecting modernity, or one can see them as being in the cultural vanguard, participants in the attempt to shape a new worldview. While there may be legitimacy to both interpretations, I believe the latter view allows for a more complex and interesting analysis. It is true that new paradigm groups reject certain aspects of contemporary culture, but they are also *transforming* many elements of the secular worldview in highly innovative ways. One might identify these Christians as "postmodern primitivists," for they acknowledge and utilize many aspects of postmodern culture, yet they find in the biblical tradition—in particular, the "primitive Christianity" of the first century—an underpinning for a radical spirituality that undermines the cynicism and fragmentation of many postmodern theorists.

Two Useful Guides

At many points in the following analysis, William James's perspective on religion and his classic lectures on *The Varieties of Religious Experience* serve as a reference point.[28] James rejected what he called "medical materialism," the attempt to explain away religious experience by identifying physiological correlates of mysticism or other religious experiences. He disagreed with the mind-body dualism that assumes religious experience is not also a physical sensation. Furthermore, he argued that all religious philosophy is based on religious experience and that doctrine and dogma are derivative "secondary accretions." For James, religious experience is the foundation of religious life, and prayer is the lifeline of ongoing communication with God.

James's framework is attractive for several reasons. First, many of the accounts of religious experience found in our research are similar to case studies reported in his lectures. Anyone prepared to dismiss our reports of divine encounters out of hand must also reckon with James, a rather formidable philosophical foe. Second, James comes to his conclusions as something of an agnostic, with no particular brief to argue except that religious experience is part of everyday life for many people and thus should be taken seriously. In a similar fashion, my approach does not stem from a personal commitment to the groups described in this book, although I admit to being fascinated by them. Third, to a limited degree I embrace James's pragmatism. Like James, I am interested in the "fruits" of religious experience rather than merely its roots (i.e., whether God or the Holy Spirit is the *actual source* of what is experienced is not going to be settled in the pages of this book). I judge the efficacy of conversion experiences on the grounds of whether they help people to be productive citizens, better fathers and mothers, and more responsible spouses.

One extrapolation from James's theory is my contention that denominational growth or decline is linked to the vitality of religious experience. I believe that churches (as well as synagogues and mosques) that provide access to the sacred at a deep level are more likely to grow and expand in membership, while those that do not offer life-changing, affective religious experience tend, over time, to decline and eventually die. According to this formulation, ritually oriented churches, including those that are part of mainline denominations, will grow *if* congregants within these churches are encountering the sacred in profound ways. On the other hand, if ritual has become removed from religious experience, functioning in James's terms as mere secondary accretion, then decline is inevitable.

While this extrapolation is consistent with James, he would never have linked religious experience with church growth and decline because of his hostility to institutional religion. James defined religion as something that occurs in solitude. But I am much more sanguine than James about institutional expressions of religion and in fact believe that this is the primary way in which religion has an impact on human culture. Furthermore, James was seemingly blind to the powerful ways in which communal worship can mediate religious experience. In contrast, I believe that religious experience always occurs within a cultural context and people inevitably seek to join others in collectively celebrating the source of their experience.

The famous German sociologist Max Weber serves as a useful counterbalance to James, in that he views religion institutionally rather than individually, although he, like James, acknowledges an important role for primal, unfettered religious encounters.[29] According to Weber, most of the great religions have been founded by charismatic leaders— the Buddha, Jesus, Mohammed—who had profound religious encounters or revelations that reordered their understanding of life's meaning.

Before gathering a following, these prophetic figures felt a need to seek truth at its deepest level. The institutional forms of religion that surrounded them seemed sterile and all too human in serving the professional and power needs of the priestly class. These soon-to-become-prophets rejected the religion of their heritage, but rather than remaining agnostic, they searched for the reality that originally empowered the religious forms, which now seemed so dead and wooden to them. In the desert of their self-renunciation and quest for meaning, these individuals encountered a reality that, when they began speaking of it (or modeled it in their behavior), filled the deep void experienced by others in their society. In time, a band of disciples formed around them.

In the early years of the movement, Weber explained, the charismatic prophet and his disciples typically lived communally and out of one purse. There were few, if any, rules; little organization; and an absence of hierarchy among the followers. However, after the inevitable death of the charismatic leader, the movement tended to routinize. Within a few years, the prophet's oral teachings were written down and became sacred—infallible "holy writ." The fellowship of disciples became structured into a priestly class with different offices. Rituals (including reenactments of some of the prophet's acts) developed to contain and dispense the "truth" associated with the leader. What was so direct, spontaneous, and immediate in the first generation of the movement became formalized, ritualized, and in time bureaucratized. Weber labeled this process the "routinization of charisma."

According to Weber, the routinization of charisma is not merely inevitable but absolutely necessary if a movement is to survive after the departure of the founding leader. However, a balance must be achieved between structure and substance. When routinized forms and procedures substitute for the primal religious experience that empowered the founder and his or her disciples, then a religion dies or simply becomes the indentured servant of the state, continuing to exist, not because of the personal meaning derived from the message, but because of the subsidy provided by the politicians whose pronouncements the priestly class sanctifies. It is this problematic routinization and bureaucratization that new paradigm churches are addressing, doing what reformers have always done: appealing to the early teachings of the charismatic prophet and claiming the social organization of the early disciples as the model for how the contemporary church (temple, mosque) should be structured.[30]

The next chapter tells the story of how Calvary Chapel, the Vineyard Fellowship, and Hope Chapel began and identifies some of the "ripple effects" of these congregations on the American religious economy. Subsequent chapters examine specific aspects of the experience of new paradigm Christians. The final chapter knits these observations together into a theory regarding religious change and renewal, and makes some forecasts for new paradigm churches as well as mainline denominations.

CHAPTER 2

Hippies, Beach Baptisms, and Healings

A History of Three Movements

If the individual stories of the growth of Calvary, Vineyard, and Hope are remarkable, the reasons why these three movements have grown are not. The movements have followed some simple principles, probably quite unselfconsciously, that have guided the growth of religious movements throughout human history.

To understand this growth, one must first articulate the function of religion—as distinct from the mission of other institutions in society. Although sociologists debate how religion should be defined, most suggest that the task of religion is to provide meaning, meaning that orders one's life and gives one a sense of an ultimate purpose—a reason for being, a sense of hope, and a destiny to fulfill. The assumption undergirding this definition is that all human beings, in all times and places, need to order their lives according to some scheme of ultimate meanings. Depending on the theorist, this meaning framework may be viewed as an ideology or simply as a set of beliefs. And, again depending on the theorist—as well as the cultural setting—these beliefs may be relatively formalized or embodied in ritual forms that are acted out symbolically. The point is this: if a religion is not providing individuals with a strong sense of personal meaning—and personal meaning is often encapsulated in the collective purpose of a group—then it declines. Churches, temples, and mosques are not social clubs, entertainment centers, or recreation sites, even though they may provide a strong sense of community and serve a number of ancillary human needs. Fundamental to any healthy, expanding religious institution is that it gives individuals a powerful sense of life's purpose.

Here it is important to recognize that different generations and different subcultures contend with different meaning issues, and as we have moved from primitive, to modern, to postmodern societies the gaps between generations and various subcultures have increased. In this regard, leaders of religious institutions who do not understand their church's market niche and the particular audience to whom they are communicating will typically fail in their mission. Although this marketplace language may seem jarring, the point is not to commercialize religion, but rather to underline that society is not homogeneous and all people's needs are not the same. A diffuse message will not be heard, especially in contemporary society, because while the desire for ultimate meaning may be universal, beliefs and values are contextualized and experienced quite differently depending on one's age, education, race or ethnicity, and cultural background.

In highly segmented societies, such as contemporary America, the message and the medium in which it is presented are interwoven. For example, identical song lyrics will communicate very different meanings depending on whether they are voiced by a rock band or by a choir accompanied by an organ. Likewise, the physical structure that serves as the "envelope" for the message will communicate differently depending on whether it is a Gothic-style stone structure or a converted warehouse devoid of religious symbolism. And the same message will be experienced differently if it is "preached" or "taught" and if the speaker wears clerical garb or shorts and a T-shirt. Simply put, if the message is going to communicate with an intended audience, it must be culturally appropriate—that is, the medium for the message must relate to the everyday experience of the audience.

In contemporary society individuals have options in selecting the values that orient their lives. Many constraints of the past, such as following the religious tradition of one's family, no longer apply. Someone who grew up in the Presbyterian church, but finds that it no longer speaks to his or her life situation and needs, is likely to explore another alternative. This is a lesson that business firms have learned all too well in recent years: brand loyalty lasts only so long as the product is competitive. The cynical view of some religionists is that we have collapsed into a nation of narcissists, seeking only to indulge our fantasies and pleasures. Indeed, there may be a grain of truth to this accusation. But there is a more constructive way to view the freedom of choice and accompanying pluralism in contemporary religion. Applied to the restructuring of American Protestantism, it is that churches that find culturally appropriate ways to meet people's felt needs for ultimate meaning will succeed, and those that do not will fail.

Calvary Chapel

Although I had learned to expect surprises in this research, I was still shocked when I walked into Calvary Chapel Costa Mesa on a Monday night and found 2,300 teenagers gathered to study the Bible. Every seat in the main auditorium was full, and teens were sitting on the carpeted floor; one girl was lying down, propped up on her elbows, as if watching TV in her living room. Sitting in front of me was a young woman wearing a T-shirt that said on the back, "Born to be wild." I observed an equal mix of boys and girls. This was Orange County, known for its political conservatism, and it was a different generation of high school students from that of the mid-sixties, when Calvary Chapel was founded. Almost everyone seemed to possess the clean-cut, tanned good looks of people enjoying an affluent lifestyle.

The music was good; in fact, very good! One might expect to pay handsomely at a concert to hear a band this professional. For some of the songs, the audience joined the band in singing. For others, they clapped, danced in place, or tapped a foot in time with the music. The lead guitarist stopped at one point and sermonized about what constitutes true Christianity, saying, "We're not singing about religion tonight; we're talking about a relationship with Jesus." There were a few whistles of approval to this statement, and the band then started playing "I'll walk down that aisle and believe it today." After about forty minutes the band ended with "Amazing Grace," and the entire audience stood and joined them.

Greg Laurie, an early convert to the Calvary movement and now pastor of a 10,000-member congregation of his own, had driven from Riverside, California, to speak. His topic was the story of the Samaritan woman whom Jesus met at the well and who finally confessed that she had been married not once but five times. Laurie told these teens that some of them had an appointment with Jesus tonight, just like the Samaritan woman. He said that when he gave his heart to Jesus, he had no idea beforehand that this was what he was going to do.

Deep down inside everyone has a thirst for God, claimed Laurie, just as the Samaritan woman did. Laurie stated that we try to cover over that thirst by seeking short-lived pleasures. But sex outside marriage, drugs, new clothes—none of these diversions is enough; they are followed by a continuing desire for something more. All of Laurie's images pointed to a quest for something that is solid and permanent and that, unlike material things, fills the emptiness many of us feel in our quiet moments.

Laurie echoed the statement of the lead guitarist: "The answer is not religion; it is a relationship with Jesus." He then did a little denomination bashing, arguing that there are no holy buildings, that instead the people are the church. He questioned churches that go "up" instead of "out," and the audience clapped when he said, "We could just as easily meet for church in a park or at the beach." The only issue, he emphasized, is whether Christ is living inside you, and he noted the pointlessness of claiming identity as a Baptist or Presbyterian.

The sermon continued for another twenty-five minutes, with repeated references to the Samaritan woman. In his closing comments, Laurie looked directly at his audience and asked, "What are you doing to fill that void in your life? Are you looking for the perfect man or woman to satisfy your deepest longings? Are you attempting to fill that emptiness with possessions? This is your chance, like the Samaritan woman, to reach out to Jesus. He is wanting to come into your life right now. Jesus will forgive you for your failures. He is the water of life." Right on cue, the band began to play in the background as Laurie announced that those without Jesus could come forward and give their lives to God tonight.

Laurie then stepped back from the lectern, and the band picked up the tempo. First one, then dozens of teenagers made their way out of their seats to the front of the auditorium. Included in this assemblage were couples holding hands, young men wearing surfer T-shirts, and girls in halter tops. For each new convert the audience applauded. I even heard a few whistles of approval. When the forward flow had abated, Laurie stepped back to the lectern and led these newly committed Christians in a short prayer in which they acknowledged their sins and asked Jesus to take control of their lives. Laurie instructed the audience to wait a few minutes for their friends who had come forward, because he wanted to give each new convert a Bible and some literature. The mood was joyous. The band leader turned the amplifier up another notch, and the community celebrated its new members and their profession of faith.

A few weeks later, I made the hour-long drive once again to investigate weekday events at Calvary Chapel Costa Mesa. It was Wednesday night, and the place was buzzing with activity. Several hundred women, maybe more, were meeting for Bible study in small groups. In addition, about 400 people had gathered in the main auditorium for the regular Wednesday night teaching on prophecy led by Chuck Missler. The college and career group was meeting in the fellowship hall, with about 250 present, and it interested me that during announcement time the leader listed approximately ten different ministry groups, including an "accountability" group for men. I was also intrigued to note that the lights were turned low during the worship period, much as they might be at a club frequented by young people.

As I wandered around the church campus, I saw Vietnamese participants in a Bible study group, a classroom full of single parents, and Calvary's equivalent of an Alcoholics Anonymous meeting. It was obvious that Calvary had an interest group for any need.

A similar bevy of programs occurred on other nights of the week. On a Thursday evening, for example, I visited Chuck Smith's Bible study, which had 800 to 900 people present. I noticed that some participants had multicolored pencils, with which they marked their Bibles according to a coding system. I was intrigued with Smith's examples of God leading in strange ways. The dead car battery, the flat tire, he said, may be God's way of protecting you from danger—"nothing happens accidentally." Smith's suggested response to such events is to ask, "God, what are you trying to tell me?" I also noticed that Smith dismissed attempts to intellectualize the faith: "God doesn't care what seminary you went to."

One Tuesday evening I went to Oden Fong's Bible study. It was not as well attended as Smith's, but I suspect that in this smorgasbord of church offerings Fong may have his own clientele. He is a very skilled musician, and the worship was rather mystical. I saw more people raising their hands during worship than is usual at Calvary, and there seemed to be more openness to charismatic gifts at this meeting. Later in an interview Fong explained that he was heavily involved with drugs before he walked down the aisle at one of the early Calvary Chapel concerts. His experiences with cocaine and LSD had exposed him to the possibility of "alternative realities." For him, "tongues speaking" and other encounters with the Holy Spirit seem congruent with a religion that does not dichotomize mind and body.

Sunday morning worship at Costa Mesa is more formal than in many of the other Calvary Chapels. Chuck Smith wears a suit. Some old-style hymns are mixed in with the usual Calvary Chapel choruses. Young children are not allowed at the service. Anyone who leaves the auditorium during the teaching portion of the service is not permitted to return in order to avoid disrupting others. On the other hand, the service retains a casual character. A loudspeaker carries the sound to people sitting on lawn chairs on the patio outside the main auditorium. The service is also piped into the gymnasium, and a few hundred people may be sitting there on bleachers, some with their kids crawling around as if the seats were a jungle gym.

The programs at Calvary Chapel Costa Mesa are obviously highly evolved. But this complex offering of services had a relatively humble beginning thirty years ago.

HISTORY OF THE CALVARY MOVEMENT

For the early part of his career, Chuck Smith was a pastor in the Foursquare Gospel denomination. He attended the church's Bible college and as a young pastor attempted to conform to all the strategies of church growth, including dozens of denominationally sponsored contests to bring the largest number of new converts into his church. But he grew disenchanted with the "hype" surrounding institutional Christianity and, in spite of winning first place in one of these contests, decided to break his affiliation with the Foursquare church. "I did not fit within the denomination," explains Smith, "and so I was wanting out. But the longer you stay in, and the more seniority you get, the harder it is to escape."[1]

After investigating several other denominations, Smith concluded that his criticisms of the Foursquare were, in fact, endemic to all denominations: "I saw them as ultimately coming under control of those who are not necessarily the most spiritual men. A man who is truly spiritual is going to be satisfied and happy wherever God has called him." In Smith's analysis, it is power-oriented people who end up leading denominations, and "once they have achieved a position of power, then they become protective and they want to protect themselves in this position of power." As Smith explains, "They do that by surrounding themselves with weaker men and by eliminating all those who are a threat to their position." In his view, the most promising leaders are typically marginalized by the denomination because of the threat they pose to the ensconced leadership; those in power then consolidate their position by creating rules that strip subordinate churches of their independence. Quoting one of his mentors, Smith observes: "The more spiritual a man is, the less denominational he becomes."

Tired of denominational structure and strategy, Smith started Corona Christian Center in the early sixties. It grew rapidly, requiring the church to move to new quarters to accommodate the increasing attendance. In the midst of this success, he received an invitation to pastor a struggling church of twenty-five members in nearby Costa Mesa. Rationally, it made no sense to leave the vital church he had started for Calvary Chapel, a church that seemed about to close. But there was a factor in Smith's life—his belief in the guidance of the Holy Spirit—that made self-interested calculation inconsequential. Initially, Kay Smith opposed her husband's answering this pastoral call, but one evening she greeted her husband as he returned from an evening Bible study by saying, "Honey, I've been in prayer and God has really spoken to my heart. The Lord has made it clear that I'm to submit to you."[2]

So in 1965 Chuck Smith started pastoring Calvary Chapel, meeting with two dozen discouraged people. Drawing on his experience of fixing up homes he had owned, Smith got the congregation to let him modernize the interior of the church. They also agreed to pay for broadcasting his Bible studies on the radio. Within a short time, Smith had to go off the air because the church could not accommodate all the new people he was attracting. Smith made an agreement with a Lutheran church to use their much bigger facility on Sunday afternoons, when it was not otherwise occupied. Soon this church was also packed. Looking for an even larger building, the church leaders submitted a minimum-level bid on a public school that had been declared surplus property. To their great surprise, they became the owners of Greenville School.

However, what changed the future of Calvary Chapel more than any change in location was Smith's decision to minister to the so-called hippies in the beach areas surrounding Costa Mesa. Smith began to meet some of the early converts of the Jesus movement through his college-age daughter. Initially repulsed by their long hair, beards, and politics, he was stunned by the inner transformations occurring in these young people and their zeal for sharing their new faith.

Several of these early converts needed a place to live, so the Smiths invited them into their own home. But in May 1968, after their residence became overcrowded, Smith rented a two-bedroom house for youths making a transition from drugs to Jesus. At the end of the first week, 21 new Christians were living in the house, and a week later there were 35, with one person sleeping in the bathtub. Before long there was a network of these Jesus houses, including a hotel in Riverside, California, where 65 young people were baptized in a fishpond in the second week of its occupancy. That first summer, 500 people converted in Riverside alone, and active ministries were spreading throughout southern California and northward to Oregon.

Meanwhile, the church leaders built a new chapel on the Greenville School property, assuming that 300 seats would be the ideal size. But the first Sunday, every seat was taken. The next Sunday they added 50 folding chairs in the foyer. Before long they were offering triple services, with people sitting on the floor, in the aisles, and in adjoining rooms. Finally, they doubled their seating capacity by moving out the side walls, but before long they could not accommodate everyone even with 500 extra chairs set up on the patio. This growth forced them to exercise considerable faith: they bought eleven acres of property a few blocks away for $300,000.

"We immediately put in the parking lot," says Smith, "and bought a big, old circus tent to accommodate the people before winter. We set 1,600 chairs in that circus tent and planned double services. The Saturday night before opening on Sunday morning, we had a prayer meeting. After the prayer meeting some of the fellows went over and stood on the platform. The men were finishing the lights and getting everything all set. I looked out at that sea of folding chairs. I had never seen so many folding chairs in all my life! I turned to Duane [a volunteer] and asked, 'How long do you suppose it will take the Lord to fill this place?' He looked at his watch and said, 'I'd say just about eleven hours.'"[3]

By the next winter they had built an addition onto the back of the tent to accommodate another 400 chairs. In 1974 they finally built a permanent sanctuary that seats 2,300 people. Within three weeks of opening the new building, they were holding triple services. A short time later they built Fellowship Hall to seat 700 people and piped in closed-circuit television. The push to expand might have continued if Smith had not begun to mentor young converts to start Calvary Chapels in their own neighboring cities. Instead of commuting to Calvary Costa Mesa, people could now experience a similar style of worship in their local communities. And so the Calvary Chapel movement was born.

Of the over 600 Calvary Chapels worldwide, some of the largest churches were started by "sons" of Chuck Smith: young converts who observed the low-key leadership of the person who nurtured their new-found faith. Some of these churches took the name Calvary Chapel, but not all.[4] Smith was not attempting to create a denomination; rather, what emerged was a loose fellowship of like-minded people. Statistics in the early 1990s put weekly attendance at San Diego's Horizon Christian Fellowship at 6,500, Riverside's Harvest Christian Fellowship at 9,000, Covina/Diamond Bar's Calvary Chapel Golden Springs at 8,500, Downey's Calvary Chapel at 12,000, Albuquerque's Calvary Chapel at 7,300, and New York's Calvary Chapel Finger Lakes at 4,500.

Not all Calvary Chapels are mega-size congregations. The median congregation has 138 people in attendance on a typical Sunday morning, according to the 200 Calvary Chapel pastors who responded to our survey. A quarter of the churches were founded in the two years before the survey, and three-quarters a dozen or fewer years ago. Although there are a number of large congregations within the Calvary fold, this is a relatively young movement that is continually planting new churches. The median budget of a congregation in the early 1990s was $70,000. Three-quarters of the groups were meeting in rented space, although many of them had a growing building fund. For seven out of ten congregations, the current pastor was the first and only minister.

Chuck Smith's view on planting churches is highly pragmatic. Converts who feel a call to the ministry, and who have spent enough time around the church to understand the philosophy of Calvary Chapel, are sent on their way with prayer and a blessing—but seldom with money. Those who are genuinely called to ministry, Smith reasons, will have a congregation that can support them in a few years; if this does not occur, then God probably has some other intention for them. In Smith's view, external financial support often keeps young pastors from relying on God as completely as they should. Nevertheless, with consensus from his board of elders, Smith has frequently lent money to churches that are overflowing with people and need to purchase property and/or build a place to worship. These loans, however, are always short-term so that congregations maintain their autonomy.

Independence is a hallmark of the relationship between the Costa Mesa mother church and the many Calvary Chapels born out of it. Each church is separately incorporated, and there is virtually no reporting back to Costa Mesa, except for the friendly phone calls that might occur between a father and his sons. As the movement has grown, the numerous mega-size churches have planted many "offspring," and the relationship of these new congregations is not directly to Costa Mesa, but to the congregation where the pastor was mentored. There is no attempt to centralize authority or offer programmatic materials. Every church is free to print its own curricular materials for Sunday school and other programs. Many of the mega-size congregations have their own pastor training schools, and there is no ambition to create a Calvary

Chapel seminary. This is a movement built on relationships, not centralized authority or formal reporting structures.

Asked about what is preventing a movement the size of Calvary from becoming a denomination, Smith emphatically answers, "Me," and then clarifies how a relationally based movement was ensured "by being fiercely independent and implanting this independence in them [the offspring churches]; by each of them incorporating independently; by not requiring reports; by keeping the affiliation [of churches] just a very loose affiliation." He states that there are no requirements, no calls, no letters from headquarters, unless there are major deviations from Calvary Chapel philosophy, at which point there might be a call from "Dad" to inquire what is going on. Calvary Chapel doctrine, if it can be called that, is simple. On many points there can be diversity of opinion so long as the centrality of scripture is maintained, along with such fundamental Christian beliefs as the deity of Christ and the resurrection of Jesus.

Smith explains that Calvary Chapel fits somewhere in the broad spectrum between Baptists and Pentecostals. He indicates that he believes in the gifts of the spirit, as do charismatic Christians, but that they should never be the focus of worship. As with Baptists, says Smith, teaching the Bible is the central goal of worship, although in private and small group meetings (as opposed to the larger worship services) the gifts of tongues, healing, word of knowledge, and prophecy are practiced as specified in Saint Paul's instructions to the early Christian church. He claims to be an "evangelical" but winces slightly at the label "fundamentalist" because of the authoritarianism and strict rules, as well as the defensiveness, associated with that tradition. Rather than drawing a hard line on who is "in" and who is "out," he says that membership in the Calvary movement is a matter of whether you are "fellowshipping" (in regular communication) with us or not.

The trademark of the doctrine of Chuck Smith and all Calvary Chapels is their verse-by-verse exposition of the Bible. In his years with the Foursquare denomination, Smith reports, he was a "topical" preacher, jumping from one passage to another as he sought to cover the major concepts and doctrines of Christianity. Every sermon was an effort to prepare, and after about two years of preaching he had to change churches to avoid repeating himself. Since abandoning this "hodgepodging" around the Bible, he has, in his words, been "cruising."[5] Sometimes he takes a few verses and other times a few chapters, but Smith's approach and that of most Calvary pastors is to teach consecutively through the Bible, book by book. Smith's goal is to have "the best fed sheep" in the church. In his view, healthy sheep will want to share their faith with others, helping the flock reproduce.

Although Calvary Chapel has not developed systematic doctrine to which all pastors must subscribe, many of them have spent hundreds of hours listening to Chuck Smith's Bible study tapes. The "Word for Today" tape catalog contains 1,000 different titles of Old and New Testament commentaries, in-depth studies, and Sunday morning sermons delivered by Chuck Smith. Tens of thousands of these tapes have been given away to overseas missionaries and to people who have requested them; otherwise, they are sold for a nominal amount and may be ordered individually or as a set. Many of the pastors of the larger churches have created their own tapes, so church members can listen to their own pastor on tape while commuting to work. As a result of modern tape-duplicating technology, it is often possible to pick up a copy of the pastor's sermon on the way out of church on Sunday morning. Committed members may opt for audio- or videotapes packaged into topical sets and sold in special cases.

The music that has been produced since the early days of the Jesus movement is another trademark of Calvary Chapel. Although one can still hear traditional hymns at some Calvary Chapels, especially Costa Mesa, a new generation of Christian music was introduced by Calvary-sponsored groups such as Love Song, The Children of the Day, The Way, Gentle Faith, Country Faith, and others. Using contemporary instrumentation similar to what one might hear at a rock concert, these groups have written lyrics that express their perception of an encounter with Jesus. This contemporary music has been vital to the Calvary movement: without it, how many young people would have bothered to listen to the movement's relatively conservative biblical teaching?

Calvary Chapel can be viewed as the pioneer of new paradigm churches. Hope Chapel has similar denominational roots in the International Church of the Foursquare Gospel through its founder, Ralph Moore.

Hope Chapel

I had been visiting new paradigm churches in southern California for several months before I had an opportunity to observe a baptism. After driving an hour from my home in Pasadena, I arrived ten minutes late at the announced site in Hermosa Beach, fearing that I might have missed the opening moments of the ceremony. I checked through the turnstile at the "Seaside Lagoon," where, to my surprise, my parking pass was validated by a member of Hope Chapel, and I immediately entered a large public park. On one end were sand volleyball courts; on the other, a grass area with picnic tables and barbecues. In the center was a saltwater lagoon with a roped-off swimming area, children's wading pool, and floating platform.

Concerned that I was late, I looked for the baptism and instead saw hundreds of people enjoying Sunday afternoon at the beach. I smelled cooking hamburgers and chicken. Children were playing in the water. Adults were sprawled on the sand talking. Most of the tables were already filled, so mothers were spreading tablecloths on the grass. Everyone was in shorts, sundresses, or bathing suits, and I suddenly felt overdressed in my long pants. I also felt mildly awkward, as if I were crashing someone's family picnic. But it was a warm evening with the sea breezes blowing, and after a few minutes I joined the many members of Hope Chapel on the sand.

I got out my notebook and began writing a few observations. It was difficult to separate church members from other sun worshipers, but I estimated that there might be 500 to 600 people who were part of the Hope Chapel community. The mean age was early thirties, although there were plenty of teenagers, numerous babies crawling on the grass, and an occasional graying head. Most people were white, although I observed several African Americans and a few Asian Americans. It looked like a fairly middle-class crowd, even though the surroundings were affluent, with the adjoining harbor filled with luxury sailboats.

After about fifteen minutes I saw the pastor, Zac Nazarian, walk through the turnstile with his family. Tall, tanned, wearing shorts, he obviously felt at home on the beach. Every few yards he stopped to greet someone. An hour later, as families were cleaning up the remains of their picnic dinners, a microphone and small stage area were set up, and someone with an amplified guitar began leading people in typical Hope Chapel songs. After about twenty minutes of the crowd singing, Nazarian took the microphone. To his right was a line of some seventy people waiting to be baptized. They were both male and female, of all ages and shapes. Nazarian invited them one by one to the microphone to give their names and say a few words about themselves. The audience clapped after each person's statement. I found myself surprised at how relaxed the speakers were as they shared a brief testimony. One person had been "saved" just three hours before; a couple in their sixties, baptized in the Presbyterian church as children, were now "rededicating their lives to Christ" as a result of finding Hope Chapel. Perhaps a third of those being baptized were former Catholics. A majority said that they had committed themselves to Jesus within the last several months. The dominant refrain was, "I was doing things my way, and now I want to give everything to Jesus and follow him."

People seemed to enjoy sharing their testimonies. Several cited drugs or divorce as the precipitating factor that brought them to Hope Chapel. Others talked about a general feeling of emptiness and commented on the family warmth they found the very first time they came to Hope Chapel. As they were talking, I flashed back to another baptismal scene, the one recorded in the Synoptic Gospels when John baptizes people at the River Jordan, and I began to wonder if those first-century converts might have said something similar to the seventy people I had just heard give witness. However, before I could reflect further, it was time to head down to the lagoon for the official act of immersion. Two rows of converts lined up, and several pastors in their swimsuits waded waist-deep into the water. One by one, individuals were tipped backwards by the two pastors at both stations. I could not hear what was said, but I did notice the flash from a camera as each person was lifted back onto her or his feet.

As I drove home that evening I found myself deep in thought about the differences between the baptisms I had just witnessed and the sacrament of baptism in my own Episcopal church. I also contemplated the relaxed and joyous style of the people. They seemed to be having fun! Their religion might be filled with commitment, but it was not at the expense of celebration. I didn't sense, even among the youth, that they were there out of obligation. They seemed to have found something that was giving their lives an important new focus. I wondered how many of these individuals would be in a mainline church if they were not at Hope Chapel.

THE HISTORY OF HOPE CHAPEL

Except for the generational difference, there are striking parallels between Ralph Moore, the founder of Hope Chapel, and Chuck Smith, the founder of Calvary Chapel. Smith is clearly the elder statesman, old enough to be Moore's father, but their pedigree is similar. Both grew up in the International Church of the Foursquare Gospel founded by the evangelist and healer Aimee Semple McPherson. Both went to L.I.F.E. Bible College, a Foursquare-sponsored school. Both were mentored by Nathaniel M. Van Cleave, a respected professor at L.I.F.E. and a senior figure in the Foursquare movement. Both served as pastors in the Foursquare denomination. Although Smith left the denomination and Moore remains a loyal member, it was Smith who influenced Moore to teach through the Bible, verse by verse and chapter by chapter.

From age six, Ralph Moore fought against the feeling that he was destined to become a pastor. Finally, at age seventeen, he had to choose whether to pursue architecture, a field that spoke strongly to his creative talents, or to attend the denominational college. After thirty days of reading ten chapters of the Bible each day, he acknowledged the pastoral call and somewhat grudgingly headed to Los Angeles from Portland, Oregon. It was there that he met Professor Van Cleave as well as Jack Hayford, the dean of students.[6] It was Hayford who challenged Moore's rebellious attitude and told him he should run for student body president rather than complain about the school, a challenge he accepted.

After graduation Moore was serving as an assistant pastor in a Foursquare church when one day, he says, he heard God speak aloud to him in a crowded restaurant telling him that he should take the pastorate of a small Foursquare church in Redondo Beach, California. The church held only seventy-two people and offered parking for just a few cars, but even this structure seemed too large for the small congregation. The timing of this divine direction was not good: Moore's wife was pregnant and had quit her job, and their only savings were earmarked for the down payment on a house. At first even Dr. Van Cleave, his former professor and then district supervisor for the denomination, tried to talk him out of the decision. But when Moore told Van Cleave about God speaking audibly to him, Van Cleave gave Moore his blessing. In September 1971, Ralph Moore, his wife, and his newborn son, along with a few relatives and friends, pulled a few chairs into a circle to worship together at the Redondo Beach church.

Frustrated that no one was coming to his church, Moore assessed the neighborhood and decided that the group no other church was reaching was young, single adults. So he began taking out newspaper ads and distributing flyers targeted to this population. But the church exploded with growth when he persuaded a Christian philanthropist to fund the purchase of 20,000 copies of David Wilkerson's book *The Cross and the Switchblade*. To each book, members of Moore's fledgling congregation attached a little sticker that said, "Need Help? Call Hope Chapel," giving Moore's home telephone number as a 24-hour hotline. Congregants gave away the books in front of schools, at the beach, and in jails.

The next few months were some of the most exciting in his life, reports Moore. Before long the congregation had to knock out the walls that enclosed several small classrooms, and, by also eliminating the church office and baptistery, they were able to crowd 200 people into the church. This expansion was followed by double services, buying a house nearby for additional Sunday school classroom space, and erecting a 14-foot-square tin lawn shed to accommodate more people. Then the church moved to a community center for Sunday services, and before long it was so packed that people were sitting on stacked tumbling mats in the rear and looking inside through windows and open doors.

Clearly, larger and more permanent facilities were needed, so Moore and members of his growing congregation canvassed the area. "We tried to buy four or five other churches and only got them mad at us in the process," reminisces Moore. "We looked at industrial space, at vacant supermarkets, and got into a race with the Federal government for a huge warehouse. We tried to buy a high school and junior high school. You name it, we knew the size of the property and how much it cost. We knew everything about every chunk of land in the South Bay."[7] The piece of property Moore kept revisiting was a bankrupt bowling alley in nearby Hermosa Beach that had been vandalized and gutted; it was about 30 percent larger than a football field.

At first the congregation wrote a letter to the owner suggesting that he donate the property as a tax write-off. As might be expected, they didn't even receive a response. Eventually the property was auctioned. Although Moore negotiated a loan with the Foursquare denomination for a preset amount, it was not sufficient to match the bid from the developer of a racquetball sports center. However, the city would not give the new buyer engineering approval for this renovation, and the members of Hope Chapel ended up with the property, which they still occupy. Their current auditorium seats only 800 people, so to accommodate the 2,500 who come to services on a typical weekend, they have Friday, Saturday, and Sunday night services, as well as worship Sunday morning at both the bowling alley location and a nearby community auditorium. They are now attempting to purchase the supermarket that adjoins their property.

Ralph Moore is no longer the pastor, however. Inspired by a vision that he believed was a direct revelation from God, Moore left the

Hermosa Beach church in 1983 to start a new Hope Chapel in Hawaii, the thirtieth church to issue from the Hermosa Beach congregation in twelve years. The first week they met under a tree in Kailua Beach Park, with sixty-four people present. According to Moore, "You should have seen the place! Beach chairs and boogie boards were piled everywhere. We brought tons of food, and ice chests abounded. It looked more like a company picnic than a church meeting."[8] Currently, Hope Chapel Kaneohe has an average of 1,400 people attending each weekend. The congregation has started another twenty churches in the Hawaiian Islands and elsewhere. Although Moore's church is still meeting in rented space on a public school campus, it has purchased property and hopes to begin construction shortly. Unlike the California congregation that Moore left, this church is only about 30 percent white; the majority are of Asian and Pacific Islander descent.

Central to the life of both the Hermosa Beach and Kaneohe congregations are "MiniChurches." Members and staff alike assert that these meetings are the core experience of their Christian life, and that the large group weekend services are secondary in importance. In these small group meetings people are nurtured in their religious faith, and leadership is developed. Each group has a "shepherd" and an understudy, and if the group grows too large, threatening its intimacy, then the understudy becomes the shepherd and the existing leader starts a new MiniChurch. Through this process, hundreds of people are trained. Furthermore, it becomes apparent which individuals have the gift to shepherd and proliferate small groups, and these are the people who commonly become the pastors of new Hope Chapel churches.

Ralph Moore's principal self-image is not as a charismatic leader, but as someone who is gifted at training and equipping others to do the work of ministry. He is drawn to rebellious, natural leaders—like himself in college—whose leadership abilities can be channeled and developed. His strategy is to work with these individuals and then send them off with a segment of his congregation to create another church. While this means that his church is constantly losing leaders, their departure creates the opportunity for newcomers to fill their shoes. Thus, Moore sent his strongest assistant, John Honald, along with 200 members of his church, to start a new ministry on another part of the island. In two years, this new church has more than doubled in size, and, equally important, Moore's church has more than replaced the 200 people it lost.

The church that Moore founded in Hermosa Beach is prospering under the leadership of Zac Nazarian, a former pharmacist who started coming to Hope Chapel after his marriage dissolved and he was desperately seeking a new way of life. Earlier, following his graduation from the University of Southern California, Nazarian traveled through Europe and Asia on the "Hashish Trail." He then opened a pharmacy in Kona, Hawaii, where he sold legitimate drugs by day but operated a marijuana farm in the mountains by night. A natural entrepreneur, he went from the drug business (both legal and illegal) into a rapidly expanding pyramid-style sales business, but then his life fell apart. He came home one day to find his wife gone and everything cleaned out of the house, including the telephone. Although he had been a Catholic, Nazarian now turned to Hope Chapel, which he had attended several times at the urging of his former spouse. Immediately he began to establish a new way of life, compulsively studying the Bible and attending multiple services on Sunday, plus every service that he could find on weekdays. Ralph Moore describes Nazarian as a voracious learner. When Moore was looking for his own replacement several years later, he turned to Nazarian. In retrospect, Moore says that Nazarian's organizational skills took the church to a new level, one that the "pioneer" Moore says he personally could not have achieved.

Compared with Calvary Chapel and the Vineyard Fellowship, Hope Chapel may occupy a theological middle ground. Whereas Calvary relegates the expression of charismatic gifts to the private realm of personal prayer and the Vineyard welcomes the gifts of tongues and healing in public worship, Hope Chapel channels these charismatic expressions into the MiniChurch or the prayer room but does not encourage them in public worship. Hope also seems to occupy a middle ground denominationally, electing to remain a part of the International Church of the Foursquare Gospel but snubbing some of the routinized expectations of denominational life. The position we heard expressed more than once is that "it is easier to ask for forgiveness than permission" in negotiating what are often perceived to be archaic rules and bylaws (even though the denomination is less than eighty years old). Clearly it is personal loyalty to individuals in the church that keeps Ralph Moore attached to the Foursquare denomination, but one wonders what the growth rate of the Hope movement would have been without this umbrella covering. In spite of its impressive spawning of fifty churches in only two decades, Hope Chapel's growth is no match for the proliferation in Calvary during the same period. Nor does it come close to the growth of the Vineyard Christian Fellowship, which has its own distinctive story.

The Vineyard Christian Fellowship

My initial visit to the Vineyard happened to be the first Sunday that the Anaheim Vineyard was meeting in its new "interim" facility, a huge white tent in a newly blacktopped parking lot that seated nearly 3,000 people. In the background stood a warehouse-like facility that was being renovated into office space and an auditorium. Across the street was a Mercedes-Benz dealership, and on both sides industrial buildings stretched several blocks. The August breeze wafted through the tent, cooling the several thousand people sitting on folding chairs on the artificial grass carpeting. Behind the tent, temporary trailers housed the children's programs. Between the tent and trailers, a kiosk offered coffee and donuts as well as literature describing various kinship groups and programs.

Sitting in the tent, I was surrounded by people in their mid-twenties to early thirties and their numerous babies and toddlers, but I also noted a surprising number of older people. At the front of the tent was a stage, filled with amplifiers, speakers, and microphones. The worship leader, a man in his late thirties, said a brief prayer welcoming the Holy Spirit into our presence, and then the band began to play. There were three female vocalists at separate microphones, someone on bass guitar, a drummer, two people playing acoustic guitars, and an individual playing keyboards. The sound was melodic; indeed, there was a distinct sweetness to their soft rock music. But this band was not "performing"; they were worshiping, and the congregation sang with them, as the lyrics were projected onto a side of the tent.

From my vantage point on the aisle, I watched as people closed their eyes, some with hands outstretched. They seemed oblivious to anyone else; they appeared to sink deep within the recesses of their own consciousness. People sat, stood, knelt, or raised their hands as the spirit moved them. I found myself thinking of the worship I had observed at Taizé, France, where tens of thousands of young people journey annually to join the robed brothers in chanting worship three times a day. The power of music to communicate, to mediate the sacred is something that my fellow sociologists have too long ignored. What struck me was that these people were not singing *about* God, they were singing *to* God, and something seemed to be reaching back to them—or stirring deep within their individual psyches, or maybe both. I pondered whether it made sense to draw sharp distinctions between sacred or secular, spirit or psyche.

At the end of nearly forty minutes, offering baskets were passed without comment, and then a tall man in his mid-forties stood in the audience and issued a prophecy. I could not make out the exact content, but there were references to several scriptures, and the people around him seemed respectful. Then John Wimber mounted the stage, and a simple lectern was lifted into place. Wimber, overweight and in his sixties, was wearing a polo shirt. In a quiet voice he said that several years ago he had had a vision of this very tent and had even made a drawing of it. The implication, that we were witnesses to a prophecy fulfilled, did not seem to surprise the Vineyard members.

Wimber's message was straight-line evangelical teaching, as nearly as I could tell. Stylistically, he showed a certain self-deprecating humor; one quickly realized that this man was not perfect. He disclosed that God speaks to him and through him, but not because he is saintly; that like everyone else, he is a sinner who is grateful for the cross of Jesus, which heals his brokenness. Indeed, he pointed out, the difference between Christians and other people is that Christians know that they are not perfect but nevertheless attempt to live up to high standards. Wimber's sermon seemed unrehearsed, but biblical in tone and references. He communicated best when he did not refer to his notes.

At the close of the sermon Wimber mentioned that he was seeing "sevens" all around him, and he interpreted this to mean that seven people were to give their hearts to God that morning. He then issued a rather standard invitation for salvation, and six people walked forward. But where was the seventh? Wimber looked to his left and said that he saw a "glow" in that portion of the audience; in a few moments a person sitting there stood up and joined the other six in front. I was skeptical, but for the believers in the audience this was an obvious confirmation of Wimber's vision.

I then observed something that was to recur at all my subsequent visits to the Anaheim Vineyard. As the band played softly, small groups of people formed all over the tent, including several dozen people who came to the front. It was "ministry time," and in an extraordinarily natural way people prayed for those who expressed a need. What was remarkable to me was the way that human touch was incorporated into this ritual moment and the fact that healing power was put in the hands of the people—to minister to each other—rather than reserved for those with clerical status. After briefly inquiring about the person's needs, a member of the ministry team, or in some cases just a friend, put a hand on the other's shoulder, or sometimes the forehead, and prayed for that person.

On a number of occasions I observed people shaking, sometimes quite uncontrollably, while they were being prayed for. Their hands might tremble slightly, or their entire bodies might move, as if possessed—presumably by what they interpreted to be the Holy Spirit. I drew a parallel to the "spirit" possession described in anthropology texts, yet I was surprised at how natural all this seemed—even in an industrial park across from a Mercedes dealership. The cynical outsider might dismiss this as "primitive" behavior. But why, I asked myself, should we believe the body is disengaged from the spirit? Perhaps we have lost something in our dualistic Western approach to reality. Who is to say that we have advanced by transferring all feelings and emotions to the mind?

THE HISTORY OF THE VINEYARD

The roots of the Vineyard are somewhat more complex and tangled than the relatively straightforward history of the growth of Calvary and Hope Chapels.[9] Kenn Gulliksen started the first Vineyard church in 1974 and can properly be credited as the founder of the Vineyard. Since 1982, however, John Wimber has provided leadership for the Vineyard movement as a distinct organizational entity; he is the founder of the mother church in Anaheim and is known worldwide as the current spokesman of the Vineyard movement. Although Gulliksen served as the overseer of Vineyard churches in the United States until 1992, he disagreed with the denominational direction of the Vineyard under Wimber's leadership and left the movement to start a new church, Metrowest, which is independent from the Association of Vineyard Churches.

Gulliksen grew up Lutheran and had a conversion experience at age fourteen. Three years later, at a church summer camp, Gulliksen and many of the other teenagers present spoke in tongues, and, as a result of their testimonies, several hundred youngsters had dramatic conversion experiences in the next few months. Following high school, Gul-liksen entered the U.S. Air Force and spent four years in Alaska. When he returned, the Jesus movement was in full swing, and he became as-sociated with Calvary Chapel, where he was ordained as a pastor in 1971. Shortly thereafter he left for El Paso, Texas, to lead a Calvary-style ministry called the Jesus Chapels. This work grew rapidly, in part from the migration of people from a mainline church. As Gulliksen re-calls: "Our greatest success was with the upper . . . Episcopalians across town. They started coming to the Bible studies, and they started want-ing more of the Lord, more of the Holy Spirit. One night eighty of them showed up, including the rector. We prayed for them and they all were filled with the Holy Spirit; many of them spoke in tongues, including the rector. It revolutionized this Episcopal church, so that they in turn went out and planted a church. It was just awesome."

After several years in El Paso, Gulliksen and his wife, Joni, returned to Costa Mesa, where they were part of the Calvary ministry for a brief period before they launched the first Vineyard. According to Gulliksen, "It started with five people in Chuck Girard's house in July 1974. It im-mediately exploded. Frankly, this may sound very unhumble and very arrogant, but we fully expected it because the one thing that we learned at Calvary was how to have vision. We fully expected that we would have a huge church, just because that was the vision that Chuck [Smith] in-stilled in us, and that we had experienced in El Paso. So there was not a doubt that this thing was going to happen." As Gulliksen explains: "I also knew how to teach the Bible by then. I played guitar and sat on a stool and led some worship and taught the Bible, answered questions in homes, and at the end invited anyone who wanted to receive Christ to come for prayer, which they did in droves. So we kept having to move from place to place to place to place." In addition to growing to several thousand people in weekly attendance at this church, another half dozen Vineyards (associated with Calvary Chapel) were started.

Meanwhile, the other root of the Vineyard was forming. John Wim-ber, born in 1934 in Kirksville, Missouri, of hillbilly stock, had moved to Yorba Linda, California. He was ambitious, and while he never lost his compassion for the poor, he wanted a different lifestyle from that of his parents. By age fifteen he had become a semiprofessional musician, and by age eighteen he was earning a living as a professional artist. By 1963 Wimber had recorded several albums that sold extremely well, and he had every reason to think that his affluence would continue to in-crease. At the time, however, his marriage to Carol, the daughter of a physician, was on the rocks. Faced with this conflict, Wimber, a self-described third-generation pagan, listened attentively when his friend Dick Hine talked about his conversion to Christ.

Wimber followed Hine into an Evangelical Friends church in Yorba Linda, which nurtured his new faith. Describing the influence of this Quaker church on his current beliefs, Wimber states: "Some of the people who mentored me were deeply committed to Quaker values and practices, and I committed myself to them. And so I am not a culture-current Quaker—I do not hold a lot of the views that many of them would espouse today—but I am nevertheless thoroughly committed to Quaker theology and practice in its ethos. I would probably be more of a seventeenth-century Quaker in that I have been very impacted early on by George Fox and by some of the early writers who expounded and established the Quaker movement." Wimber explains that his Quaker roots are particularly reflected in his concern with the poor and his commitment to social justice. However, he rejects what he views as the Platonic metaphysics of much of Quaker mysticism and instead firmly professes a biblical worldview.

For a number of years, Wimber was a faithful member of this Friends church, teaching Bible studies in his home and leading an adult Sunday school class. Indeed, his interest in the church blossomed after his conversion, and for three years in the mid-seventies he served as a church growth consultant for the Fuller Evangelistic Association, visiting as many as 2,000 different churches. This experience was harnessed in 1976, when he attended Sunday evening "afterglows" in a home. These events included members of the Friends church, but they soon exploded with growth and became too charismatic in character to remain part of the Friends church. So on May 10, 1977, a group of people from the "afterglows" gathered for their first formal meeting in the Masonic lodge across the street from the Friends church. This facility rapidly filled, and over the next few years, with John Wimber as its pastor and Carl Tuttle leading worship, the church moved from one rented school auditorium to another, growing in size to about 1,500 people in five years. Wimber associated this congregation with the growing movement of Calvary Chapel churches, and they were known as Calvary Chapel of Yorba Linda.

At a fateful meeting in 1982, Chuck Smith gathered together some of the pastors of the larger Calvary Chapels. Kenn Gulliksen and John Wimber were both present, along with Mike McIntosh, Greg Laurie,

Jeff Johnson, Raul Reis, and several others who would go on to pastor huge congregations. Some of these young pastors immediately put Wimber on the hot seat for the exercise of charismatic gifts in his church. In spite of Chuck Smith's background in the Foursquare church, he deemphasized overt expression of tongues, prophecy, and healing in public worship. Smith, Gulliksen, and Wimber have essentially the same recollections of this meeting. After interrogation by some of the other pastors, Wimber suggested changing the name of his congregation. Smith concurred and noted that Wimber's emphasis on the gifts of the Holy Spirit had many parallels to what was occurring at Gulliksen's Vineyard church. A friendship had already developed between Wimber and Gulliksen, so the match seemed perfect, and thus the Vineyard movement was born in 1982 as an organizational entity separate from Calvary Chapel.

The way in which John Wimber assumed leadership of the fledgling Vineyard movement is a story in itself. Gulliksen explains that in 1982 he felt overwhelmed trying to oversee the handful of Vineyards that existed at the time. He was working fourteen hours a day and felt he needed another fourteen hours to respond to all the demands on him. In addition, he had a young family that he was neglecting. In his words, "I was over the edge and didn't know what to do. I was ready for an emotional breakdown." For Gulliksen, "John was like a savior in a fat man's body for me at the time."

As Gulliksen recalls, "When John came, we had really no organization apart from a deep love for one another and a relationship." Gulliksen had always been a "pioneer," not a "homesteader," and he saw his gift as the ability to plant new churches and then give them to someone else to tend. In fact, in 1983, the year after Wimber took over the leadership, Gulliksen went to Newport Beach and started another Vineyard, which quickly grew to 1,400 people.

What was probably not anticipated at the 1982 meeting was that not only would the existing eight Vineyard Fellowships merge, but another thirty Calvary Chapels would join this new Vineyard movement. Over the next few years, according to Smith, a number of additional Calvary Chapels decided to affiliate with the Vineyard.

Pinpointing the differences between the two movements, Gulliksen explains that the thirty Calvarys that initially joined the Vineyard "were pastored by people who were hungry for more of the Holy Spirit in their own churches, in their own lives. They were more risk takers, possibly more pioneering, and they were people who had had previous relation-ships with John." The main line of demarcation between the two move-ments is their attitude toward the gifts of the spirit.[10]

Since 1982 the Vineyard movement has been largely associated with John Wimber. The movement has grown dramatically since the early eighties and now has 400 churches in the United States and almost 200 churches abroad (including Canada). Embracing Christianity wherever he finds it, Wimber mixes comfortably with Catholics, Anglicans, and some of the mainline denominations in America. He has given enormous energy to "renewal" (healing) conferences in England, Scotland, Ire-land, South Africa, New Zealand, Australia, Germany, France, Canada, and various Scandinavian countries. Indeed, he is probably better known in England than in the United States, with as many as 10,000 people at-tending his conferences there.

Some of the most vital Anglican churches in England are those that have been "Wimberized," meaning that the clergy, after attending Wimber-led conferences, have taken the gifts of healing and tongues back to their congregations. Until recently, Wimber had actually dis-couraged new Vineyards from being planted in England and some other countries because he did not want to compete with mainline denomi-nations. However, this policy has now changed, and Vineyards are sprouting up in England, Austria, Germany, and elsewhere.

Our survey of pastors in the early nineties showed that the median Vineyard Fellowship has 150 members, slightly more than the median Calvary, with 138. The Vineyard budgets are correspondingly higher ($91,000 vs. $70,000). A more significant difference, however, is in the number of congregations "adopted" from another denomination or movement, such as Assemblies of God that decided to become Vine-yards. Thirty-five percent of the Vineyards, compared with 13 percent of the Calvary Chapels, are adoptions. Many of these adoptions have re-sulted from pastors of other denominations attending a Wimber renewal conference. The Vineyard movement does not have as many mega-size congregations as Calvary, a difference that may, in part, reflect the rela-tive ages of the two movements; the large Calvary Chapels mostly be-gan in the 1970s, before the Vineyard was clearly identified as a move-ment. On the other hand, while Vineyards have tended to emphasize healing, Calvary Chapels have emphasized evangelism, with a concomi-tant emphasis on growth.

The Vineyard now identifies itself as a denomination, whereas Cal-vary Chapel prefers to view itself as a close-knit fellowship of churches. In declaring the Vineyard a denomination, Wimber has had to overcome the nearly phobic reaction of many baby boomer pastors to the idea of denominationalism. This term conjures up images of control, structure, and bureaucracy that are antithetical to their values. These pastors joined the Vineyard because it was culturally current, flexible, and continually innovating. When, at a pastors conference in 1988, the movement seemed on the verge of formalizing as a denomination, several highly respected leaders reported prophecies and dreams that temporarily purged the idea. Wimber came away from this conference with a strong feeling that the Vineyard movement should die, and for the next two or three years did much soul-searching about its future. He now interprets the ideology of independence as a reflection of baby boomer immaturity (i.e., resisting accountability), and he is moving to create regional overseers and more centralized reporting while maintaining a movement that is relationally, rather than bureaucratically, oriented.[11]

Drawing on his experience as a church growth consultant, Wimber fears that the baby boomer church that he helped to set up is in danger of losing its cultural currency, especially for the "baby busters," the generation born after the birthrate began to decline in the early sixties. In his view, churches should always seek a delicate balance among the *message,* the *model,* and the *market.* Wimber believes that the message remains the same: he firmly identifies himself as an evangelical with strong moorings in the Reformation. However, he contends, the model embodying the message must be sensitive to the market. Just as worship at the mainline denominations is currently trapped in seventeenth- and eighteenth-century models, worship at the Vineyard, grounded in the music of the 1960s, may sound hopelessly outdated to young members. In response to this potential datedness, the Vineyard aims to plant 500 churches led by baby buster pastors in the next decade.

Comparisons

Calvary, Hope, and the Vineyard have their own personalities. Calvary is a pioneer in reaching out to a generation of youth alienated from and basically untouched by existing churches. In contrast, Hope Chapel is a "movement within a denomination," striking out in new directions but maintaining loyalty to the community that nurtured the founder in his youth. The Vineyard is probably the most experimental of the three movements, exploring new modes of worship that break with traditional models of mind-body separation.

Nevertheless, there are decided similarities among these groups. All three have abandoned traditional styles of music and worship; they are reaching out in novel ways to people who might feel uncomfortable entering a mainstream church. And in all three groups individuals report powerful, life-changing experiences of the sacred. Learning dogma is less important than finding the Holy Spirit in day-to-day life.

These new paradigm churches are growing, while mainline churches are declining, because they address the issue of meaning for their audience in culturally appropriate ways. When Greg Laurie preaches, he identifies the void that teenagers feel in their lives. Zac Nazarian has his pulse on the fear of cultural decay that many teens and young families feel, and he addresses these anxieties in unambiguous ways, symbolized in the act of baptism and entry into a "new life." John Wimber comprehends people's deep need to be healed, physically and spiritually, and he responds to many individuals' frustration with the medical model by teaching them to "touch" each other in the name of Jesus.

All of this occurs in buildings that do not look like churches. Worship is led by people who do not dress or look like traditional clergy. The boundaries between the sacred and profane, as well as between clergy and laity, are dissolved as ordinary people take on the work of ministry. At another time and place, a different approach might be appropriate. But the target audience of these churches is people for whom *religion* is a hollow word. If the message is to make sense, it needs to be embodied in new forms.

CHAPTER 3

Transforming Your Life

The Process of Conversion

In the early 1990s Greg Laurie—with the backing of Chuck Smith and Calvary Costa Mesa—began organizing public "crusades" in various amphitheaters and stadiums. These events, which can last several days, have drawn hundreds of thousands of people and resulted in tens of thousands of converts. I attended one of the early Harvest Crusades, held in the Pacific Amphitheatre in Orange County, California. The posters, bumper stickers, and literature advertising the crusade were brightly colored and very contemporary in design, as were the T-shirts that many people wore. There was no charge for entering the crowded parking lot; Chuck Smith believes that "the gospel is free," and by offering free parking, Calvary shows it is not trying to generate money with these events.

In contrast to the demographics of the Monday evening Bible study described in the previous chapter, the average age of people attending the Harvest Crusade was mid-twenties to early thirties. As I walked across the parking lot the first night of the crusade, I noticed many young families entering the outdoor amphitheater, the parents hand-in-hand, with children romping next to them. But there were also many teens, young couples, and even a smattering of gray heads. Fifteen minutes from starting time, the amphitheater was already jammed, and people were filling the grassy knoll behind the regular seating. The atmosphere was carnival-like and the audience as anticipatory as fans awaiting a Madonna concert. Most of the people present were already part of the "born-again" family and had come to celebrate their Christian commitment, but they had brought their secular neighbors, friends, and family members.[1]

The Harvest Crusade certainly had a concertlike feel. Well-known Christian bands were there to perform, including the black-hatted Dennis Agajanian with his country-style guitar. Seated on the platform were also some well-chosen Calvary Chapel pastors, who had come to "testify" how Jesus had changed their lives. These practiced speakers knew their Generation X and baby boomer audiences well. In addition, there was a bevy of counselors trained for the crusade—people who, one on one, could answer questions and provide literature to the anticipated hundreds who would leave their seats to "accept Christ" at the close of each crusade evening. Every detail of the event had been thought through. High-amp speakers stood ready to project the contemporary music to the 10,000 or so people present. A special seating section offered signing for the hearing impaired, and simultaneous translation was available in both Korean and Spanish for the growing minority population in Orange County.

By the final night of the crusade, which was held in Anaheim Stadium, the audience had increased in size, and nearly 50,000 gathered to hear the testimony offered by Raul Reis, the pastor of a mega-size Calvary Chapel in southern California.

His father was an alcoholic and abusive to his mother, so Reis and his mother fled Mexico and came to the United States. As a teenager, he was angry and bitter, preoccupied with thoughts of killing his father. In his later teen years he got into lots of trouble and was given the choice of going to Vietnam or jail. He chose Vietnam; he arrived there on December 25 and went into combat on the 26th. He vented his anger on the Vietnamese—"I took pleasure in killing," he recalled—but he also saw thirty of his friends die. After ten months of duty he was psychotic, threatened to kill the psychiatrist in Vietnam who examined him, and was taken, shackled, to a hospital in Oakland, California.

When he was released, Reis met Sharon, a missionary's daughter; he got her pregnant and then married her. Continuing the same pattern of spousal abuse as his father, he was ready one night, five years and three children later, to murder his family and then commit suicide. But, Reis told the audience, God intervened in his life. As he was contemplating how to end his life, quite by chance he flipped the TV channel and became fascinated by a bald-headed man, who turned out to be Chuck Smith, talking about the Bible. According to Reis, this was one of the first times he had heard about the love of Christ: "After twenty-four years of hate, I began to weep. I prayed, 'Jesus, if you are real, come into my life.'" He then got into his car and drove to where Smith was preaching, went forward, and "committed himself to Christ."

This testimony was followed by several more Christian rock artists. The crowd seemed to relax, clapping and identifying with the casually dressed performers. For the nonreligious, the presentation showed that accepting Jesus doesn't require wearing a polyester suit and singing from a hymnal. In fact, a number of the performers first won recognition as secular musicians before committing their lives to Jesus. Their lyrics had changed, but not the tempo of their music.

Finally Chuck Smith came to the podium and said, "The decision you make tonight is the most important decision you will ever make, for it goes beyond your life. It is a decision for all eternity."

Greg Laurie followed up by announcing, "You have an appointment with God tonight," just as he had at the Monday night Bible study for teens at Costa Mesa. He then told the crowd to think about what happens after death. After citing some statistics about the number of people who believe in heaven, he quoted Billy Graham's statement that "Only those who are prepared to die are really ready to live." This quotation was flashed on the scoreboard to emphasize the point. Mixing references to *Newsweek* with quotes from Woody Allen ("Hell is the future abode of all the people who personally annoy me"), he maintained the attention of the large crowd, while also getting them to think beyond the moment. Putting aside the humor, he stressed: "You're responsible for sending yourself to hell, not God." When he said, "Your last breath on earth can be your first breath in heaven," people cheered and applauded.

The emptiness that individuals feel is because of their sins, Laurie explained, but the good news is that Christ died for these sins, and forgiveness is available to all who acknowledge him. At this point Laurie extended an invitation for those who wanted to join the family of God to come forward. In the next few minutes, thousands of people got up and headed for the playing field, until it was gridlocked with converts.

According to statistics from this and other crusades that Laurie has done, approximately one out of every twenty to thirty people present goes forward for salvation. Out of these, maybe 10 percent seriously pursue the commitment they make. These statistics do not discourage Laurie and others connected with the crusade. Nevertheless, Laurie feels that his true calling is as a pastor, not an evangelist, and that the real growth in the church occurs because "well-fed sheep reproduce."

In other words, it is the week-by-week teaching of the Bible in his own church that he views as his real calling. "Healthy sheep"—those who are well schooled in the Bible—bear witness to their friends; they also attract people to Christianity because of the quality of their lives and the love they express.

A Calvary Chapel in Upstate New York

After about a year of doing research on new paradigm churches in southern California, my research assistants and I gave a preliminary report on our findings at a professional meeting of sociologists of religion. The audience was clearly fascinated by the presentation, but they were also skeptical about the extent of the phenomenon. During the question period more than one of my colleagues implied that we were documenting a phenomenon that was strictly West Coast. After all, wasn't California, and particularly southern California, the hotbed of crazy cults, weird sects, and new religious movements?

After the conference I told Brenda Brasher, one of my two research assistants, "Find me a large Calvary Chapel on the East Coast. We're going to go visit it!" She found one in Farmington, New York, near the Finger Lakes, with about 3,000 people attending every Sunday. There would be no surfers, and the influence of Calvary Costa Mesa would be remote. With the permission of the pastor, Bil Gollatin, Brenda and I flew east to observe weekend services and then to interview staff and members during the early part of the week.

As we drove away from Rochester in our rented car, the landscape became more rural. From a demographic standpoint, I thought, "There couldn't be a more unlikely place to find a Calvary-style mega-church." We arrived at the church late Saturday afternoon. A youth conference was being held, and the sanctuary was filled with about 500 junior high students from Calvary as well as surrounding churches. The guest speaker, Dawson McAllister, had brought with him Todd Procter, a teen-idol singer in his early twenties. Together they talked to the kids about the hole in their lives, the feeling that something was missing. At the end of the evening session, dozens upon dozens of preteens came forward to surrender themselves to Jesus.

The following morning, I attended several Sunday services, which were vintage Calvary: the music, the understated biblical message by Pastor Bil, and the casual atmosphere. During the next few days we interviewed a number of people. I want to share several of their stories, beginning with that of Bil Gollatin.

THE SENIOR PASTOR

Bil Gollatin was born in 1937 in a steel-producing city on Lake Erie. His parents were hardworking providers, but both enjoyed partying and drinking, and his home life as a child was tumultuous. Bil's goal in high school was to be a professional athlete. He consistently was selected for all-star teams—until the summer of his junior year. "I was working on a farm in the summer," he recollects, "and my leg got caught in a hay elevator and it was destroyed, cutting my toes, crushing my foot, breaking my leg in seven places from the knee to the ankle. That was the end of athletics for me."

An A student throughout high school, Bil went on to college, but his motivation was seriously affected. "I just had anger for some reason in me," he reflects, "and I remember I started fighting a lot. I beat a guy up in our fraternity pretty badly and he almost lost his eye. . . . I found out that he had gone to a lawyer and they were going to sue me and bring charges, so I left school and joined the Marine Corps."

Bil married Rosemary, a Catholic and recent graduate of a nursing program, when he finished his two-year tour as a Marine. They immediately had a child, and Bil began to drink heavily and hang out with a group of sports-minded guys. He hated his job working indoors in a clothing store, and after filing for bankruptcy and being bailed out of jail several times by his wife, he decided it was time for a change. He told his wife, who had just given birth to their second child, that they were going to move from Ohio to Florida, where he could work on the construction of the new Disney World. With their Volkswagen bug piled high with possessions, Bil turned right when they hit Route 66 and headed toward California, not Florida. He had heard of the hippie movement and, to the protests of his wife, drove directly to Laguna Beach, the mecca of Timothy Leary and other gurus of the drug culture.

Bil quickly found a job in construction, but just as rapidly was introduced to drugs. He thought marijuana and later LSD were much better than alcohol. "I dropped out," he says. "I wasn't wearing shoes anymore. I went down to Baja on weekends." While his wife worked as a nurse at a local hospital and was the responsible adult in the household, he adopted the hippie lifestyle, long hair and all. "I didn't do it as a statement . . . an act of rebellion," he claims. "It wasn't that at all with me.

I just felt so free, out from all the pressure of having to achieve and make money. The whole material thing to me was false."

But a crisis occurred at the end of a trip to Mexico with some buddies. They had spent a week living on the beaches experimenting with mescaline, hash, and LSD. "On the way back," recalls Bil, "one of the guys had a hash pipe in my glove compartment and they [the border patrol] got us through residue and paraphernalia, and since the car was registered in my name they kept me, threw me in jail in San Diego, and they [his buddies] left." To his disappointment, "Not one of them lifted a finger to help me or anything. That kind of jolted me to reality, because everyone was going around, 'Peace brother,' and that whole phony scene." After paying a $500 bond to get out of jail, he returned home. There, inspired by the example of a Christian work associate who seemed sincere in all of his dealings, Bil reminisces: "I just started reading my Bible, staying home, and watching the kids." No one actively proselytized him. He followed an individual quest, but one that was highlighted by some unusual mystical experiences.

One day Bil went up to a graveyard on a hill overlooking the ocean and, while reading his Bible, had a strong sensation that the United States was going to be destroyed. As he describes it: "I drove up into the graveyard and I am sitting there on the hillside and as I look up toward Long Beach I see the whole coastline go up, like in nuclear explosions, and I was just shocked. I didn't know what to say. I didn't know who to tell." He adds: "It was a vision, and I just saw it and I knew that somehow America was going to be judged or destroyed. I didn't know who to tell. And see, I didn't know what was happening to me. I never had the Bible taught to me. I never went to a church where you heard the scriptures or knew about the Holy Spirit."

A short time after this experience Bil had a revelation in which Jesus appeared to him. Struggling to explain what he witnessed, he simply says that Jesus looked absolutely real, alive. "I came home to Rosemary," he remembers, "and told her, 'The end of the world is coming and Jesus is coming back.' I didn't know that much about scriptures— I just had read the book of Revelations and I read Matthew—and I just told her, 'Jesus is coming back. I can't explain it, honey, but I know he is real. He is the Lord.' . . . She's looking at me and she was thinking, 'Boy, he went over the edge this time.'"

A few days later Bil found himself in a psychiatric hospital, placed there by his wife, and he vividly recalls a fellow patient coming up to him and saying, "Don't worry. We'll be out of here pretty soon. *I'm*

Jesus." Because of his own religious perceptions, he was diagnosed as a paranoid schizophrenic (with a God fixation). However, after several weeks he was released from the hospital, and shortly thereafter picked up a hitchhiker who thanked him by saying, "Praise Jesus, have a good day." According to Bil, "After he got out of the car and stepped up on the curb, I was stunned. Something happened in my heart. I said, 'That sounds wonderful.' It did something to me, so I said, 'Why did you say that?' And he said, 'Well, I am a Christian.' I said, 'Well, where do you go to church?,' because he looked just like me and I thought he didn't look like he could go to church. He said, 'I go to the hippie church.' I said, 'The hippie church? Where's that?' He said, 'It is called Calvary. It is over in Costa Mesa on Sunflower Avenue.'"

This fleeting encounter took Bil on a search: "I eventually got there and I walked in. I said, 'I've got to talk to somebody about Jesus,' and it was Chuck [Smith]. I said, 'You know the world's coming to an end. Everybody thinks I'm nuts and I know Jesus is real. I've got to talk to somebody.' Chuck got a big grin on his face and said, 'Follow me.' I spent the rest of the day with him in his office."

The next Sunday Bil showed up at Calvary Chapel to discover that he had been talking with the minister himself. As he listened to the sermon, he found himself exclaiming silently, "I'm home. I found what I've been looking for all of my life." According to Bil, it was not the charisma of Chuck Smith, it was simply what he was teaching: "There was no guile, nothing phony. I knew-what-I-knew-what-I-knew. You can't explain that; you just know. That was it." Almost immediately, Bil became the carpenter, custodian, and handyman around Calvary. He remembers pouring the blacktop when they purchased the property for the current location, erecting the pipe for the tent, and building the patio cover over the picnic tables.

Rosemary Gollatin offers a slightly different memory of her husband's conversion: "I would go to work and talk about him, saying, 'Oh my gosh. Now he's into religion. First it is LSD and then it's marijuana. I can't keep up with him. It's one thing, and now it's Jesus.' It was just too bizarre for me to even understand. I couldn't figure out what he was doing, what was going on. All I saw was instability and another fad, another thing he was going to do. But one thing I knew was that God was changing him. I could tell that there was a definite change. He was having a desire to go to work, he was having a desire to stay sober, he didn't have a desire to drink anymore. His whole concept of living was entirely different after he met Christ." Suspicious of his religious change, however, Rosemary waited two years before she herself went to Calvary Chapel and joined Bil in his religious commitment.

THE CHILDREN'S PASTOR

Mike Sasso is the youth pastor at the Calvary Chapel that Bil Gollatin pastors. I met him when I visited one of the Sunday evening programs for younger children: a muscular, street-smart-looking fellow talking to the children about Jesus, picking them up and setting them on his knee, including a shy newcomer to the class who by the end of the hour kept bounding onto his lap. Why, I wondered, was he spending his time here on a Sunday night, rather than raising hell in a local bar? I was also intrigued by this group's pianist, who looked like a ski bum just off the slopes, but had an amazingly light touch as he played a song about Noah and the animals entering the ark.

Like Bil Gollatin, Mike Sasso was a drug abuser before his conversion experience. He told me that he got involved in drugs at a relatively early age, saying: "I ran into the wrong guys in Boy Scouts. Bronx Boy Scouts don't generally plan on camping. And I started to eat some pills. It was a big thing. Everyone in the neighborhood was doing it. It was the sixties and these things were available and, the next thing I know, I enjoyed it. I got into more and more of that lifestyle." He regularly used marijuana, uppers, methadone, and heroin, but in spite of his habit he finished high school and went to college on an athletic scholarship. However, in the middle of his freshman year he was in a serious auto accident that ended his football career, and he spent many weeks recovering from a fractured skull. For a brief period he quit using drugs, but when he returned to college he immediately started again and sold various narcotics.

Mike was working a construction job to pay for his schooling at the University of Nebraska. He had switched from his premed major because of the demands of the curriculum, but despite his habit was relatively functional. One evening, as he was relaxing in his apartment, Mike heard a knock on the door. As he tells it, "A man came in—a little bald-headed guy. He came in and asked me if I knew who Jesus was. And I told him, 'I sure do. Would you like a beer?' . . . He walked in—it was really weird—and Jesus stepped into my life. Before that, I had no understanding. I didn't know anything about the gospel. I can't remember anyone sharing anything about Jesus."

Declining the beer, his guest asked him if he *really* knew who Jesus was. Mike retorted, "Sure, and there is a number [marijuana cigarette] in the ashtray if you would like to light it up." And then on this fellow's urging, Mike recounted the Christmas story, drawing on his childhood memories in the Catholic church. When Mike finished, his guest asked, "Well, do you have a *relationship* with him?" And Mike replied, "No, anybody could tell you that God doesn't have relationships with people like me." Reflecting on his feelings at the time, Mike recalls: "I was really mad. He had no right bringing this up. I was ushering him to the door and he asked me if I had fear: If I died, where would I go? This seemed real irrelevant to me. I was nineteen, and I wasn't planning on dying."

After a few more exchanges about eternal life, Mike succeeded in removing this intruder. "I was really strung out and really needed to get rid of this guy," he remembers. "And as I shoved him out the door he gave me a tract that was like a million pages with six-point type. But it was perfect: because I was addicted to methadone, which leaves you somewhat functional; I wasn't going to sleep that whole night. So I sat up all night and I read this million-page tract. Somewhere in the evening I reached the end, and it was all about this personal relationship with Jesus, and I know it had a lot of things about the Gospel of John in it. By the end, I prayed the prayer. I wept and I saw that God has something to do with people like me. And I slept for a long time."

Like many of the people we interviewed, Mike became a zealous evangelist immediately after his conversion. As he describes it: "The next day, I got up. I called my girlfriend, and I told her to come over, that I had to tell her about something that happened to me. I told her about Jesus. She thought I had really fallen off the deep end. I had my friends over. I lined them all up on the couch, and I said, 'Listen to what happened to me.' And in my own ignorance, of course, I passed pot around and I am telling them all about this."

Several weeks later, Mike was arrested for his earlier drug dealing. He uttered a "foxhole" prayer, which the Lord answered; but by the time he was cleared of charges he was destitute. Forced to drop out of school, he was unemployed, and homeless. While surviving on the streets, he continued to announce his newfound Christianity. Then one day someone confronted him, asking: "If you're a Christian . . . where's your Bible?" This question took him back: "I didn't have one. So I went and got myself a Bible and went into a Christian bookstore. I proceeded to write a check for an account that had been closed for two months. The guy said, 'We don't take checks.' I said, 'Gee, I just met Jesus, and I was really into having a Bible.' He said, 'In this case, we'll take a check.' So I bought this thirteen-dollar Bible, and as I cleared the outside of the bookstore, I went to the corner and he is yelling behind me, 'Come back here! Come back here!' And I am thinking, 'I am snagged.' So I walked back, and he handed me the check back. He said, 'Jesus told me to give you this.'"

Like many of those we interviewed, Mike immersed himself in the New Testament. He was not part of a church; rather, his Bible reading was completely self-motivated as he tried to comprehend his conversion experience. In fact, he tried going to some churches, but he felt he was not welcome because of his long-haired, "spacey" appearance.

Needing employment, he applied for a custodial job in a complex of doctors' offices. "As I went in," he says, "I heard that they were going to polygraph us. I thought, 'Well, I am dead. There is no job here. I guess I'll leave.' But I didn't, and I thought I would try it. I remember reading that morning the scripture in Ephesians that said to lie no more, but to work hard and to tell the truth. I thought, 'All right. I'll do it.'"

"I went in," Mike continues, "sat down, and some big redneck guy from Louisiana hooked me up to the machine and asked all the pertinent questions: your name, do you drive a car, do you take drugs, have you ever been arrested, have you ever stolen anything from your employer? Most of my answers were 'yes.' At the end of the first round of questions he turned the machine off and he came around and he looked at me and he said, 'Now tell me, do you still do these things, son?' And I looked at him and I said: 'No. I met Jesus Christ four months ago. And I *still* don't do these things.' And he said, 'I am going to ask you this series again. Is that all right?' I said, 'Sure.' And we went through the whole series of questions and his last three were: 'Is Jesus Christ your Lord? Do you read a Bible?' And another question about Jesus. He turned the thing off and unhooked me. As I went out I asked, 'Well, how did I do?', and he said, 'You go on downstairs, and you tell "so and so" to give you the floor buffer. It pays a nickel an hour more.'"

THE CUSTODIAN

Chris Burton (not his real name) says that he started mainlining drugs at the age of fourteen and was an addict until his conversion at age twenty-five. "My family had renounced me as part of their family circle," he remarks. "I was no longer invited to family gatherings because of my condition. I was basically stoned all the time. Anything was expected if I came to your house—anywhere from finding me on the bathroom floor passed out with a needle stuck in my arm to freaking out on whatever drug I was taking or literally destroying your house because I smoked Angel dust. I shot heroine, I did LSD, I sniffed gasoline at one point. I just didn't care. There was no remorse for what I did. There was no care for what I did to myself; there was no such thing as caring about an eternal destination. I basically just wanted to get high, and I did anything I could to obtain that." Because he had had three drug overdoses, he notes, "My parents had taken out a burial insurance policy on me. They considered me dead already. I was down to about ninety-five pounds at the age of twenty-five."

To support his habit, Chris also sold drugs. He was supplied with illicit prescription drugs by a team of doctors. "There were probably a half a dozen doctors that were in it together," he explains, "and they took a lot of welfare people, which meant money in the hand real easy. They sold their pharmaceutical drugs to us as patients on a scale that they never had to pay. They paid, say, seven cents for a hit of morphine, and they sold it to us for seven dollars, and at a prescription of a hundred, that's seven hundred dollars a prescription. We would take the drugs, one hit that we paid seven dollars for we would sell for thirty-five dollars a hit on the street. So it was a very profitable thing to get into, for us and the doctors. I reached a high level with the doctors. I was considered a five-star patient."

Chris ended up in jail, but only after his life had been threatened by a cocaine dealer to whom he owed several thousand dollars. It was there that he called out to God. "I picked up a New Testament that was in jail," he recalls. "I started reading in it, and I believed in God because I grew up in somewhat of a Baptist background, but never really had a personal experience [of God]. I just said, 'God, if you're real, get me out of this.' I didn't want God just to get me out of jail. I wanted God to get me out of this life I was living, and I truly mean that and he knows I meant it, because it was kind of like . . . the last door that I could even try and open up or even go to before I called it quits."

Shortly after this prayer he found himself in court: "I went to face the judge, and I had talked to my warden, and I said, 'You know what, I really want to turn over a new leaf.' Of course, that doesn't go over with the judge—he's heard that before. They said, 'We'd like you to go through a drug program.' 'Whatever, I just don't want to go to prison.' So I sat in jail and I'd begin to pray, 'Lord, help me. I don't know what to do. I don't want to go back out in the streets.'" He knew that his parents would not visit him in jail, and he found his so-called friends did not show up, even to bring him a pack of cigarettes. But some Christians from a traditional denomination visited him, and when he was released they sent him to a Calvary Chapel pastor, Bil Gollatin. Bil and Rosemary Gollatin took Chris into their own home.

"Now you've got to remember the state that I was in," says Chris. "He [Bil Gollatin] knew that I just got out of jail. Believe me, there were times I thought, 'I could rip off the church, I could rip off him,' but the love that I was experiencing, I couldn't do that. I couldn't do that to these people. And I really believed at the time that this was my last chance; God was giving me my last chance in this life. So I did what I could, as weak as I was. I just showed up like a dead corpse, basically, because that's all I had left, to Bible studies, and I listened to Bil teach the Word of God, plainly and simply. . . . I could literally not think and talk at the same time, and I honestly mean that. Because of my drug overdoses, I believe I had burned out a few circuits."

The process of healing was not instantaneous: "I started out as a janitor. I was willing to do anything that God wanted me to do. If God wanted me to clean toilets, I would do it because my life was starting to come clear in a sense that there had to be more to life than what I was doing. God started opening up my eyes to his love through people, and I would spend hours reading the Word of God on my own personal time. I was experiencing a presence of love like I had never experienced. A high, if I can call it that, like I had never experienced. There was just nothing like it. And I don't even like to compare it as a high because it was something that is so fulfilling that drugs can't even measure up to, and it has continued on in my life for ten years as a born-again Christian."

A YOUTH MEETING

Not all converts, of course, are ex-hippie drug addicts. I selected these three accounts because they illustrate dramatic recoveries from devastated lives. However, a large number of people seek salvation from lesser problems: generalized stress, feelings of failure and inadequacy, confusion about appropriate moral standards, and sometimes simply a gnawing sense that there must be something more. These issues confront children as well as adults, and Bil Gollatin's church makes special efforts to reach out to troubled youth.

Dawson McAllister, the speaker at the weekend junior high conference at Bil Gollatin's church, is the author of twenty books, speaks regularly to youth around the country, and has a nationally syndicated radio show that invites kids to call in and talk about their problems. At this particular meeting, he was accompanied by Todd Procter, a blond, red-cheeked, and handsome musician in his early twenties—the perfect countermodel to the long-haired, drugged-out, sex-crazed MTV star. Procter sang to the background of prerecorded tracks, making this a relatively inexpensive, but nonetheless impressive, performance.

The last Saturday evening meeting I attended began with a comedy routine by one of the leaders of the group. He wore his bill cap backwards, had on a B.U.M. sweatshirt, and knew how to communicate with kids, using rather sacrilegious anecdotes to point out that one does not have to be sanctimonious to be a Christian. Todd Procter followed this warm-up routine with several songs, interspersed with scripture quotations. After emphasizing that Christians are not wimps, he asked, "Are you ashamed?" and his audience shouted back, "No." Procter then sang "I am not ashamed" to further defuse any anxiety these preteens might feel about being a Christian and "being weird." Next, playing on the Pepsi commercial, he chanted, "Jesus is the right one, baby," and the audience responded, "Uh, huh." He then sang an Elvis-style melody about Jesus being the "real thing."

When Dawson McAllister mounted the platform, I noticed that he did not use a podium. As he told me later, a podium distances him from his audience, and kids need to feel that the speaker is touchable and vulnerable, not a "holier-than-thou" preacher. Also, "You need to communicate to them that you are not afraid of them," he said. In the afternoon he had worn jeans and a Gold's Gym T-shirt, but now he had put on a sweatshirt with Jesus on the cross.

McAllister began his talk by saying, "Tonight I am going to give many of you a chance to make a decision for Christ. You are as lost as an Easter egg. You're religious, and you're lost. Baptism doesn't make you a Christian. You need an intimate relationship with Jesus." For the next twenty minutes he described Jesus' death on a cross, hung between two thieves, and he said that the cross of Jesus Christ demands a response: "Jesus paid for your sins; now you need to give your life to him."

From the examples he offered, it was obvious that McAllister believes in a literal hell, and he did not hesitate to tell these students that it is a dark place, devoid of all light. Heaven, according to McAllister, is also a real place—not just a symbol of hope, as the liberals might have it— and to keep it a place of purity, it was necessary for Jesus to expiate the sins of the world by dying on the cross. However, McAllister's fundamental appeal did not concern heaven or hell, but whether "you are sick and tired of the way you are living." Giving your life to Christ, he said, provides an alternative path.

With this declaration, taped music began to play in the background; adult counselors went to the back of the auditorium; and McAllister prayed, "Lord, give them the courage to come." Then he addressed the youngsters: "What you feel in the pit of your stomach is not what you ate tonight. It is the Holy Spirit. Come on. Don't sit there now." In response, nearly fifty kids came to the front of the auditorium. At least three-quarters of them were girls. The music continued to play, and McAllister waited, saying: "Is this it? I don't think so." Three or four more young people got out of their seats, then another five or six. It was a dramatic moment, and McAllister concluded it by saying, "Let's give these people a hand. They made the right decision tonight." All the students then sang, "Our God is an awesome God," clapping in time with the music and clearly feeling proud of their Christianity.

Cultural Relevance

From our interviews it is apparent that the cultural relevance of new paradigm churches, including their contemporary style of evangelism, plays an important role in their growth and the strength of their members' conversion experiences. As Greg Laurie explained in discussing the Harvest Crusades: "If they [nonbelievers] are going to reject the message I preach, let them reject it, but let them reject the message and not all the peripheral things that are secondary." By being culturally current, new paradigm churches aim to keep nonbelievers from feeling alienated by any style of dress or ritual associated with Christianity; instead, they want any objections to stem from the content of the teachings, which they refuse to compromise. In other words, while culturally current worship unquestionably attracts people to new paradigm churches, it is equally important to stress that conversion experiences focus on the *message* and not simply the *form* of Christianity.

A somewhat comical expression of the tendency to mistake *message* and *form* was reported by Chris, the drug addict described earlier: "When I got out [of prison] I figured, 'Well, I better cut my hair and clean up,' because I wanted to please God. I would do anything at that time to get out of my lifestyle. I cut my hair, trimmed up a little bit, and I had got some polyester stuff to put on and I came up here and I met the pastor. I wasn't sure this guy was a pastor because he had on a Hawaiian shirt, blue jeans, was barefoot, and I'm still waiting to meet the pastor, the preacher."

Chris continued, "Then I was introduced to Bil and it was just something different. There was something different, not necessarily about Bil in himself, but the peace and the love that I had never experienced before and I wanted that. I wanted that in my life. I wanted that to be a part of my life to the point that I could give it to other people. I was tired of taking from people. I wanted to give and I knew that I wanted that in my life. He never prayed with me; Bil never prayed with me. He and his wife, Rosemary, just loved me like their own son. I'll never forget that. There were things that they've done: they would buy me shoes; they would take me out to dinner; spend money on me. I wasn't used to that. What I grew up in, if somebody did something like that for you, there was a catch, and I couldn't quite figure out why these people were doing it other than the fact they told me that they loved me and that Jesus loved me and I never understood that."

In short, the focus of new paradigm churches is on internal transformation as opposed to change in external appearance. As one of the Calvary Chapel individuals we interviewed said: "I come to church dressed anyway that I want to. If I have an earring, that's cool. No one looks down on me. . . . People with pink mohawks and bobby pins for earrings, that's just the way they are on the outside; they're reaching out for love." As for nonbelievers, he advised: "Let's just meet people where they're at, and then minister to them. And then if there are changes in their life that need to be made, drugs or alcohol or something like that, well, it's the Holy Spirit that's gonna do that. Not us." His current experience, he indicated, contrasted with his religious upbringing: "I was an Episcopalian as a little boy, and you walk into church and you're immediately supposed to put a look of fear on your face. It's uncomfortable and I didn't like going to church when I was a kid. I felt very intimidated there." Calvary Chapel, on the other hand, seems "neutral territory," without any foreign religious culture.

This viewpoint is not only common to Calvary Chapel members. A member of the Vineyard described why he invites fellow-workers to church: "I feel very comfortable asking people to come to this church that I rub elbows with at work, that swear, that drink beer, whatever. I feel very comfortable asking them to come, knowing that they're not going to feel like they're in a different world, an entirely different world. When they hear the message, they're going to know a different world, but when they come in, they're going to feel like, right away, 'I don't feel out of place.' On the other hand, I know they're going to get a message that's going to pierce their heart."

Similar views were echoed in other interviews. Referring to his first visit to a Hope Chapel, one young adult stated: "I thought it was great. I thought here is a church where you didn't have to wear a suit, or look a certain way, or say certain things. I felt very accepted, and I felt an atmosphere of acceptance. But I wasn't ready to make a decision to follow Jesus at that time. But I had a real positive experience. And it stuck with me." He went on to say, "I never knew it was possible that I could go to a church and wear shorts, and the pastor would wear shorts, and it was okay. So I guess it was the casualness and acceptance that drew me in that way."

Casual clothing and culturally current music do not in themselves create the connection that makes people want to follow Jesus. A recurrent theme in our conversations was that the people encountered in new paradigm churches are somehow different from ordinary associates and friends. The term *real* frequently surfaced as a way of describing these Christians who seemed to lack the defensiveness and egocentricity that is so much a part of the human condition. New paradigm churchgoers, it was claimed, understood themselves as "sinners," as people who needed the grace of God and were not self-sufficient. For one convert, the men he met were unlike any he had ever met before. In his words, "there was something unusual about these men, and these were men that could express their love openly, not in a macho way, but there was a genuine love that was unconditional, and I now understand it was the love of Jesus." Another interviewee described his initial impressions of new paradigm Christians in this way: "I sensed people that were real. . . . In some churches there's a facade. They may or may not intentionally do it. Or you're already categorized as this sort of person or that sort of person. When I came here, it was just real people, and they were transparent. And that was just really refreshing. And there was no pressure put on me to sign a card or stand up or anything like that. The leadership here gave me the ability to meet God where I was at, or God met me where I was at."

Catholics Finding the Light

An important aspect of the appeal of new paradigm churches came out in our interviews with former Roman Catholics. According to our congregational surveys, 28 percent of new paradigm churchgoers were raised as Catholics. In our interviews many of these former Catholics reflected positively on their upbringing and indicated that they were taught the fundamental truths of the Christian faith. But—except for those who had been part of the Catholic charismatic movement—none had developed a "relationship" with God. Religion consisted principally in attending mass and observing certain rituals in their homes, they said. Prayer was formal; doctrine and creeds were taught, but not the Bible. Absent from their experience of Catholicism was the intimacy with God that they found in new paradigm churches. In addition, occasionally a person mentioned feeling rejected by the Catholic church because of a divorce, abortion, or other violation of church teaching. While these behaviors are not condoned by new paradigm pastors, the Catholics we interviewed reported that they did not feel condemned when they started worshiping at a Hope, Calvary, or Vineyard church.

John Honald, a pastor of a new but rapidly growing Hope Chapel in Hawaii, illustrates in somewhat dramatic form some of the characteristics of these converts. He grew up in Catholic schools in Hawaii and not only served as an altar boy but also was regularly president of his class and eventually student body president of his parochial high school. Religion was a meaningful part of that experience. "I spent a lot of time with the Catholic priests," he told us, "and I think it's kind of a norm for kids when they go through that, when you spend a lot of time in a Catholic school, that you think about becoming a priest. Since I was a little kid, I was always amazed, I was kind of awestruck with, I guess for the sake of a better word, with the *majesty* of the church." After a day at the beach, John would enter the side door of the church: "I'd slip in and just kind of stare at the cross of Jesus. In the Catholic church you're taught that when that little candle is on inside of the tabernacle that God is there, so I'd always check the candle."

Although John seriously contemplated the priesthood in high school, he "also liked the ladies in high school, and so that was the end of that!" He continued to participate in church-related activities, including various retreats, but his life was anything but consistent with church teachings. From high school, where he actually failed his senior year, he went, with the help of his bishop, to Santa Clara University, a private Catholic college in California. For the next two years, according to John, "I rowed intercollegiate crew, drank a lot of beer, went out with a lot of ladies, and I think I passed three classes in two years." While he was there, however, he met a "born-again" Christian (actually a Jew by heritage) who witnessed to him relentlessly.

In John's words: "I had just found out that I was kicked out of college. It was one o'clock in the morning and I was just walking around the campus. I'm walking upstairs to the dorm. He [his born-again friend] meets me at the stairs and he just very dramatically goes, 'God told me to meet you here. I got to talk with you about your relationship with God.' So we both went to my room, and I go, 'You've got something with Jesus that I don't.' He goes, 'You gotta invite him in, and you gotta ask him into your heart, and gotta accept him as your Lord and Savior.' And I did that. We prayed. All I remember is we were holding hands, and I haven't ever experienced this with anybody, but there was a bright flash of something in that room when I accepted the Lord. I didn't realize, but the Bible says, 'To much is given, much is asked.' I look back and I go, 'God was setting me up, because he had plans for me and he brought me here dramatically.'"

When he returned to Hawaii, John went to talk with his bishop about his born-again experience: "He just said, 'Well, you don't need that. Get right back into church.' They put me right in charge of their youth group, but here I was drinking with these high school kids, going out and doing terrible things with some of them. By terrible, it's just that we were having sex and doing weird things."

John's conscience bothered him, however, because as he put it: "I have the Lord now, so I'm going through these incredible pangs of guilt." Eventually, on the recommendation of a young woman he met from the mainland, John attended Hope Chapel—only three weeks after the church had been started in Hawaii. Ralph Moore immediately spotted his leadership potential when John started a Bible study group, which met under a tree at a local school and grew to forty-five people by the end of the semester. Within five months Moore had invited him to join the staff of the church as the singles minister.

Other former Catholics told us similar stories. Typically they encountered someone who was a born-again Christian. Often they had quit going to church, but found themselves attracted to the relationship these individuals claimed to have with Jesus. They then attended a service or meeting that caught their attention, in part because worship was so different from what they had previously experienced. One individual said, "Being in the Catholic church we were taught who Jesus was, that he was the son of God, that he died on the cross for our sins, that he made a way for us to reach heaven and gain salvation. But in knowing who he was, the Catholic church never taught us we could know him." It is this intimate relationship with God that former Catholics note as the distinctive difference between their early experience in a hierarchically and ritually oriented church and their present experience in an informal and spiritually populist new paradigm church.

The Conversion Experience

Conversion is a normative experience for participants in new paradigm churches. In our congregational surveys, 93 percent of the respondents said that they were certain they had been "born again," and another 5 percent thought that they had been. Among age groups, the highest incidence of conversion was for individuals between sixteen and twenty years of age, although over half of our respondents said that they were "born again" as adults.[2] Several other patterns emerge from analyzing conversion accounts from our interviews, as well as reading hundreds of descriptions of the born-again experience on the survey forms submitted to us.

DESIRE FOR A NEW LIFE

As the previous examples imply, conversion never occurs in a vacuum; there are always predisposing factors. In many analyses of conversion by psychologists and sociologists, the efficacy of the conversion experience is reduced to the *needs* that precede conversion, as if describing the origin of the event would explain it away.[3] Yet, when converts describe their conversion experiences, it is precisely their needs and their desire for a new life that are at issue. For the convert, being "needy" is the rationale for conversion, not a reason to dismiss it, as is implied by the deprivation theorists.

Indeed, converts tend to be quite analytical in describing their preconversion life. In some instances, a string of events drove them to question their lifestyle. For example, one individual stated that he was deeply troubled by the divorce of his parents. A short time after the divorce his mother died. He was then drafted into military duty in Vietnam, where a number of people in his battalion died, and while still in the marines he received a "Dear John" letter from his girlfriend. In short, he was barraged with death, failed relationships, and instability.

Sometimes the sequence of precipitating factors is more mundane but nevertheless equally significant for the convert. For example, a Calvary Chapel member told us how his life felt out of control: he was married and had small children, but he was drinking every evening, had regular affairs on the weekends, and was generally irresponsible. He stated, "Inside I knew that I was really a rat." The turning point was when his wife had an affair and he physically abused her and then contemplated killing himself and the entire family.

A number of people began using drugs recreationally and for a while enjoyed them, but at some point realized that their dependency was ruining their lives, and they were ready for a radical change. A few had entered a drug rehabilitation program that helped them to reach out for a power beyond themselves, but others simply realized that they were helpless, dependent, and in need.

More typical, however, were functional individuals with jobs, marriage partners, and children who nevertheless said that their lives felt "empty"— a term I heard frequently. In every case, some litany of problems in the person's background or current life could be elaborated: divorced parents, an abortion that left feelings of guilt, the death or terminal illness of a loved one, a friendship that suddenly seemed devoid of commitment, a marriage that went awry. These might be described as the conditions of contemporary existence—there was nothing unique about our sample.

TRIGGER EVENTS

The routes to conversion are diverse, ranging from solitary religious quests to large group crusades. For Mike Sasso, the trigger was a random visit by a complete stranger, who surely must have felt that he failed in his mission; and yet the tract that he left behind was the turning point in Mike's life. Bil Gollatin and several other individuals cited above began to read the Bible on their own, and only later joined a religious community. What we did *not* find were people on a sustained intellectual quest, who, through some logical process of comparing religious alternatives, had a revelatory experience. Certainly such philosophically based conversions occur—and these are the individuals most likely to publish books about their experiences—but intellectually based calculations about the superiority of Christianity over other world religions were rare in our interviews. What might be said is that because Christian symbols are part of the acculturation of most Americans, when there is a strong desire for lifestyle change—accompanied by the right triggering events—individuals readily seize on the Christian story as a guide for interpreting their existence.

The influence of acculturation can be seen in a chance event that precipitated one conversion. The individual casually asked a coworker, "Do you want to smoke a joint?" and was startled by the reply, "No, I get high on Jesus." If the potential convert had not already had a reservoir of Christian understanding with which to interpret this comment, it is unlikely that the remark would have triggered the reaction it did.

For other individuals, the trigger event was not a momentary meeting but a sustained relationship with an individual, such as a spouse or parent. Several people reported that a husband or wife had a born-again experience, and they then watched to see whether this was one more aberrant experiment or whether there would be some lifestyle change. When the altered pattern of behavior sustained itself—particularly abstinence from drugs—they decided to check out the church the spouse was attending.

I also interviewed converts who stated that they wandered into a church, perhaps seeking something, and were surprised by what they found. One individual said that he used to go to a Bible study with a jug of wine in hand to argue with the "Jesus freaks." He said that he was not particularly convinced by what they said, but he was struck by the fact that "they literally practiced what they preached." Another person said that he visited a Pentecostal church, not knowing what to expect. During his visit several people embraced him and said, "I love you." His response to this display of affection was, "I wish my own parents could have done that."

Finally, several people described revelatory moments before their conversion experiences. A woman with several young children who had been having an extramarital affair reported that, while having an abortion, she suddenly realized that she needed to change her life radically, and on returning home she asked her husband, who was a new convert, if she could go to church with him. Another convert said he was struck in the face by a drinking buddy in a barroom brawl and suddenly recognized the artificiality of his friendships, which then sent him on a search for a different way of life.

These trigger events—whether an abortion, a chance visit to a church, or a random conversation—would not have precipitated conversion if the individual had not already been seeking a change in his or her way of life. In addition to being motivated by human need, the person was already receptive to Christian ideas, as suggested by the absence of intellectual debate regarding the truth of Christianity before conversion. As a result, conversion was often precipitated by relatively minor events or experiences.

TURNING POINTS

Theological descriptions of conversion often represent the born-again experience as instantaneous: one moment an individual is a "sinner" and the next moment he or she is "saved." Our interviews reveal a somewhat different process. Indeed, while some people do describe dramatic moments of epiphany, most point to a longer process in which the individual's "will" and intentions are transformed.

Nevertheless, many converts report a "turning point," when the process of character transformation begins. Typically this is a prayer, often very untutored, in which the person confesses that his or her life is a failure, that a self-sufficient approach to existence is not working, and that he or she needs help. While sometimes these prayers conform to a tract formula, such as the "sinner's prayer," they are equally likely to be prayers "launched out into nothingness," as one person put it. These prayers are cries for help, admissions of personal failure, and statements of desire to live a God-centered rather than self-centered life.

Several interviewees, who had uttered their prayers while "high" or inebriated, reported that they instantaneously—and, in their view, somewhat miraculously—became sober. One individual, for example, stated: "And immediately as I said that [sinner's prayer] I came off the drugs, which was really weird. What was going on here? And I felt a lifting of my soul and just a cleansing. And I went, 'What? This is happening.'" When he arrived home, he flushed all his drugs down the toilet; his wife, he said, thought he had "flipped."

Other individuals report a considerable outpouring of emotion, often weeping, in response to some combined sense of relief and release. One person expressed it this way: "I felt lighter, physically lighter. I was crying and weeping. . . . It was like it [the weight of her past] was unloaded off of me." These turning-point experiences typically included a cathartic moment, later described as forgiveness, when the new converts felt absolved of their failures and were hopeful, sometimes ecstatically so, that yielding themselves to God might bring a different future.

In some of the literature on conversion, the experience is formulated somewhat simplistically as a switching of worldviews without any real attention to the hard task of character transformation.[4] Our interviews suggest that a change in beliefs is only one aspect of conversion. The true turning point is the decision to relinquish one's will—to turn from being self-oriented, seeking personal status and pleasure, to being God-centered. At this turning point, it was seldom clear to the individuals what was involved in committing themselves to God. Indeed, the nearly frenetic desire to read the Bible after such an experience can perhaps best be understood as an attempt to understand what it would mean to lead a God-centered life. In short, beliefs and theory appear to follow rather than precede profound religious experiences.

The Postconversion Lifestyle

As we have seen, the immediate circumstances surrounding pivotal conversion experiences are often random and coincidental. However, conversion is a longer-term process, going beyond the specific turning-point experience. The character transformations initiated by these conversion experiences often are molded within religious communities of one sort or another. Individuals who described a solitary religious conversion frequently reported bouncing from one church to another in search of a community that understood their experiences and in which they felt at ease. Perhaps not surprisingly, these individuals often lasted only a Sunday or two in mainline churches. Hippies and former drug addicts mentioned feeling unwelcome in formal, dressed-up environments. Others, with more mainstream lifestyles, found their reports of conversion experiences dismissed at liberal mainline churches. It was often in Pentecostal and charismatic churches that these individuals first discovered a community that accepted them and acknowledged their experiences.

Whatever their route to conversion, the following process typically unfolds for new believers. The Bible becomes the normative lens through which the world is viewed. New converts often saturate themselves with biblical narratives and images, and within a few months superimpose these symbolic forms on all of their everyday experiences. Most converts become involved in home Bible studies, so that new friendships with like-minded people frequently complement or replace their preconversion social network.

At the core of these acculturation experiences is a radical change in focus from being self-directed to being God-directed. This refocusing of one's "center of value" is perhaps best understood as a basic openness to direction, or leading, by the Holy Spirit. In any case, many of these converts reveal a decided deemphasis on "self" as typically understood within the psychological literature on *self*-fulfillment. The model instead is one of *servanthood*. At a practical level, there is considerable emphasis on personal discipline and responsibility, particularly to one's family.

Indeed, words such as *discipleship* and *accountability* are heard at every turn within these movements. More mature Christians *disciple* younger converts, and *accountability* to one's spiritual mentor or home fellowship group runs at radical odds with the individualistic ethic of contemporary America. The feelings of chaos and emptiness that characterize the preconversion state are replaced with order and normative demands in the postconversion lifestyle. While this image of membership may seem repressive to outsiders, the reported experience is quite different. These movements are not legalistic in the typical fundamentalist sense of being rule-oriented. They maintain an emphasis on spontaneity, cultural currency, and "spirit leading" that challenges the routinization of organizational form.

Interpreting Conversion

Conversion accounts such as those described in this chapter are often dismissed, not simply by skeptical philosophers of religion, but also—and sometimes even more vociferously—by those within the mainline churches who associate conversion with fundamentalism. The common assumption of critics both within and outside the religious fold is that conversion is an escapist, emotionally manipulated experience.[5] To be "born again" is politically and intellectually incorrect. Much of the academic literature on conversion buttresses this perception, associating conversion with theories of cultural strain, social deprivation, social influence, or resolution of childhood trauma. The integrity of the conversion experience is attacked by explaining it in terms of external social or cultural factors—especially forces associated with social change—or individuals' "need" to adopt or construct a meaning system. What much of the literature ignores is the individual convert's interpretation of his or her experience.

As already indicated, William James offers a valuable counterview to the reductionism of many interpreters. In the opening pages of *The Varieties of Religious Experience,* he attacks the tendency toward "medical materialism," which, for example, would reduce Saint Paul's vision on the road to Damascus to a manifestation of epilepsy.[6] James is much more interested in the "fruits" of conversion than in its "roots." In my opinion, by taking James's pragmatic approach, one can appreciate that many members of new paradigm churches are leading productive lives as a result of the "turning point" that they associate with conversion.

Conversion appears to be a quest for something more profound in human experience. Whether one posits a "religious urge" as fundamental to human nature, or whether conversion reflects finite human beings, ravaged by problems and inadequacies, reaching for the supernatural, our conversion reports reflect the search for something that transcends physical survival and sensate fulfillment. In more extreme examples, conversion is accompanied by visions and experiences that clearly stem from high levels of human consciousness and thus deserve careful scrutiny.

Many of those we interviewed spoke of having a "relationship" with God or Jesus as a result of their conversion experiences. Whether Jesus or God exists as some ontological entity with which one can have a relationship is certainly not going to be settled here; however, there is no doubt that new paradigm Christians, such as Bil Gollatin, Mike Sasso, and Chris Burton, developed an intimate, functional relationship with someone or something that changed their lives. It is possible that what they call Jesus or God is an element of themselves, which they psychologically project and then establish a relationship with. And it is possible that what they repeatedly refer to as the "Holy Spirit" is simply the deep voice of conscience calling them to a higher state of being than physically based pleasure seeking. But what is important is the experience, whether it is identified by words drawn from the Christian tradition (e.g., "born again" or "filled with the Holy Spirit") or terms coined by social scientists, drawing on Greek mythology.

Conversion and Church Growth

Conversion experiences are an important element in, but not a complete explanation for, the growth of new paradigm churches. In our congregational surveys, 37 percent said that their conversion experiences occurred in a Calvary, Vineyard, or Hope Chapel. Six out of ten respondents had conversion experiences in other settings, but eventually joined one of the three new paradigm churches we studied, presumably because they were drawn to the style of worship and community life within these churches.

Whatever else conversion may imply, within new paradigm churches it refers to individuals having a "personal relationship" with God. Although such language is normative in most fundamentalist and evangelical churches, it is not stressed to the same degree in many liberal Protestant and Catholic churches. Here it is important to note that over a quarter of those who responded to the survey had Catholic backgrounds, and over 10 percent grew up in liberal Protestant homes. Another 13 percent had no church affiliation as youth and therefore presumably were not exposed to conversion rhetoric. In contrast, slightly over a third of the respondents had fundamentalist or evangelical backgrounds, in which conversion rhetoric would have been common.

Our survey also reveals that before their conversion, many individuals were pursuing lifestyles at odds with the values affirmed by members of new paradigm churches. For example, a quarter of our respondents said that they had often used marijuana or drugs in the past. An equal number said that they had often abused alcohol. And over a third said that they had engaged in a lot of premarital sex. Interestingly, the pastors of new paradigm churches reported such preconversion behavior even more frequently than their members. So perhaps it is understandable why these pastors communicate so well with people seeking to turn their lives around.

If I may be permitted to apply a market analysis to something as personal as conversion, several points suggest themselves.[7] First, conversions are not going to occur unless a church affirms their efficacy and regularly provides occasions that trigger their occurrence. While this may seem self-evident, mainline churches are not going to grow through conversion if they do not affirm "born-again" experiences; if they do grow, it will be for other reasons, such as the appeal of their social outreach programs, the beauty of their formal worship, or the quality of their children's programs. In contrast to many mainline churches, new paradigm churches are highly conversion-oriented; they believe that they have an answer to people's felt needs, and this conviction is perhaps intensified by the fact that so many of the pastors have drug addiction and other vices in their backgrounds. These pastors understand firsthand the needs of people with such trouble-filled lifestyles, and they have the vocabulary to communicate, at a very personal level, the solution to these individuals' problems.

Second, when they look for religious establishments where they can pursue the transformation triggered by conversion, individuals gravitate toward communities with some cultural resonance for them. Baby boomers and the twentysomething generation are probably not going to seek out highly routinized, bureaucratic institutions that were stylized in another era, as evident in their music, for example. Within the religious economy, one would expect Calvary Chapels, Vineyard Fellowships, Hope Chapels and similar new paradigm churches to attract larger numbers of people than religious establishments that have been slow to incorporate cultural change.

Third, converts are going to maintain loyalty to institutions that rigorously pursue the task of life transformation—if, indeed, that is what they are seeking—and they will have only marginal loyalty, if any, to religious institutions pursuing other agendas, such as social problems in other parts of the world. New paradigm churches are "high-demand" institutions, however relaxed and contemporary their music and organizational structure may appear. They provide a structure of mentoring and accountability for individuals who are serious about the tough challenge of changing their lives.

To summarize, using market terminology, the growth of new paradigm churches can be attributed to several factors. They have developed a new market constituency by attracting people who were not consumers before (i.e., individuals who were nonbelievers or unaffiliated). They also attract people from other religious markets (e.g., Catholic or liberal Protestant)—markets that do not offer, at least as manifestly, a structure for radical conversion and self-transformation. In addition, they attract members from other conversion-oriented groups (e.g., Pentecostal and various evangelical and fundamentalist churches) that are less culturally current, as measured by worship and organizational style. For all these congregants, they invite consumer loyalty by nurturing them, week by week, in the prolonged process of self-transformation.

CHAPTER 4

Beyond Rationality

Democratizing Access to the Sacred

New paradigm houses of worship seldom have steeples. More frequently they are converted warehouses, former grocery stores, leased stores in shopping malls, rented school auditoriums, or public meeting rooms. Their worship spaces are devoid of symbols, except for the abstract image of a dove that one finds, for example, in Calvary Chapels. Stained-glass images, statues of religious saints, candles, and icons are all products of a church that has undergone routinization; such symbols point to sacred moments of past religious history as a substitute for contemporaneous religious experience.

New paradigm Christians have democratized the sacred, making it available to all, regardless of their theological education and training. Consequently, there is no need for new paradigm pastors to parade religious symbols in orchestrated rituals. Rather, they invite their congregants to dine with them at the banquet table of the sacred. There is no hierarchy. The only distinctions among people are those dictated by various functions of servanthood; hence, some are called to be pastors and others deacons, elders, and prophets, but all people, church members believe, have equal status before God.

Nowhere is this democratization of the sacred more evident than in the music sung in new paradigm churches. It is populist, written by common people whose lives have been transformed. And it is contemporary, drawing on the musical forms of popular culture. Social movements, both secular and religious, have often been accompanied by a radical shift in musical expression. Music reflects the deep unconscious structures of a culture, and correspondingly, the music of social change movements signals discord with these routinized structures. Movement music simultaneously symbolizes a break with the old mores and provides a source of cohesion for those choosing the new way.

Self-Made Tunesmiths

Dramatic changes in musical style also occurred during the Second Great Awakening. Analyzing this period of American religious history from 1800 to 1830, historian Nathan Hatch states: "At the turn of the nineteenth century a groundswell of self-made tunesmiths, indifferent to authorized hymnody, created their own simple verses and set them to rousing popular tunes." He says that the music for these songs was borrowed indiscriminately from "a wide variety of secular tunes of love, war, homesickness, piracy, robbery, and murder."[1] The established churches of the time (e.g., the Episcopalians, Presbyterians, and Congregationalists) viewed these religious "ditties" as vulgar street songs, unfit for respectable religion. But this musical innovation was, of course, a protest against the dreary and theologically laden prose of the establishment hymns, which failed to express the vital religious experience of members of the rapidly growing dissident churches of the period.

Movements such as Methodism (which began in England) were propagated as much through song as through preaching.[2] The hymns written by John and Charles Wesley used everyday language that was accessible to all social classes, and their hymnal, which went through thirty-five editions by 1805, played an important role in communicating a new set of religious values. In Methodist camp meetings the music was often even more expressive than the hymns sung in church, reflecting the musical culture of the people attracted to these meetings. Except for the content of the lyrics, one might easily have thought that songs were issuing from a tavern or bar. As Hatch states: "Methodist revivalism removed elitist constraints on music by accepting spontaneous song, exuberant shouting, and unrestrained music enthusiasm as natural to a vibrant spiritual community."[3]

The gospel music expression of the Second Great Awakening broke with religious musical conventions of the time as a way of protesting the sterility of organized, establishment religion. The new music written by individuals within these movements sought to connect with the everyday experience of people. Hatch says, "Tunes that succeeded were catchy and contagious—the kind that could be hummed or whistled behind the plow or at the anvil."[4] In this regard, they were in stark contrast to hymns with complicated lyrics and melodies, more suited to performance by choirs than to singing in the fields and streets.

The music that emerged during this period was not, for the most part, written by theologians or educated clergy. Instead, ordinary people wrote music that addressed problems that they faced on a daily basis.[5] The musical monopoly of established religionists was challenged by people who drew directly on their personal experience of the sacred. However vulgar these songs may have appeared to the theologically sophisticated, they reflected the everyday connection between the sacred and ordinary life that many new converts were experiencing.

Although the Second Great Awakening represented a powerful flowering of religious folk music, it is by no means unique in Christian history. Martin Luther is often quoted as saying: if music is the handmaiden of theology, why should the devil have all the good tunes?[6] Indeed, many of Luther's hymns were written in the vernacular and set to barroom melodies. At the time of the Reformation these songs represented a decided break with churchly musical convention. Sung today they represent establishment religion, just as the hymns of Charles Wesley do. Each transformation of religious culture, then, is accompanied by new music, and the very songs that create revolutions and aid the cohesion of a social movement will later represent the established cultural tradition to be overthrown.

The Megaphone for the Movement

It should not be surprising that the Jesus movement of the sixties was accompanied by a radical break with churchly religious convention. Hippies who had found Jesus did not retune their guitars; they simply started writing lyrics that reflected the joys and struggles of their born-again experience. The genius of a pastor like Chuck Smith is that he welcomed these hippies into the church to play their music. Not only was it all right to wear sandals (or no shoes at all) to church, but Smith also gave these young converts a stage for their music, with Sunday night performances and concerts. The bands that the audience liked, he invited back to play again. And as the Jesus movement began to build, Smith helped establish a record company, Maranatha Music, to distribute the music of these young artists.

However much the Bible-oriented teaching of Chuck Smith and other founders of this movement might have resonated with the members of a drug-satiated culture, it was the music that drew tens of thousands of young people. The music signaled that this was not religion as usual. People were getting high—on life, love, and Jesus—and this message was communicated in music that was culturally relevant. Marshall McLuhan's famous maxim that "the medium is the message" was at least partly true. People knew they did not want the religion that went with stained glass and pipe organs, but a long-haired hippie strumming a guitar and singing about Jesus' love sent a different message.

According to Chuck Fromm, who was involved with Maranatha Music from its early days, the most powerful and enduring songs were written by nonprofessionals from the depths of their own experience. They were truckers, former strippers, and housewives who wanted to share their love of God and wrote songs such as "Father I Adore You," "Seek Ye First," and "Glorify Thy Name." As the movement developed, the songs became more sophisticated. Secular recording companies realized that there was a growing market for Christian music and signed some of the better talent. But in Fromm's view, it was the songwriters and singers with a very direct and personal message who really communicated with their audience.

Fromm describes Maranatha Music as the megaphone for the Calvary movement. Their tapes and records were shipped across the country and around the world. Radio stations started to play this new music and found that it had an audience. In Fromm's opinion, every social movement has its own "sound," and the Jesus movement was marked by the guitar and a culturally current rhythm. Young people could imagine Jesus playing a guitar in a way that they could not picture him at a pipe organ or leading a choir. Fromm believes that you can tell how vibrant a social movement is by the vitality of its music. If a movement (or for that matter a local church) lacks a signature sound, he suggests, then it undoubtedly lacks cohesion at a foundational level.

Kevin Springer, a key figure in the Vineyard Fellowship, supports Chuck Fromm's emphasis on the role of music in the emergence of this new religious movement. "You don't understand the Vineyard if you don't understand the worship music," he states. "That is probably the greatest contributor to the growth and advancement of the Vineyard movement. More than healing, more than books, more than tapes. It's

Vineyard music. That's my experience based on what people tell me. John Wimber, if he's really technically trained at anything, it's as a musician. He's the one who developed and set the tone to the music that's gone all over the world and touched Christians from all kinds of traditions."

As we interviewed worship leaders at Calvary, Vineyard, and Hope churches, it became evident that they know each other's music and often typecast it in similar ways. Vineyard music, for example, is viewed as intimate and worship-oriented; Calvary music is identified as more upbeat and praise-oriented. Within a given church, there are typically also identifiable styles that reflect the various worship bands. For example, the morning worship team may be "mellower" in tone (utilizing acoustic guitars), whereas the evening worship team may be rock- or jazz-oriented (utilizing electric guitars). Youth bands (say, of high school students) are almost always "harder," with more of a rock edge to their music, while the adult bands are more sixties-oriented. And sometimes the same music is played differently depending on the region of the country. For example, a worship leader from a Vineyard in Chicago told us that southern California Vineyard music is just too mellow for their taste, so they rearrange it with a stronger beat and a more urban, "bluesy" flavor.

What is distinctive, however, is that these groups are constantly writing new music. Most of the music played on a Sunday is probably no more than three or four years old. Obviously this constant innovation keeps the music fresh and distinctive. Many churches develop their own sound because most of the music is written by individuals within their own congregation. Thus, even the casual observer may note congregations that reflect a black gospel tonality, or a New Age style of arrangement, or the imprint of a particular artist, such as James Taylor, who has influenced the worship leader.

In spite of the stress on cultural currency, several people we interviewed noted the difficulty of incorporating some music styles, such as punk rock, into worship. Both Chuck Smith and John Wimber stated that the sensuality and violence that characterize music of the last decade are simply not congruent with Christian values, and consequently they are struggling with building a bridge to the current generation of youth. Sixties music tended to be "message" music, which lent itself to adaptation to Christian lyrics. MTV-style music, on the other hand, relies heavily on visual representations (often of sex and violence) that are inconsistent with the Christian ethic. Nevertheless, in our interviews pastors expressed an openness to understanding the Generation X culture of the nineties and to connecting with it whenever possible. For example, one pastor told us that his own teenage son goes to "Biker James's" church, where they do "slam dancing" in between listening to fundamentalist, hellfire-and-brimstone preaching.

Some new paradigm pastors are beginning to worry that their music has lost its contemporary edge. Christian bands are focusing too much on the Christian marketplace and are not connecting with youth who are nonbelievers. Within three decades Christian music has already become routinized, reaching an audience mainly of fellow Christians. In the opinion of pastors such as Tom Stipe in Denver, this limitation is dangerous, and he is committed to developing bands that will play in secular venues. He believes there is a role for message-oriented music that is not saturated with Christian imagery and can be played in secular clubs. He approves of such Christian artists as Amy Grant, whose albums are not restricted to overtly Christian songs. Value-based music produced by Christians has a definite role within the secular marketplace in planting ideas that churches can eventually harvest. While some people within new paradigm churches are writing music for a secular audience, most of the music that is currently being written is intended for use in the worship setting.

Singing, Teaching, Prayer

Regardless of the Vineyard one enters, the pattern of worship is similar. The service opens with a brief prayer, inviting the people to enter into the presence of God. Then for the next thirty to forty minutes, a worship team comprised of several vocalists and a small band of musicians leads the people in singing worship songs. The lyrics are simple and are projected onto a screen or wall where all can see them. There are no hymnals or prayer books to occupy one's hands. Posture is a matter of personal preference and changes as individuals respond to their spiritual yearnings. Looking around the audience, one may see some people standing with arms raised, and others sitting. On some faces, tears trickle down cheeks; others possess a radiant smile. This period of worship is a time of both great interiority and divine connection.

Approximately the first third to half of each service is devoted to singing. Then, as the band leaves the stage, ushers silently pass offering baskets, without fanfare and often without any announcement. Baby boomers are tired of associating religion and money—hence, the nearly offhand way in which the collection is taken. For the next thirty to forty minutes, the pastor shares his reflections on a passage of scripture, often drawing on his own personal experiences as a way of relating to the concerns of the audience. The style is informal, not oratorical. This is a congregation in which pastor and members, together, are making their way toward a deeper relationship with God.

In the Vineyard the period of teaching ends with an invitation for individuals who desire prayer to come forward. This is the third and last element of the service. Without the drama that surrounds the invitation for people to come for salvation at Calvary Chapel, there is something very gentle and caring about "ministry time" in the Vineyard. A lay member of the church who is part of the "ministry team" joins each individual who has come for prayer. Quietly, this lay minister asks what the person's need is and then often places his or her hand on the other's shoulder (individuals typically are matched with someone of the same sex). In a large church dozens of these paired groupings may occur, beginning with those who come to the front and then growing in clusters around the church, as more and more people pray for each other.

The three elements of the service—singing, teaching, prayer—are intertwined. The singing, or worship, portion of the service provides an extended period for the individual to commune with God, with the music triggering entry into a level of consciousness in which everyday defensiveness is abandoned. Feelings of ecstatic union with the sacred are often mixed with access to emotions that need healing. These feelings, typically raw and undigested, are given shape and interpretation during the teaching period of the service. However, it is during the third part of the service, the ministry time (in the case of the Vineyard), that these emotions are dealt with tangibly in prayer and through human touch. In some churches, this is the time when new converts come forward to "receive Christ," when their past is contextualized in terms of Jesus' death on the cross for their sins, and a counselor helps mediate a new lifestyle based on biblical teachings.

Adoring the Lord

According to new paradigm members, the purpose of worship is to express love, praise, and thankfulness to God. Vineyard music is distinctive in that the lyrics are often intended as a form of prayer or direct personal communication with God. Contrasting the Vineyard worship approach with that of mainline churches, one worship leader emphasized: "We direct most of our songs *to* God as opposed to singing *about* God." And, indeed, there is something personal and intimate about Vineyard worship. Rather than the focus being on the group on stage, the worship team is merely the medium, and not the focus, for conversations with God.

In interviewing worship leaders, we asked them to explain the planning behind worship. Many of the large churches have four or five worship teams, and although considerable energy is devoted to music within new paradigm churches, worship leaders stressed that worship is not intended to be a performance. For example, a Vineyard pastor said, "My goal as a worship leader is to point people to Jesus, but I want to go there too. I see leading worship as an experience in worship: I'm going towards God, and I am asking and inviting the people to come along with me." A Calvary worship leader expressed the same idea: "The key thing for me is that I go out there with every intention of being transparent. I don't want them to see me." Another Calvary worship leader summarized his conviction that the goal of worship is to give the priesthood to the people: "We're not up here to be your representatives to God. You have your own communion with God." Gesturing, he declared, "Here, you do it!"

At the Vineyard, worship is a time to praise God and to offer oneself to him in service. This process cannot be hurried. The normal preoccupations that so dominate and structure our thinking and worrying need to recede from consciousness; only then can the deeper connections be made. One individual said that, at first, thirty to forty minutes of worship seemed too long, but then exclaimed: "It was like God kind of drew me and taught me how to worship. How to be intimate in that way with him. I loved it because the songs were so simple. I'm not a great singer, and I can't remember wordy songs. For me, it was kind of a teaching time, learning to be intimate to that degree. They began to draw me, and after a short time [of attending] it was like, 'You mean it's over already?'"

In new paradigm churches, worship may be viewed as a form of sacred lovemaking, transcending the routinized rituals that so often structure the human-divine communication. In new paradigm churches, unlike mainline churches, no one tells you when to kneel, sit, recite, or read. Worship proceeds without scripture reading, recitation of creeds, offerings, and all the other busyness that dominates the typical service. A Calvary worship leader said, "My goal is to see people who are 'gone,' who are with the Lord, who are just adoring the Lord. . . . What I want to see is people who have 'checked out' and who are with the Lord, who are communing with God in the spirit, who have made the 'connection.'"

Many people told us that in the act of worshiping, they find their defenses and pretenses of everyday life vanish. They said that in communing with God, who knows the secrets of the human heart, feelings and emotions surface that are otherwise buried. Sometimes they get in touch with deep wounds inflicted by others; other times they return to personal failures that have been rationalized and repressed. Connecting with these memories and feelings and giving them to God for healing are important byproducts of worship.

Sprinkled throughout our interviews were comments that something in worship frequently evokes tears and extremely deep emotions. A typical statement was: "The first three months I came to the Vineyard I cried through the worship. I still do at times." Another person added more texture to her response, saying, "Often, when I first came, I would cry and cry, as if a dam were loosening." One individual described his experience of inviting a guest to worship. "My brother-in-law [who normally attends a mainline evangelical church] came to a service a few months ago, and walked in Sunday night and stood there and the worship started and he was standing there, and he's a real stoic kind of guy, a businessman you know, and I turned over and I looked at him, and I realized that he was crying. He said, 'I don't know what's going on. I don't know why I'm reacting like this.'"

When we asked a Vineyard pastor about these spontaneous tears during worship, he prefaced his answer with another example: "A person who was here the other day was talking about the first time he came to the Vineyard years ago, and he was a coke-head and his life was a mess, and somebody drove him to church and he just walked out almost every time after about fifteen or twenty minutes of worship. He just was going to sob, and he didn't even know what it was. He'd just walk in, and he'd feel *that thing*." "That thing," the pastor explained, is not simply the music, it is also the way that people respond in worship, their "simplicity and the sincerity." He expanded: "There is just this incredible sincerity you see in people. When you look around, you see a certain sweetness. I think it just touches some sort of a heart-chord."

The tears may also be part of a healing experience. Recalling a particularly vivid moment of worship, a Vineyard member said: "One time a girl had a song from the Lord and started singing it, and immediately the Lord just put my father there in front of me, and just healed some things right there in that service. I mean, I couldn't stop crying. I was so embarrassed. I didn't want to cry. I had tears just pouring down my face. I was sobbing." Another respondent echoed similar feelings: "When I'm worshiping God I often experience feelings from issues that I've tried to bury or avoid. When I pray and take those issues to the Lord I often feel a release from the anxieties, fears, hurts." Still another person said that the openness of the worship leads to an opening of her own emotions. She frequently prays, "Lord, I am here to meet you," and in this unguarded state various issues emerge, which she then deals with in prayer or after the service during the ministry period.

One of the individuals just cited, attempting to explain these powerful moments, argued strenuously, "It's not an emotional thing. Do you understand what I am saying? It's a spiritual thing as opposed to an emotional thing." To underline the difference between an emotional and spiritual experience, he offered this contrast: "You know how your emotions are all caught up within you, and you have this burning, or churning, or grief, or whatever? This [worship] is something completely different. It is almost like a peace, a joy, and a sorrow all mixed together, and you are not necessarily crying, although you have tears running down your face. You feel this welling up. I guess that's the only way to describe it. This tremendous welling up."

Certainly not everyone cries during worship, but many experience deep and highly complex emotions. In the congregational surveys people frequently reported feeling joy, peace, love, gratitude, intimacy, happiness, and delight during worship. But nearly as often, people spoke of brokenness, pain, sorrow, repentance, and memories of wrongs that they had committed without retribution. It is as if the potential for joy—nurtured by the Christian perception that Jesus offers unconditional love and acceptance—allowed them to acknowledge the underside of their lives, the ugliness that they usually attempted to hide from view. Here, worship has its intended and *express* functions—to praise and honor God the Creator—but also equally important *latent* functions, which operate at a deeply personal level in reordering the worshiper's unconscious life.

It is obvious from our congregational surveys that worship is what draws people to new paradigm churches. The attraction for many people may be the contemporary music and the "comfortable" feeling of the service. However, many other places offer culturally current music, so this is not in itself the basis for the commitments people make.

Rather, it is the deep encounter with the sacred—in believers' words, an experience of the Holy Spirit—that appears to account for the growth of new paradigm churches. By stating this, I do not mean to demean other worship styles. Cultural currency can certainly mean many things, depending on one's background. For some, organs and choirs may be the medium that opens their consciousness to the sacred. But whatever style of worship resonates for the individual, it is the experience of the holy (i.e., the sacred, the numinous, God) that distinguishes religious worship from experiences at a rock concert or an evening at the local bar or a nightclub.

Interpreting Worship Experience

William James and various theorists who have studied human consciousness are helpful in conceptualizing what occurs in worship. The model that James and others suggest is that human consciousness has many different levels, or what James calls "subuniverses" of meaning.[7] There is a difference, says James, between the state of *everyday* consciousness (in which one brushes teeth, does household chores, or interacts socially with people) and the *dream* state of deep sleep. In addition, everyday consciousness and the dream state both differ from such subuniverses of meaning as *scientific reflection,* the *fantasy* world associated with a good novel or movie, or the states of consciousness associated with *laughter* or *play.* According to James, *religion* is a distinct province of meaning alongside these other subuniverses of consciousness and is as subjectively real (at least while we are in that subuniverse) as any of the others. During the course of a day or even a few minutes, we are constantly moving in our consciousness from one subuniverse to another.

James argues that various stimuli trigger us to jump from one state of consciousness to another. For example, the "reality" of the fantasy world we are in while watching a movie is challenged when someone shouts "Fire!" And lapsing into a dream state during a boring lecture at a scientific conference may suddenly transport one into a world that is as real as the discussion of subatomic particles. Along these lines, music may play a strong role in triggering one's consciousness during a Vineyard worship service, so that one momentarily leaves the world of everyday reality (and all its tensions and conflicts) and enters into a different state of consciousness, experiencing the reality of holiness, purity, and all-embracing love. During worship one may go in and out of this religious subuniverse, just as the scientist may move in and out of the realm of scientific abstraction while toiling at her or his desk.[8]

James's point is that consciousness has many layers or levels. The basepoint to which one always returns is the subuniverse of everyday life. Nevertheless, the priority given to it does not minimize the reality or importance of the others: they are simply *different* realities, each one carrying its own internal logic. Thus, the distinct states of consciousness experienced while dreaming, fantasizing, playing, and being absorbed in an artistic creation are certainly as real and important as the basepoint of everyday consciousness. Each of these subuniverses is governed by its own mode of discourse and style of cognition, and what makes sense in one may seem absurd in another. Indeed, this very incongruity provides an invigorating tension between the sacred and profane worlds. Within the everyday world, for example, violence and warfare may be inevitable, but this does not invalidate the vision of peace and harmony that may fill the religious subuniverse of meaning. The religious person (whether Christian, Muslim, Hindu, or Jew) leads a "counterpointal" life in which the differing "realities" of the sacred and profane worlds intersect—often rather strikingly in worship.

In traditional religion a variety of triggers have evolved to aid the movement from the profane to the sacred realm. These triggers include practices as diverse as fasting, chanting, and pilgrimages. Conventional religious services also draw on a kind of symphony of interacting symbols as triggering devices. The church architecture, stained glass, statues, frescoes, incense, candles, and all the liturgical activities may play an important role in guiding the shift from everyday to religious consciousness. But for many baby boomers and Generation Xers, these conventional triggers to religious consciousness no longer work because they are associated with images of false or dead establishment religion.

Reformist religion has the choice of scrapping the old symbols or trying to resuscitate them. New paradigm churches have taken the former approach, by and large. They meet in buildings that do not look religious; they have abandoned almost all of the conventional artistic symbols of the Christian church; and they have opted for a very simple style of worship. In the very emptiness of these worship places, music becomes central as a triggering device. Music connects to very deep strata in human consciousness; the interaction between performer and listener is nonrational and "right brain" rather than rational, objectively verifiable, and "left brain." Yet the music that triggers religious consciousness is culturally specific and historically relative. It makes sense that the

music that speaks to the baby boom generation is music utilizing the instruments and melodies of their age. Gregorian chant may work in one
century and not in another, and the Christian rock music of the 1990s
may have little cultural resonance in the next millennium.

According to James, people who reject the reality of the subuniverse
of religion have simply chosen to limit their horizons of what it means
to be human. James's book *Varieties of Religious Experience* is testimony
to the multiplicity of different experiences that people have had, including life-changing conversions and worldview-shattering mystical visions. Among these various experiences of the religious life, the "gifts
of the spirit" are not uncommon in new paradigm churches.

The Gifts of the Spirit

In the book of First Corinthians, the apostle Paul de-
scribes the various gifts of the spirit practiced in the first-century Christian church: "For to one is given by the Spirit the *word of wisdom;* to another the *word of knowledge* by the same Spirit; to another the *working
of miracles;* to another *prophecy;* to another *discerning of spirits;* to another divers kinds of *tongues;* to another the *interpretation of tongues;*
but all these worketh that one and the selfsame Spirit, dividing to every
man severally as he will."[9] As literal interpreters of the Bible, new paradigm Christians, unlike some fundamentalists, believe that these gifts of
the spirit are as appropriate now as they were in the early church. So
long as these gifts are exercised decently and in order, as Paul instructed,
they have a role in the life of the Christian community.

The gift of tongues may manifest itself in several ways. The original
expression was at the so-called Day of Pentecost, when the book of Acts
reports: "And suddenly there came a sound from heaven as of a rushing
mighty wind, and it filled all the house where they were sitting. And there
appeared unto them cloven tongues like as of fire, and it sat upon each
of them. And they were all filled with the Holy Ghost, and began to speak
with other tongues, as the Spirit gave them utterance. And there were
dwelling at Jerusalem Jews, devout men, out of every nation under
heaven. Now when this was noised abroad, the multitude came together,
and were confounded, because that every man heard them speak in his
own language. And they were all amazed and marvelled, saying one to
another, Behold, are not all these which speak Galileans?"[10]

The phenomenon of ecstatic speech is not unique to the early Christian community or to contemporary Pentecostalists or charismatics. In many different cultures people have entered into trance states where they engage in dissociated speech. The term *glossolalia* is used to refer to unintelligible vocalizations, whereas the term *xenoglossy* describes speaking an actual language that is unknown to the speaker. The events described in the second chapter of Acts refer to xenoglossy, for observers heard members of the Christian community speaking in a recognizable foreign language, but one they presumably did not know. In contrast, the "prayer language" or tongues speaking heard during a typical Pentecostal worship service (or spoken in private devotions) is glossolalia, although occasionally an outsider claims to have heard their own native tongue (e.g., Chinese or an African dialect). *Cryptomnesia* is the ability in a trance state to recall a language that one has heard but never actually learned.[11]

In our congregational surveys of Calvary, Vineyard, and Hope members, 41 percent indicated that they often speak in tongues (presumably glossolalia), 13 percent said that they have spoken in tongues a few times, and 4 percent said they had done so once. Vineyard Fellowship respondents were much more likely to cite tongues as part of their religious experience than either Calvary or Hope Chapel members. To a large extent this difference reflects the varying emphases placed on tongues by the leadership. Chuck Smith and Ralph Moore, who share a Foursquare denominational background, are skeptical of exuberant expressions of tongues. Moore says that his congregation is encouraged to raise their hands in worship, but there is an awareness that tongues speaking may frighten off newcomers. Even in the many Vineyard services that we attended, while tongues may be heard more frequently in worship, public exercise of the gift is most likely to occur in healing conferences and in small group meetings. Indeed, all three groups place more emphasis on tongues as a form of private prayer than as a normal part of public worship. When tongues *are* spoken publicly, there is an attempt to follow Paul's instruction that an interpretation should be given.

While new paradigm churches embrace the gifts of the spirit, they do not necessarily identify with the American Pentecostal movement, which dates to the Azusa Street revivals in 1906 in Los Angeles. They attempt to distance themselves from the televangelists and others who make speaking in tongues central to the Christian experience. Rather, tongues is viewed as one of many gifts, and it is secondary to the gift of charity as expressed in the famous thirteenth chapter of First Corinthians:

"Though I speak with the tongues of men and of angels, and have not charity, I am become as sounding brass, or a tinkling cymbal. And though I have the gift of prophecy, and understand all mysteries and all knowledge; and though I have all faith, so that I could remove mountains, and have not charity, I am nothing."[12] Nevertheless, with the mentioned qualifications, tongues are normative for many people in new paradigm churches. The same, of course, is true in many non-Christian religions, as the literature on trance and "spirit possession" so amply documents.[13]

The pastor of a large Calvary Chapel told us of his encounter with this gift of the spirit after his conversion. He had been very involved in the drug culture and identified with Lonnie Frisbee, an important figure in the early history of the Jesus movement.[14] As he described it: "So Lonnie was there and he was preaching. I related to him right away: beard and long hair. Hey, this guy's got something to say. So I listened to him. He says there's this baptism of the Holy Spirit that you need to have. I said, 'Well, I've got Jesus, I guess I need this. All right.' So I went up there, and they brought me in this little room and prayed for me. I'll never forget it. Lonnie lays his hands on me. I went right down. I just fell on the ground. I started crying and laughing at the same time—had an incredible emotional experience. I was out of control. I was just lying there, speaking in tongues. Lonnie [finally] came over to me and says, 'You can get up now.' I was really emotionally out of control, but I was loving it. It was like a deliverance."

This was in the early days of the Calvary movement, and, according to this pastor, Chuck Smith felt uncomfortable with the emotionalism of such experiences. He remembered Smith saying something like: "Let's stop this falling down emotional stuff. Let's get down to finding out what the Bible says, and then we'll go on with the gifts." Yet this pastor remarked about his own experience: "That was a real, I would say, pivotal point in my whole life, with the baptism of the Holy Spirit. That just knocked me right down and got me right up and, I mean, I was on fire from then on out. It hasn't stopped."

Experiences of this intensity are common at Vineyard healing conferences, but there is a definite effort in the other movements, as well as some Vineyard churches, to contain these experiences by channeling them to "afterglow" meetings. Sometimes these meetings are held after the Sunday evening service, and in some churches there is a regular night, perhaps once a month, when people are invited to be baptized by the Holy Spirit. Only converts are asked to these meetings, where those in attendance invite the Holy Spirit to manifest himself. In these smaller group settings (including home fellowship meetings), it is not unusual for people to speak in tongues for the first time, for a prophecy to be heard, or for someone to experience physical healing as a result of prayer. Thirty-eight percent of the Calvary, Vineyard, and Hope members we surveyed indicated that they had often prayed for someone by laying hands on them. Thirty-one percent said that they had been prayed for by another member of the church. And almost half of our respondents claimed to have been miraculously healed.[15] An even higher percentage (65 percent) said that they have experienced emotional healing.

On a personal level, many people utilize tongues as a form of individual prayer. One Hope Chapel pastor delineated the uses of tongues and then described his own practice of praying in tongues: "There are three manifestations of the gift of tongues. One of them is in the form of a prayer language where one speaks to God, gives praise to God. The other two manifestations are in the general assembly, in the church. One of those is the sign in tongues, which is followed by an interpretation, which you see a number of times throughout [the New Testament book of] Acts. The third one is where somebody speaks in tongues and it is understood by the recipients—by the people in the congregation, and that has been demonstrated in Acts, too, where foreigners were being spoken to in their own language." In his view, "Tongues is an unlearned language. You don't understand what you're saying when you're speaking it. It's done, or should be done, at times of spiritual submission to the Lord's work in your life." He sees speaking in tongues "as a wonderful way to extend your prayer capability, because quite often, if I'm praying in English, I run out of words to pray and I don't feel that I've finished praying. I can continue in tongues, and I can pray for an hour in tongues. There's no restriction at all. When I pray in tongues I am edified, it lifts me up."

A careful reading of Acts, First Corinthians, and portions of the Gospels reveals that Holy Spirit possession was a normal experience for some members of the early church, along with miraculous healings, exorcisms, visions, dreams, prophecies, and other works of the Holy Spirit. Ecstatic experience is the nerve that energizes religion, but there are always ongoing battles (especially by the priestly class) to control it, and frequently order and intellect win out over primal religious experience, or what the theologian Rudolf Otto called the "mysterium tremendum"—that awe-inspiring encounter with the sacred that is beyond description in human language.[16] The essence of religion is to be seized ("possessed") by something outside oneself, and when this no longer occurs, worship becomes rote, boring, and an optional human activity.

Given the influence of psychoanalysis on our culture, these nonrational encounters with the sacred are often viewed as psychotic episodes. However, we found no evidence that the people who have these experiences are psychologically unhealthy or dysfunctional.[17] Indeed, quite the opposite might be argued, namely, that people who experience altered states of consciousness may be psychologically *healthier* than those who remain confined in the limited perspective of the rational, empirical world.[18] Without venturing a definitive opinion on this issue, one can say that the experiences of members of these movements seem very similar to accounts of visitations of the Holy Spirit offered in the New Testament book of Acts; moreover, their dreams and visions parallel the many examples of these phenomena given in the Hebrew scriptures. Rather than dismiss these experiences a priori, perhaps we should acknowledge that religious people of all times, of all ages, and, very likely, of all traditions have had mysterious encounters with the sacred that the rational mind, and more particularly, Enlightenment science, simply cannot comprehend.

Clearly, for many people worship and singing help to trigger entry into a different state of consciousness.[19] People who pray in tongues are accessing a realm of consciousness different from the subuniverses of everyday life or scientific reflection. The same is true of people who hear voices or receive visions. Within a community of faith, it is not surprising that people attempt to name the source of these experiences, or that as Christians, like those in the early Christian community, they identify these experiences with the Holy Spirit, who is believed to have appeared after Jesus' ascension into heaven.

BEYOND A SHADOW OF A DOUBT

Steve was the head of a large advertising department when he met a salesman, Jim (not his real name), who had been "born again" six months earlier at a Calvary Chapel service and was instantly cured of a severe alcohol addiction. Steve described his early encounters with Jim: "He would come into my office maybe two or three times a week, and he would tell me about Jesus, but there was something about him that was different from all the other Christians I had ever met. He was happy! He always had a grin on his face, and there was joy that I'd never seen, [a joy] in his heart that I'd never had in mine." After observing Jim for a while, he remembered thinking: "I want what that guy's got." Steve, however, was a Jew by heritage; he thought of Jesus as a prophet, but he had never seriously considered becoming a Christian until the following experience.

Steve's back was giving him great discomfort and he was in considerable pain when Jim stopped by Steve's office one day. Jim told Steve that he had been driving around Anaheim when the Lord spoke to him and told him to come and pray for Steve. Steve's response was one of incredulity, "God speaks to you?" And Jim replied, "Yeah, he speaks to his friends," and then Jim asked if Steve would object if he prayed for Steve's back. In desperation, and feeling that it couldn't hurt, Steve agreed. "So," according to Steve,

he put a chair in the middle of my office and told me to take off my shoes. So I took off my shoes. And he said, "Stretch your legs out," and he said, "See how one leg is longer than the other?" And he said, "Now I'm gonna pray and I'm gonna ask God to straighten out your legs, because your hip is in a weird position." So I said, "Okay." So he closed the door to my office and I'm sitting in the chair, my shoes off. I've got my socks on, and I closed my eyes and I'm just sitting in the chair, and he started praying. He started speaking in tongues. I'd only heard tongues once before in my life. My mother-in-law had shared with me about her prayer life, and I didn't know what that was. I didn't even know who the Holy Spirit was at the time, even though I had read parts of the Bible.

So he starts speaking in tongues, and then he says to me—and I've got my eyes closed—and he says, "Do you believe that Jesus Christ is the Son of God?" In my mind I said, "God, if Jesus Christ is really your son, you're gonna have to prove it to me beyond a shadow of a doubt." At that instant he [Jim] touched the toe to my right foot. I had my legs up like this on the chair. [And] as soon as he touched my toe, this fire went up my leg, went down my left leg, went up my torso, into my arms and in my face. It was like a blowtorch was running through my body inside, you know, blowtorching inside of my skin. The fire was so intense that I thought I was gonna die. I felt like I'm going to become incontinent, that I might have a bowel movement, it's so intense. And then, all of a sudden, and I can't explain it any other way, and it's never happened to me since—I felt, for a second of time, the love that God has for humanity, and this love welled up inside of me, a love I'd never experienced before and never experienced again, this compassion for humanity, not for the guy in the room, but for the whole world, and like, I had a vision of every person on the earth, every color, the Chinese, the Japanese, the blacks, the whites, everybody, and I had, in an instant of time, I don't even know how long it took, but this love. I had love for every person on the face of the earth. And it started coming, like in a wave, over my body. The waves started getting stronger and stronger and stronger, more intense, until in my mind I was saying, "I'm gonna die." I couldn't handle this love. I started to cry and in my mind I said, "God. Stop. I can't handle this."

Steve then fell off his chair, onto the floor:

I'm lying on the floor, and out of my mouth is coming, "I love you, Jesus, thank you, Jesus." And in my mind, I'm going, "Wait a minute, Steve. Do you realize what's coming out of your mouth?" And I'm trying to analyze what's coming out of my mouth, and I'm so happy, and I don't know why I'm so happy other than the fact of this love of humanity. So Jim helped me up from the floor and I had a sofa, and I lay down on my sofa in my office, and I looked at him and I could hardly move my mouth, and I said, "Jim, what's happened?" It felt like "I'm having a drug experience," but yet there was no drug. And I remember thinking, "This is the greatest high I've ever had."

When Jim explained, "You just got filled with the Holy Ghost," Steve replied, "The holy what?" And Jim said, "The Holy Spirit, Steve. Go home and read the book of John and the book of Acts." So when he arrived home, Steve said: "I grabbed the Bible off of the shelf, King James version, which I hadn't opened in quite a long time. I read the book of John and the book of Acts, and I went, 'Oh, my Lord. What happened to them 2,000 years ago just happened to me!'" His back pain was gone.

Steve's experience is not unique. A seminary student in his mid-twenties told us that in a worship service the Holy Spirit came upon him "with ferocious intensity." He said, "I had never experienced anything like this in my entire life. There was a possibility in my mind that I could actually die right there on the spot." In his case, it felt as if God had a hand on the inside as well as the outside of his body: "I was literally being crushed to death." He interpreted this experience as being in the "grip of God," and he related it to the accounts of first-century Christians who were accused of being drunk but instead were filled with the Holy Spirit. For this young man and others, such experiences, even if they occur only once in a lifetime, are clearly unforgettable, serving as significant reference points in understanding the power of God.

A number of individuals also told us about hearing God speak to them. In several instances people heard a voice, and in one case the communication was visual. One Vineyard member said, "It was right at the end of my second year at Princeton: I woke up one morning and there were—it's almost embarrassing to say this because most people look at you so incredulously—but there were fiery letters across the field of vision that were about this high that said 'Seminary.' I went, 'Oh, God wants me to go to a seminary.' It was just a no-brainer." Other individuals described extremely visual dreams that gave specific instructions about future plans. Indeed, we were told, in new paradigm churches the pastor often waits for a congregation member to receive the same spirit-initiated vision the pastor has already received—for example, that the congregant should lead a particular ministry or enter full-time ministry.

Living under the Freudian paradigm, we tend to interpret dreams and visions as expressions of subconscious wishes and desires, and certainly the examples just cited are amenable to such an interpretation. On the other hand, there is a long tradition of sacred visitations in dreams as well as in the waking state, and I prefer to highlight the continuity between the religious experiences of new paradigm Christians and those of past ages than to debunk these experiences through modern psycho-analytic theory. More specifically, whatever may be occurring at a sub-conscious level, these dreams and visions are turning-point experiences for people who affirm that God is a living presence in their lives. Far from sensationalizing these sacred encounters, the people we inter-viewed seemed caught by surprise; indeed, my impression was that the unanticipated quality of the experience was what made it so powerful.

God or Drugs?

Worrying about the roots of religious experience may quickly dissolve into reductionism, dismissing the integrity of the experi-ence by explaining it away in terms of its antecedents. The dilemmas associated with interpreting religious encounters, especially those con-nected to drug use, are raised forcefully by the experience of one of the early converts to the Calvary movement who, at the time, was heavily into cocaine. The following account could probably be interpreted as a drug-induced experience, but does that invalidate the spiritual en-counter? William James would strenuously argue that it does not.

"So I snorted this whole vial," this man recollected, "and I sat down because I knew that it would be a real rush, and it started to come on, that familiar feeling of a tightening in your throat, and the taste that goes through your system. Everything started to break down. And I knew it was stronger than anything that I had done before and it was hitting my system faster. And so I put myself down into a half-lotus position and started doing a chant to center myself so I wouldn't go crazy."

What followed was a definite near-death experience, similar to those described in many case studies:

Something happened and I started to convulse. I started to sort of foam at the mouth and my heart started beating like really, really violently, and it was just beating harder and harder, and then I kind of doubled over and I was trying to throw up, but nothing was coming out of my mouth but foam. And I remember that my heart was beating harder and harder and I couldn't breathe. I was gasping for breath, and my friends couldn't do anything for me, and the last thing I remember was tumbling over and not being able to breathe and just feeling like the life ebbed out of me and my heart just kind of stopped. And I remember being conscious of the fact that I had died, or my bodily functions had stopped, which was confirmed to me by my friends. They said they couldn't get me going, they couldn't get me breathing, they couldn't find a pulse.

He then described his sensations: "I was a totally conscious person, but I was no longer attached to my senses. In other words, I couldn't see anything anymore. The desert had disappeared, the people had disappeared. I had a total awareness. And I remember I couldn't feel anything. I couldn't hear anything. I couldn't see anything. But I was totally conscious. And everything was totally dark because I couldn't see anything, but it wasn't like a darkness where you shut out the lights. It was a darkness where there was nothing."

But he remembered wanting to return to earth, even in this detached state of consciousness:

I started to cry out with the mantras, with the chants, focusing upon the energies of the universe, but to no avail. Then I started to summon from my soul names of Krishna, Lord Krishna, Buddha, Brahma. [But] because the nonpersonal vibrations weren't working, I started crying out to personalities. Nothing was happening. And the very last name I cried out to was Jesus, because Jesus was to me the lowest level that I had found of spirituality. I thought that Christians were just a bunch of mindless little zombies, and I didn't have a good experience of Christians at all.

But when I cried out to the name of Jesus, in the deepest part of myself I started to see flashes of light, and they got brighter and brighter and more and more numerous around me. Even though I couldn't see with my eyes, they were like flashing at my soul. And they were brighter and brighter and brighter, and then pretty soon everything became one giant bright light for a moment, and I woke up. I mean, I 'came to' in my body, and I could see that I was lying on my back, and I was looking forward at the outline of a man who seemed to be the source of the light. I looked at the light, and for half a moment I could see the image of a man, with his arms out and all this light just flowing out of that image, and right behind him the sun was shining, and the sun was like really dead in comparison to the brightness from the countenance of this man.

And I remember feeling total stark fear, like so afraid that I knew that I was in mortal danger, or I felt I was in mortal danger. All my senses told me to run. And I spun around, I covered my eyes, and I was so afraid that I actually found myself trying to burrow into the sand to get away from the sight of this being. And yet even with my back turned and my eyes closed and trying to dig my head literally into the sand I knew he could still see every single part of me. He could see through me, and in me, and my whole soul was like naked before this being. Now I remember feeling like my whole life I had always felt like I was a pretty good person. I'm pretty moral, I don't do anything to hurt anybody else. And all of a sudden, all of that meant nothing to me. I couldn't cling on to anything to make me feel comforted before his presence. And I remember I couldn't hide, I couldn't get anywhere.

I remember that I felt or heard something—you know, it's so hard to tell what happened—but I felt this voice or heard this voice that kind of moved right through my whole being, and I remember the words he said: "I am Alpha and Omega, the Beginning and the End." And that's all I remember, and it started to fade behind me. And by the time I turned around, there were just little flickers of light, and the sun was shining and the desert was there, and I was all alone. And I sat there going, "Was that a hallucination?" I mean, that was the most incredible thing that I had ever experienced. It was like, was it a vision?

He said that he sat there two more days, in a somewhat blind condition because he had lost his contact lenses. He then drove home, snorted some cocaine, and went back to everyday business. A short time later he had a conversion experience at a Calvary Chapel concert, in part, I suspect, because his drug-related vision had awakened an awareness of Jesus.

Although one might be tempted to interpret this vision as nothing more than a hallucinatory episode, such "medical materialism," as William James called it, is too easy an answer. Ironically, it ignores the fact that all experience is physiological and has its chemical correlates. If electrodes were attached to the shaved heads of monks uttering Gregorian chants, they would undoubtedly measure a change in brain wave activity, as has been demonstrated for chanting associated with transcendental meditation.[20] Those who dismiss religious experience—including both liberal religionists and skeptics—often, somewhat paradoxically, spiritualize it, refusing to acknowledge the interconnections of mind, body, and spirit.

Church historian Robert M. Anderson, a student of American Pentecostalism, argues that ecstatic experience is at the heart of many spirit-centered movements, both Christian and primitive, but he tends to see religious experience as compensatory, helping people cope with their economic and social deprivation.[21] I disagree. Functionally, religion may be viewed as psychological compensation—but, then, there are few human experiences that cannot be so interpreted, including art, opera, drama, and dance. Although Marxist and psychoanalytic perspectives are valuable, they evoke cynicism when applied too dogmatically. I believe that ecstatic religious experience can empower rather than simply compensate, that it raises people to heights they would otherwise never experience. In my view, it is an altogether natural experience, which is diminished when reductionistically attributed to either social deprivation or abnormal (psychotic) wish fulfillment.

Healing at the Vineyard

I have vivid memories of the first Vineyard healing conference I attended, which was shortly after the Anaheim Vineyard had moved into its new 3,000-seat auditorium. Although I had witnessed "ministry time" at the end of Sunday worship services, I was not prepared for the "manifestations of the spirit" that I encountered in this several-day conference. In fact, at the end of the first evening I remember returning to my car and turning on a rock-and-roll station (to which I never listen), just to ground myself again in the profanity of everyday life. I had encountered something that shook the foundations of my late-twentieth-century worldview.

That first evening session was led by "Mahesh," who was born in India, converted in Kenya, and at age twenty-five came to the United States as a student. The auditorium was filled, and worship was archetypal Vineyard: several upbeat songs at the beginning led by a lively band, and then a half-hour of extremely mellow music with people singing along to words projected on two giant screens on either side of the stage. The lyrics emphasized God's holiness and compassion, and perhaps a third of the people stood spontaneously at different moments with their hands raised in praise. Close to where I was sitting was a group from the Palo Alto area, several hundred miles away, and others had also traveled a distance to attend.

Following the worship period and a few announcements, Mahesh was introduced without fanfare, and he began his talk on "complete surrender" to God's will, interspersing throughout his message specific examples of God's healing power. Some accounts were rather dramatic, including a personal story from his work in an institution for retarded children. There, one young boy continually bashed his face against the wall. Mahesh fasted for fourteen days and then prayed for this child, who was instantly delivered of a demon and ceased his masochistic behavior. After a half hour of similarly riveting accounts, Mahesh stopped to pray, thanking God for "the anointing" of the Holy Spirit, and continuing, "We give you glory, Lord . . . Just breathe in now . . . Let the Lord Jesus refresh you." He then began to name specific physical ailments of people in the audience: "The anointing is touching a hip that needs surgery." He cited specific individuals and diseases—for example, a person with lupus who was wearing the color teal. Dozens of people started to come forward for prayer at this point, more than were named. As people gathered in the front, Mahesh continued to tell stories of people whom he had seen healed, and he called out to additional people in the audience: a woman with a dyslexic child, a man with severe migraines, someone needing arthroscopic knee surgery, a person who was HIV positive, a woman with a prolapsed uterus.

Before moving down the steps of the stage to pray for these individuals, he said, "Holy Spirit, let the anointing come now." Immediately, someone in the audience began to sob, and this seemed to unleash tears from others gathered in the front of the auditorium. People continued to stream forward for prayer, and the band started playing quietly in the background. The initial person's wailing had stopped, but I heard more sobbing, including one man who seemed overwhelmed with grief. Members of the ministry team had come forward to help pray, because clearly Mahesh was unable to pray for everyone individually. Often, when Mahesh did touch someone, the person fell backward in response and was caught by someone who seemed especially skilled at the task.

While Mahesh was praying for people, John Wimber came to the microphone. He, too, called out infirmities of various kinds. When he mentioned someone with an injured navel, however, no one responded. "I was sure the Lord said that you were over here," Wimber remarked. And he waited, joking, "Are you ashamed to stand up for your navel?" The crowd laughed. (Later, according to Wimber, someone admitted to being healed but being too embarrassed to stand up.) Wimber proceeded to cite someone with white spots on the roof of the mouth. Three people stood. He then spoke of someone with a lacerated throat, and when two people rose together, Wimber ribbed, "What have you two been doing?" There was a curious blending of profane and sacred, lightheartedness as well as ministry to profound pain.

Turning my attention from the stage, I saw a person close to me jerking violently and involuntarily. Others extended trembling hands. Then Wimber said: "While the Lord is here, this is the time to go to work. So turn to the person next to you and pray for them." These instructions increased the number of people having healing experiences. The couple next to me was praying together, and the young woman was crying. The implication of Wimber's remark was that if God was here, the congregation should take advantage of his power, and Wimber continued to encourage people by saying, "Raise your hand if you want to be prayed for."

The room seemed a laboratory for healing, where anyone could get into the act—either by being prayed for or by praying for someone else. People were moving freely around the auditorium, and I ventured over to someone who was wailing uncontrollably. A small prayer circle had gathered around her, including a woman on the periphery who had extended her hand toward the person. Wimber was silent now, except to say occasionally, "Let the power come. Come Holy Spirit." And reinforcing the laboratory notion, he said: "Learn by watching, praying, thanking God. It's okay to look around and see what God is doing."

And look I did. Dozens of people were lying prone in front of the stage. Some were shaking, others were crying, and some were still. Typically there were several people ministering to these individuals by praying for them. A line had gathered in front of Mahesh, and his touch seemed to buckle their knees and put them into a trancelike state, clearly interpreted by all concerned as an anointing by the Holy Spirit. Uncertain of what was transpiring, I kept my distance, but I did have a vivid image that something similar might have occurred when Jesus (and later his disciples) healed the sick and ministered to those possessed by demons.

By 10:30 P.M. I was exhausted, confused, and desperately in need of some interpretive framework to protect my sanity. The next day I was back, however, and I asked permission to distribute "testimony" forms to the conference participants. As I pored over these forms in subsequent weeks, I was very impressed by the reality of the issues addressed—especially the emotional pain in people's lives—even though I remained uncertain about the method of cure.

A typical testimony form statement comes from a woman who was sexually abused as a child and reported the following process of healing during the conference:

I was worshiping and praying while John Wimber was speaking on Wednesday night of the conference. I had earlier that day dealt with the forgiveness of my father for his sexual abuse and abandonment of me when I was a child, but I had never really felt the whole pain of that experience. I had only dealt with my anger.

That night as John asked the Holy Spirit to come, I felt as if I were in a trance. My eyes were closed and I at first just felt at peace. I was breathing very deeply and the spirit was comforting me.

I then had a sharp pain in my lower right abdomen, and it was constant. As the Spirit intensified I felt very hot and like an energy force was pulsing through me. A woman came over and began to pray. The Lord revealed to her my problem, and she began to command me to release my anger and bitterness.

I began to cry very hard and the more she prayed the more the Spirit intensified, and the pain in my abdomen began to decrease. She told me to give my pain to Jesus, so I lifted my hands to Jesus, and as she prayed for the pain to release, the pain began to flow up from my abdomen, out of my chest through my fingers and began to leave.

I then could feel something bubbling up in my chest, and I began to cry more intensely and scream out. I had finally released all the pain. Then she invited the Holy Spirit to fill me up, and I felt such joy, happiness, as if Jesus were holding me and he told me he would be my father and never leave.

I still feel totally on fire and tingling all over. I felt very refreshed, like a burden had been released from my soul. I couldn't stand up because my legs were shaking, but I felt so good and blessed.

One thing that is fascinating in these testimony accounts is how frequently people mentioned experiencing specific physical sensations, such as heat, tingling, electricity, palpitations of the heart, sweating, and rapid breathing. These physiological sensations were matched by ecstatic feelings of joy, peace, blissfulness, and purging (especially of past memories).

In reading the testimony responses, I was particularly struck by the number of people who said that they had been abused physically or sexually as children and reported finding release from the anger and pain of these experiences during the conference. People also spoke about their feelings of being physically abandoned as children (often by fathers), as well as their anger toward parents for lack of nurturing and cultivation of self-worth. It appears that many people were able to access extremely deep-seated memories (sometimes totally repressed until some moment during the conference) and then experience almost complete release from the pain of the past.

Many people also claimed relief from physical problems at these conferences, although this was cited less frequently on the testimony forms than emotional healing. Among the physical problems mentioned (in order of frequency) were back injuries, neck pain, breathing problems, headaches, abdominal pain, reproductive problems, and leg pain. In addition, people cited specific "spiritual" problems that were healed, ranging from lack of trust in God, to "abuse" experienced in other churches and "demonic" attack.

The testimony forms also provide a demographic portrait of those who attend Vineyard healing conferences, or at least the several where we distributed our forms.[22] Slightly less than half were from Vineyard churches, with approximately a fifth from nondenominational churches and 30 percent from denominations such as Baptist, Presbyterian, Episcopal, Assemblies of God, and Methodist (in order of frequency). In terms of childhood religious background, Catholics were most frequently represented, followed by Baptists, various nondenominational churches, Methodists, Presbyterians, and Lutherans.

Many people travel some distance to these conferences: nearly 40 percent were from outside California, and 7 percent were from foreign countries. Forty-four percent were male and 56 percent female; 88 percent were white, 7 percent Asian, 3 percent Hispanic, and 1 percent African American; 71 percent were married, 9 percent divorced, 2 percent widowed, and 16 percent single. The mean age was forty-two.

In response to our questions about religious experiences that they had had prior to attending the conference, 84 percent said that they had spoken in tongues, 86 percent had experienced emotional healing, and 74 percent said they had experienced physical healing. Yet 45 percent had never before attended a healing conference.

HOLY LAUGHTER

On the final night of the conference something happened that caught me completely by surprise but has subsequently been much debated in the religious and secular press. The worship period was routine, although I detected a distinct sweetness and power to the music. Even Wimber was wiping tears from his eyes as the podium was lifted into place for him to speak. His first comment was, "Wouldn't it be great if he [Jesus] came right now?"

Wimber's message was on the "impartation" of the Holy Spirit, and he belabored the point that "God is boss, not us." Stressing God's sovereignty, Wimber said, "We are clay and he is the potter." Running throughout his message was the idea that God does the healing, not himself, Mahesh, or other conference speakers. And to keep us honest, said Wimber, sometimes God chooses not to show up, just to demonstrate that he is in charge and that it is nothing that we do or control. Furthermore, Wimber stressed that we cannot give rational accounts of God's actions; we can only be faithful servants. While many churches have elected to ignore the practice of Jesus and the early church, he noted, Christians are instructed to heal the sick and to cast out demons—irrespective of the success rate of these activities. Addressing our natural inclination to interpret the successes and failures of healing, Wimber said that the Holy Spirit does not have our categories of success and failure, and he implied that the rational mind really cannot evaluate the work of the Holy Spirit.

When he finished the message, Wimber prayed, and then, spontaneously, first one person started laughing, then another, and another.[23] I didn't know what was occurring; no joke had been told. After a few minutes, as the laughing continued, Wimber offered an interpretive comment, saying, "It's the power of God," followed by the biblical citation, "Be not drunk with wine, but filled with the Spirit." I got out of my seat and started walking around the auditorium to find men and women laughing hysterically, some literally falling on the floor. Wimber was simply watching this spectacle, at one point encouraging, "Let it come."

After a while he asked several of the conference speakers to come and pray for specific gifts, saying, "When they pray, I want you to reach out and get whatever you want." Prayers were then offered for compassion and various spiritual "impartations." I was intrigued that one of the speakers prayed, "Make us people of heart [versus mind]. Give us humility to receive it [i.e., the gifts of the spirit]. Say 'no' to our [academic] degrees if they get in the way of our heart." I suspect he had people like me in mind. Then, after a few more prayers from the leadership, Wimber closed with a prayer of blessing, remembering those in need of food and clothing, those who are divorced, and children who are fatherless.

Spontaneously, many of the younger people in the audience formed a circle, and holding hands danced in a large circle around the auditorium. A mother with a baby stroller joined in while the band played. For another twenty minutes people celebrated, and then we left the auditorium to reenter the profane world of traffic lights, mortgage payments, and the demands of our varying places of employment.

CHAPTER 5

Living by the Bible

Social Ministry, Politics, Theology

As a lifelong Democrat and a theological liberal, I cringed slightly when I first saw the results of our congregational survey. Only 8 percent of more than 3,000 respondents had voted Democratic in the 1992 presidential election. On a broader question regarding their political inclinations, over half indicated they were "conservative" or "extremely conservative," while only 2 percent fit the corresponding categories on the liberal side of the ledger (the rest were independent or middle of the road). When I turned to the responses to the pastors survey, I was somewhat taken back to find that the overwhelming majority of clergy said that "only the followers of Jesus Christ and members of his church can be saved." This view did not sit well with my own appreciation of the multiple insights found in a variety of different religious traditions.

On the other hand, as I looked more closely at the results, I saw that some of the stereotypes about those on the "right" and "left" did not hold. For example, while new paradigm members were overwhelmingly opposed to abortion as well as homosexuality, they were strongly against racial prejudice. New paradigm members were also relatively liberal on civil liberty measures. And, in spite of their millenarian beliefs on the imminent end of the world and the return of Christ, they were heavily involved in forward-looking activities such as feeding the poor, donating for disaster relief, and caring for prisoners.

In pondering our survey results, I have become convinced that three factors must be accounted for in understanding the beliefs of new paradigm members and their pastors. The first is their commitment to "historical realism" (in contrast to the symbolic realism that most liberal theologians hold); they believe not only that the Bible is divinely inspired but that the events described in it literally occurred.[1] This perspective on the Bible explains why they believe in miracles (including the virgin birth and the physical resurrection of Jesus from the dead), affirm with Paul that women should submit to their husbands, and have a conservative sexual ethic. If something is stated explicitly in the Bible, then new paradigm pastors accept it as gospel.

Second, new paradigm members and their pastors see human selfishness—or, to use the old-fashioned term, *sin*—as the core cause of all social problems. They do not think that a few more social programs will make the streets safe, remove the menace of drugs from public schools, or reverse the breakdown of the American family. A much more fundamental change is needed, one that tackles the problem at its roots—namely, that people need to shift from serving *self* to serving *God*, and hence be "born again."

Third, converts to new paradigm groups are seeking order in a world that has left many of them struggling for meaning. According to our survey, 30 percent of congregants come from broken homes, and an equal number say their parents abused alcohol or drugs. In addition, they have struggled with their own problems. One out of three have been divorced or are currently separated; nearly half say they have gone to a professional therapist at least once (with 11 percent going "often" and 23 percent "a few times"); and, as was reported previously, a quarter said that they often used drugs prior to conversion.

Given the pain and disruption that fill the lives of new paradigm members—and they, of course, are not unique in contemporary American society—it is quite understandable that they might seek anchorage in a religious tradition where truth claims are relatively unambiguous. By saying this, I am not dismissing the theological or philosophical arguments for viewing the Bible as the authoritative, inerrant Word of God, although I do not personally hold to this view. It is also quite understandable, especially given their own experience, that new paradigm members do not think government-funded social programs will solve the deep-seated problems of our times. Our postmodern world is a fractured place of competing interest groups, discourses, and perspectives, and the desire for something that is unchanging, eternal, and divinely inspired is undoubtedly attractive, especially when one can experience it through joyful, culturally current worship forms.

In this chapter I examine what new paradigm Christians believe and the ways in which they are enacting these beliefs, beginning with descriptions of some of the social ministries of new paradigm churches. I am convinced that the *practice* of people in these churches is an important way of understanding the *meaning* of what they teach. I also look at gender roles, marriage, and raising children, as well as the political commitments of new paradigm members and their pastors. Finally, I turn to the specific theological views of new paradigm Christians.

In my opinion, the personal religious experiences of new paradigm members and their beliefs connect with the cultural tensions of the late twentieth century. Specifically, the conservative theological beliefs of new paradigm Christians are a response to a world with no stable moral center; and the conservative political views of new paradigm Christians ironically reflect countercultural attitudes toward government institutions that were cultivated in their youth (i.e., "Since government is false and hypocritical, the less government the better"). In other words, conservative religious and political views coalesce in a culture where young families and teenagers are seeking meaning and moral order.

We Need the Poor
More Than the Poor Need Us

It used to be that only liberal mainline congregations were engaged in serving the poor and dispossessed of our society, while conservative and Pentecostal churches were busy praying and worrying about personal holiness—or at least this is how the story was commonly told. Whether this account is true is for future historians to sort out. But today new paradigm churches are as busy passing out food, collecting clothes for distribution, running gang prevention programs, and providing health care as any comparable liberal churches. The primary difference between their social ministries and those of their liberal counterparts is that they believe the ultimate solution to any social problem is a "changed heart," and thus evangelism is often included in their ministry to persons in need (although not in the dogmatic way that one sometimes associates with fundamentalist-run skid row missions).

A typical activist is Monte Whittaker at the Vineyard Christian Fellowship in Anaheim, who helps lead this church's "benevolence" ministry. A program that now serves over a million meals a year had an unpretentious beginning when Monte and his wife moved to Los Angeles. They lived in a rough neighborhood, and his wife used to nurse their newborn son behind the security bars of their living room window. She wondered, Monte recalls, why people tended to walk down the center divider of the street, "and then she realized it was because they were walking on the grass, because they didn't have shoes on or they had holes in their shoes, and so they burned their feet walking on the sidewalk or the pavement. And so she began to take shoes out to them and blankets and give them things from our home." Before long, Monte and his wife were packing bag lunches to give to people and going to the park where the homeless congregated.

One night they went to the park with thirty-six dinners to distribute, but it had rained and few people were there. They gave away about a dozen bags and were wondering what to do with the rest of the food when they decided to ask for guidance. As Monte recalls: "We sat and we prayed, and I felt like the Lord was telling us we were to take the remaining food along Imperial Highway to some shacks that I had seen around there. The first family took a long time to answer the door. There were about twelve people sleeping in this little room, so they had mattresses and blankets laid out through the whole thing, so when they opened the door, they had to lift a mattress to get the door open. And so we gave them most of what we had left and then we went to the next door."

Then an event occurred that deeply affected Monte: "The next fellow, I told him in my broken Spanish, that we had free food that we were giving out, and he came back with a little baggie that had about a half inch of rice on the bottom of it. And he told me in Spanish that that was all the food he could spare because they only had another baggie about the same size left for his family, but that I was welcome to it." Immediately Monte explained that they wanted to give *him* food. But this act of generosity so moved Monte that he and some friends from the Vineyard began taking groceries on a regular basis to the parks, and in a short time they were giving out several hundred bags weekly.

What began as a few bag lunches has grown to a warehouse where surplus food is bought very cheaply, and sacks of food continue to be given away, principally to recent immigrants. Also, a program called the Lamb's Lunch has evolved in which people are served a hot meal that is followed by a time of worship. According to Monte, "We need the poor more than the poor need us. We need the poor in order to learn to become 'otherly.'" In his view, "God has blessed us because of our ministry to the poor, and much of what He [God] is doing here [at the Vineyard] is because of that."

Another program that grew spontaneously out of the conviction of a Vineyard member is the ministry to prisoners. Jack Russell (not his real name) had himself spent several short stints in jail, so he assumed that he would never be given the identification tag he needed to visit a penitentiary and evangelize. When he received his ID, he said, "This must be God," and immediately began a small Bible study. "It started out with about eight to ten guys just coming into this room staring at me," he remembers. "No motion at all. And I'm trying to give this Bible study. I didn't know whether these guys were Christians or whether they hated me or liked me." Tuesday after Tuesday he went there thinking, "What am I doing?" But in spite of feeling intimidated he thought, "You know what? God has loved me so much in this last year, and so much in my life, I just want to give something back. I'm just going to love these guys even if they stare me down. I'm just going to keep loving them and keep showing them how God loves them." Within a short period, his Bible study went from ten prisoners to sixty, and he dropped the Bible study and began to do a Vineyard-style worship for them.

Meeting in the same small room in which the Bible study started, Jack reflects: "I could have gotten mauled. But, no, God was very much there and these guys began to come alive. They knew that I loved them, they knew I was there for them. I wasn't there to put on a show for them or to do some kind of ministry that somebody's paying me to go do. They kind of began to get the message that I loved them and God loved them. I think out of that, they just opened up."

On many occasions, Jack couldn't get them to stop singing. "I wanted to bring a contemporary worship that I loved, that just freed me up," he explains. "If you have ever been down there [in jail], you would understand that these guys do not [usually] feel anything. [But] they bounce off the walls with the songs, and they get excited. They are not ashamed to worship. If you were to lock yourself in your bathroom for about six months and you walked into a Vineyard, you might just dance off the ceiling, also. So they love to worship and they don't want to stop. If we don't get it going with the guitar, they'll start the song. They don't want to stop worshiping."

Jack wants to be a pastor who gives them hope, even though they don't believe in themselves: "That's the kind of pastor I want to be to them, somebody who believes in them even though society tells them, 'You failed, you blew it, you're a mess, you've got no hope, there is no future for you, you're just going to be locked up for the next twenty years and you're going to have to join a gang to survive.' I want to be a pastor who says, 'No, you don't have to give up. Our God is bigger. I believe God has a plan for your life and a purpose for your life, even if it's behind bars for twenty years.' I just want them to be laid out [confronted by Christ] like I was."

The same church sponsors an equivalent program for women prisoners. One focus of this ministry is on pregnant women in prison, who fear that their infants will be taken away from them completely. "Newborn Connection" matches pregnant incarcerated women with licensed foster-care parents from a local church. After the baby is born, the foster parent takes the newborn to the prison once a week to allow some bonding to occur between mother and infant. Once the woman is released from prison, the former foster parent often maintains a connection with the mother and her baby. Newborn Connection is a simple idea, founded by someone whose motivation came from her own "newborn connection," a spiritual one, she says.

Another example of a formalized social ministry for pregnant women is the House of Ruth. This program was started by the wife of the pastor of a large Calvary Chapel. As a teenager, she had given her baby up for adoption and was deeply hurt by the fact that she was not able to maintain contact with the child. As a result, the goal of this program is not simply to talk women out of having abortions, although this is one motive, but to establish a connection with parents who will adopt the child and include the birth mother as part of their family.

In addition to the long list of programmatic social ministries in new paradigm churches, there are many individual acts of selfless human kindness. For example, in our interview with Kim, a member of a Calvary Chapel on the East Coast, she casually mentioned that a high school teenager had lived with her family most of the previous year. "She was fifteen and she had a baby," Kim said. "We took her through labor and delivery and she came and lived with us a year and we homeschooled [the mother] for a year." When asked why she would give of herself in this way, Kim responded: "That's what the Lord teaches us to do. It says to do unto others as you would want them to do unto you. Now if you are out there and you are hurting, do you want to sit on a street bench? Or would you rather come into somebody's warm home?" Then Kim added another wrinkle to her motivation: "It helped *us* to grow, to not be selfish, and we still would like to have more kids come live with us as the Lord lays it on our hearts."

Social ministry at new paradigm churches is deeply motivated by biblical examples. So it is not surprising that the programs I have cited deal with feeding the hungry, clothing those in need, ministering to prisoners, and assisting young single mothers (today's "widows").[2] Such services to those in need often involve invitations for them to find new life in a relationship with Jesus and, as a corollary, join a supportive community of like-minded Christians. Thus, community and ideology are both part of what new paradigm churches offer the needy.

In interviewing participants in these programs, I heard little about changing society through advocacy of new social policies. If anything, their conservative political views suggest that social welfare is the responsibility of the church, not the state. From my own perspective, I have questions about the capacity of the private sector to deal systematically with the day-to-day needs of poor people for health care, housing, and monthly income subsidies. Yet it is difficult to ignore the human good that these people are doing as they minister to individuals in concrete ways.

Gender Roles, Marriage, Children, and Sex

Although many of the social ministries of new paradigm Christians are focused on individuals, they are committed to a broader vision of societal change. Their specific target is the family, because from it, they believe, all other social institutions can be altered. The family is where values are shaped and children are molded to be productive citizens. But, unfortunately, say new paradigm Christians, the family has disintegrated as people have followed their "sinful," selfish inclinations. To counter this trend, they aim to create families that provide ordered, nurturing environments for children. From this goal follow many of their values related to gender, marriage, and sexuality.

Accepting the Bible as literal truth, new paradigm Christians accept the following statements of Paul as prescriptive: "Wives, submit yourselves unto your husbands, as unto the Lord. For the husband is the head of the wife, even as Christ is the head of the church: and he is the savior of the body. Therefore as the church is subject unto Christ, so let the wives be to their own husbands in every thing."[3] This oft-quoted passage from Paul's letter to the Ephesians is then qualified by instructions to husbands on how they should treat their wives: "Husbands, love your wives, even as Christ also loved the church, and gave himself for it. . . . So ought men to love their wives as their own bodies. He that loveth his wife loveth himself."[4]

In our interviews with members and pastors, the principle of submission was repeated by men and women alike with little qualification or apology. Indeed, they seemed to appreciate a clear chain of command. But they stressed that this submission also implies responsibility on the part of those to whom one submits. While I believe that the notion of submission could certainly be abused, women we interviewed frequently commented that submission did not mean an authoritarian relationship. For example, one woman said, "I kind of ran the family until I was thirty-six years old and we came to the Lord. I still try and do it, but I'll tell you, [now] I give him my opinion, and I persuade him in a lot of things, but when it gets right down to whether we are going to do it or not, if it's a big thing, Rick decides, but he is easy to be submissive to. He is so kind now. It is always, 'What is the best for me?'" Further clarifying why submission is palatable to her, she stated, "He has become such a different man—in the way he looks at me and the way he loves me. It's so easy to do what he asks me to do because I know it's for the best. It isn't, 'Oh, God, do I really have to do this; I really don't want to, but God says you've got to be submissive to your husband.' It doesn't work that way."

Another woman contended that a proper understanding of Paul's teaching is actually liberating for women: "You would never hear it from the Vineyard that the wife is to be at home barefoot in the kitchen taking care of the kids and cooking the meals for the husband and attending to his every need. In fact, in a lot of our ministry in the South and in the Midwest, we actually end up bringing new freedom to women in that area, because it is the only life they have ever known and we say that is not what life has to be for you. That is not the way the Lord intended it. You are supposed to have your own identity. You are supposed to be a person."

When, in a separate interview, we asked this woman's husband to explain his view of Paul's teachings, he responded: "I don't think that my wife is inferior to me in any sense of the word. I believe that God created men and women equally, but I believe he created them with different roles . . . there are some roles that God would prefer to have filled by men, and some roles for women." Nevertheless, his wife indicated that final responsibility for decision making belonged with him: "He is the ultimate decision maker in our household, although we discuss every decision, and we make them all together."

Some women are attracted to this view of husband-wife relationships by what has been called the "patriarchal bargain": they believe they get a more responsible and caring spouse when their husbands assume the role of "head" of the house.[5] In addition, some women seek legitimation for a more traditional role, one that does not require them to link their identity to a profession.[6] On the other side, this biblical interpretation of gender roles may hold an attraction beyond just power for men in today's society, especially for those who seem uncertain about their male identity. For example, one man told us that many of his peers are confused about what it means to be masculine. He claimed that this is a "fatherless" generation and therefore he and many of his male friends do not know how to be husbands or fathers. Consequently, he welcomes the normative standards inherent in a biblical view of the head of the household.[7]

The text from Ephesians is not the only one quoted by new paradigm Christians in discussions of gender roles. In a passage offering advice on how to worship, Paul tells women that they should dress modestly, without gold or pearl adornments, and then he states: "Let the woman learn in silence with all subjection. But I suffer not a woman to teach, nor to usurp authority over the man, but to be in silence."[8] This passage is quoted to explain why the senior pastors in new paradigm churches are men, yet it is also seen as justifying female leadership in the all-women groups that thrive in many new paradigm churches. Women are allowed to exhort and teach so long as only women are in attendance, but they are not permitted to preach or "usurp" the leadership of men.

Thus women sidestep Paul's prohibitions by creating women-only groups, some of which number several thousand women.[9] Supposedly, in these groups women "teach" rather than "preach," but if one looked at a transcript, it would be hard to distinguish between what a male pastor might say and the "exhortations" offered by women in these settings. While I would not defend the prohibition against women serving in a broad range of pastoral roles, I was surprised that the women I interviewed seldom raised this prohibition as a problematic issue—leading me to think that, for the moment, women-only groups are providing fulfilling leadership opportunities.[10]

Within these groups women not only "teach," but they also worship together (sometimes more expressively than they would in male company), meet in small support groups, go on retreats, and organize activities to address the specific needs of women. In this regard, women have created roles in these new paradigm churches that are, in many instances, the functional equivalents of the roles officially reserved for men. And rhetoric aside, I sometimes see more equality—at least in terms of men's shared responsibility—in new paradigm churches than I have observed in many mainline liberal churches. Men, for example, are active in children's programs, ranging from preschool on up. Also, within the family, many men appear to be taking more responsibility for child rearing than their counterparts in mainline churches.

Our survey included several questions designed to measure attitudes toward women's roles. Nearly 70 percent of our respondents approved of a married woman earning money outside the home, even if she has a husband capable of supporting her. On a more politically oriented question, three-fourths of our respondents disagreed with the statement that "women should take care of running their homes and leave running the country up to men." Although there was more ambivalence, a majority of respondents also disagreed with the statement that "men are better suited emotionally for politics than most women."

In spite of these generally liberal sentiments about gender equality, many new paradigm Christian families feel that, until children are past grade school, a mother should stay home rather than work—if the family can afford this option. In fact, 58 percent of the spouses of Calvary pastors and 48 percent of the Vineyard pastors' wives were "keeping house" rather than working at outside jobs. Nurturing children is an extremely strong value for new paradigm Christians in their attempt to rebuild the institutions of American society. Chuck Smith, for example, indicated that his wife, Kay, did not become active in leading the church's time-consuming women's program until after their youngest child had left home. Other couples told us that they were living modestly because they wanted the mother to be at home for her kids.

The most extreme sign of dedication to children is the popularity of home schooling. Our survey indicated that a number of parents were teaching their school-age children at home, an activity that places enormous demands on parents and often disproportionately on the mother. While some of the motivation for home schooling may be protecting children from the "secular values" of public schools, the stronger reason seems to be the perception that children receive a better education at home. Active networks have developed among parents doing home schooling—who often use church facilities as a meeting place—and some of the churches with day schools permit home-schooled youth to participate in their athletic programs.

In new paradigm churches this commitment to children and the family extends to marital counseling and even the initial decision to get married. Pastors apply rigorous criteria in agreeing to marry couples and require formal preparation for marriage. For example, new paradigm clergy will not marry a couple unless both individuals are committed Christians who have a "relationship" with Christ. If an unmarried couple is living together, they will frequently be asked to separate, since the church believes the Bible prohibits premarital sex. If one of the parties seeking to be married is divorced, an inquiry will be made into the grounds for the divorce, because the Bible prohibits adultery. Attempts are often made to reconcile a divorced couple, and only if these fail will remarriage within the church be sanctioned. If all of the biblical conditions for marriage are met, then the couple goes through an extensive program of premarital counseling, covering issues ranging from sexual fulfillment in marriage to management of household finances.

It is within the context of the priority given to the family by new paradigm churches that I believe one best understands the emotions surrounding abortion. More than 90 percent of our congregational respondents did not believe that abortion should be legal for married women who simply do not want to have more children, and the clergy nearly universally rejected this view. Nevertheless, I believe that this view, only marginally alluded to in the Bible, is based less on moral abhorrence to extracting fetal tissue from a woman's womb than on a strong commitment to family life and values.

On another controversial issue, homosexuality, 97 percent of our congregational respondents and nearly 100 percent of the clergy said that sexual relations between two adults of the same sex are always wrong. This strong response undoubtedly reflects the various scriptural references forbidding same-sex relations. However, I believe the vehemence of the response is also related to a perception that homosexuality is a threat to the traditional family and, implicitly, to traditional gender roles.[11]

Political Commitments

When asked to identify themselves on a political spectrum, new paradigm Christians identify as conservatives, with the pastors being even more conservative than their members.[12] When the conservative label is translated into voting behavior, members and clergy tend to prefer Republican candidates, with the clergy voting Republican somewhat more frequently than their members.

Nevertheless, our survey data suggest that pastors and congregants are not politically homogeneous. While pastors indicate a strong interest in politics and national affairs, only a quarter to a third state that they try to persuade people how to vote. Instead, many see their primary responsibility as focusing on spiritual matters rather than attempting to change political structures. However, clergy do speak out on moral issues, including racism.

In our survey, clergy strongly rejected any disposition toward prejudice. For example, 95 percent of the pastors strongly disagreed with the statement: "I would object if a member of my family wanted to bring a friend of a different race home to dinner." An equal percentage strongly disagreed with the statement: "There should be laws against marriages between minority races and whites." On these questions, clergy were slightly more inclined to oppose racism than their congregants were, but in neither case was there indication of much prejudice—at least as far as our questions went.

On civil liberties issues, pastors are consistently more progressive than their congregants. For example, 90 percent of the pastors, but only about 70 percent of their members, agreed that someone who is against churches and religion should still be allowed to make a public speech. And well over 80 percent of the pastors thought that someone who is hostile to religion should be allowed to teach in a college or university, but slightly under 60 percent of their congregants shared this view.

On all sex-related issues, new paradigm clergy and members are conservative. Half of the Vineyard pastors and about 70 percent of the Calvary pastors strongly opposed public schools teaching sex education in grades four through eight. In this regard, they were somewhat more conservative than their congregations. As indicated earlier, pastors demonstrated a nearly unanimous position against abortion and homosexuality; also, 99 percent declared it is "always wrong" to have extramarital sexual relations.

Our survey data are consistent with my experiences in dozens of worship services and with the hundreds of pieces of literature I have read. Church leaders represent conservative political values, but they differ considerably in their public expression of these values. Thus, while Chuck Smith may hand out a voter's guide indicating the positions of candidates on abortion, pornography, school prayer, and other conservative issues,[13] other Calvary pastors say little more than that Christians have a responsibility to vote. And while Zac Nazarian participates in active demonstrations at abortion clinics, the founder of Hope Chapel, Ralph Moore, shies away from Operation Rescue and other highly political activities, as does the senior pastor at the Anaheim Vineyard, Carl Tuttle.

New paradigm pastors also differ in their levels of interest in international affairs. Chuck Smith reads the *Jerusalem Post* faithfully, is a strong supporter of Israel, warns from the pulpit about anti-Israeli policies of the United States, and displays a menorah on the altar table, a practice widely copied by other Calvary Chapel pastors.[14] In contrast, when I visited the nearby Vineyard Fellowship prior to the Gulf War, I heard prophetic statements that God might use this war to punish America for its arrogance.

In most Sunday sermons, however, political references are minimized—at least in comparison to the tone in my liberal Episcopal church. The focus instead is on personal salvation, learning the grand narratives of the Bible, and praising God. This reality runs counter to the perception of many liberal church members that the "political agenda" of the religious right infiltrates every sermon. This agenda may be evident in some conservative churches—and especially in their political lobbying organizations—but it does not appear in most new paradigm churches, except, perhaps, in their opposition to abortion. Lesser refrains deal with pornography, sex education, and homosexuality. Sometimes a voice is raised against the teaching of evolution, when the creation account is not also acknowledged. But the political tone is not strident. Many new paradigm members seem too busy caring for their children and offering constructive alternatives to societal violence to engage in polemical politics. The diatribes against "secular humanism" and the political left tend to come from televangelists, radio preachers, and fundamentalist preachers with small congregations.

Empirical Christianity

My approach to interpreting theological views is pragmatic: I examine the behavior they inspire rather than focus on the actual words. It is for that reason that I have left theological considerations for the end of this chapter.

As I have said, the beliefs of new paradigm Christians do not fit easily into traditional categories. On the one hand, they may be viewed as evangelical. In this regard, these people affirm the divinity of Christ, the inspiration and infallibility of the Bible, the physical resurrection of Jesus from the dead, the virgin birth, and the literal second coming of Christ as the promised Messiah. New paradigm Christians might even be described as fundamentalists, in terms of the various propositions issued during the early part of this century to distinguish conservative and orthodox Christians from so-called modernists.

But the labels *evangelical* and *fundamentalist* refer to subcultures within the American religious economy that are different from new paradigm churches.[15] Evangelicals are typically associated with conservative mainline denominations, and fundamentalists are viewed as culture-denying reactionaries. In contrast, new paradigm churches seek to be culturally relevant in their music and organizational style, and they are quick to distinguish their services from the formalized worship patterns of churches in most evangelical denominations.

Moreover, new paradigm Christians differ from typical evangelicals or fundamentalists in their acceptance of the "gifts of the Holy Spirit." This belief might lead to the conclusion that they are Pentecostal, and yet they represent a different, "softer" form of Pentecostalism than that associated with Jimmy Swaggart or Oral Roberts. New paradigm Christians reject the posturing and greed associated with the televangelists; the Holy Spirit in their view chastens the ego rather than embellishes it.

Members of the Calvary, Hope, and Vineyard movements constitute a "new paradigm" precisely because they do not fit the traditional categories. For example, many evangelicals and fundamentalists emphasize doctrine over religious experience. New paradigm Christians, in contrast, are *doctrinal minimalists*. Their emphasis is on one's relationship with Jesus, not on whether one believes in predestination, or whether one believes that Christ will return before or after the great "tribulation" of the "end times." New paradigm Christians view doctrine as being of human origin and see it as something that too often divides the church.

Members of the liberal mainline denominations often dismiss the growth and appeal of these churches by attributing their popularity to the certitude of a rigid belief system. These new paradigm churches are interpreted as being part of a fundamentalist backlash and as therefore having nothing to say to cultural progressives. It is assumed that they exemplify a precritical, premodern mentality.

I believe this interpretation is wrong. New paradigm churches represent something qualitatively different from the standard labels of fundamentalist, evangelical, or charismatic. Far from being premodern, new paradigm Christians might in one way be viewed as cultural innovators, for they are responding to the pessimism of postmodern culture by transforming it rather than simply rejecting it in the hope of recovering a simpler, less corrupt bygone age.

One aspect of the postmodern worldview that new paradigm Christians actually appropriate is their refusal to be trapped by the rationalism of modern critical thought. Truth is not merely a cognitive exercise in reasoning; it is also rooted in experience. New paradigm Christians have taken a step beyond their liberal counterparts in that they seek a unity between mind and body rather than subjugating all knowledge to the realm of cognition. Noncognitive experiences, such as those encountered in worship and moments of religious experience (e.g., visions, speaking in tongues, prophetic utterance, and other ecstatic states), are also legitimate ways of knowing.

New paradigm Christians are pioneering a new epistemology, one that seeks to move beyond the limitations of the Enlightenment-based understanding of religion that informs most modern critics of religion (e.g., Hume, Freud, Marx) and makes room for realities that do not nicely fit within the parameters of a materialistic worldview. Detached reason, they contend, is not the only guide to things ultimate. They believe religious knowledge is to be found in worship and in the spiritual disciplines associated with prayer and meditation—that the acts of singing, praying, and studying scripture offer insight. They follow the long history within the Christian tradition of referring to these moments as the presence of the Holy Spirit. To acknowledge this dimension is not to enter with fundamentalists into a precritical worldview. Rather, as already stated, it is to disavow the hegemony of the socially constructed "rational" mind.

The certitude of new paradigm Christians seems different from the doctrinally enshrined certainty of many evangelicals and fundamentalists. The difference lies in how new paradigm Christians arrive at their conclusions. Theirs is not a deductive approach, which begins with theological propositions and ends with assent to a series of dogmatic conclusions. Instead, the process is much more experience-oriented, or inductive. Individuals typically respond to an invitation to commit their lives to Jesus (at a crusade, a worship service, or sometimes alone), and this begins a process of associating with a worshiping community of people who study the Bible, pray for guidance, yield their wills to God, and respond to the direction of the Holy Spirit.

Perhaps surprisingly, new paradigm pastors and their congregations appear more hostile to dogma than do mainline members. Rather than give topical sermons, which might tend to overemphasize dogma, most new paradigm pastors offer verse-by-verse expositions of the Bible. Over several years, members of these churches will make their way through the entire Christian Bible, from Genesis to Revelation, learning hundreds of stories of how God relates to his people and how his children struggle in the process of submitting their wills to a divine plan.

In contrast, the sermons of mainline pastors are often topical, focusing on generalized truths. In this regard, these sermons are manifestations of the routinization process so well described by Max Weber.[16] In the evolution of Christianity from the elementary relationship between Jesus and his disciples, first canonized sacred texts emerged, then interpreters of those texts, along with a whole infrastructure of priests and theologians who codified doctrine and held councils; these were followed by seminary and university professors who systematized, rationalized, and analyzed these doctrines, writing books to be read by pastors and priests and laypeople.

In contrast, new paradigm ministers are "primitivists," seeking to guide their congregations back to the original narratives on which the Christian tradition is built.[17] Verse-by-verse teaching is a safeguard against creating doctrinal orthodoxies. Furthermore, while new paradigm pastors teach the Bible and undoubtedly instill their own hermeneutic, or mode of interpretation, on the text, the layperson is also invited to read the Bible for him- or herself. The focus is not on memorizing a catechism or learning doctrinal truths. Instead, people are asked to seek narrative analogues to their own experiences.

This process of studying the Bible is further individualized by the explicit invitation to seek the guidance of the Holy Spirit during meditation on scripture. There is an assumption that God speaks through these narratives in highly personal ways. The focus is thus on what this text means to me, an individual, rather than on what doctrine it supports.

In an odd sense, the quest for the historical Jesus, as well as the more recent attempts by liberal scholars to distinguish the original teachings of Jesus from later emanations, is mired in a form of historical realism that reflects the modern rather than postmodern worldview.[18] For new paradigm Christians, the truth of the Bible is revealed in one's encounter with the narrative, not in successive efforts to dig through the sedimentation of different retellings to see whether some kernel of truth exists. Indeed, the hermeneutic of new paradigm Christians is almost the inverse of the analytic critic's interpretive method. The miraculous and the supernatural in the Bible make sense, not through detached analysis, but as one experiences similar transformations in one's own life.

Critics of these groups and cynics too often lump new paradigm believers with defensive fundamentalists. If they indeed shared many beliefs, one would expect to encounter apologists pursuing rational arguments for the miraculous. But only occasionally does one find this. More typically one encounters people who are anxious to describe what God is doing in their lives: their struggles with moral failure, the forgiveness they have experienced, the odd ways in which the Holy Spirit has told them to change their life course, and how God is providing for their needs. Occasionally, they describe healings and visions and "weird" things they cannot explain but attribute to the supernatural work of God.

In short, the epistemology of new paradigm Christians is radically different from that of those operating from a critical, Enlightenment worldview. From new paradigm Christians' perspective, the miraculous is not available to the "ideal observer," because the Holy Spirit does not conform to the standards of universalizable secular truth. They have experienced a rupture in the materialistic worldview and have opened themselves to new ways of knowing that unite head and body, cognition and feeling. New paradigm Christians operate computers and embrace technology with a vengeance, but contrary to the Enlightenment "fundamentalism" of turn-of-the century rationalist theologians (such as Rudolf Bultmann, who said that one couldn't possibly use electricity and still believe in miracles),[19] these individuals accept supernatural realities precisely because they have gone *beyond* the constraints of the "modern" worldview.

More specifically, when new paradigm Christians read about Jesus and Paul and first-century Christians casting out demons and healing people, they believe that these must be their tasks also. They read about the prophets and sages of the Old Testament seeing and hearing God in their visions, and before long they too are having these encounters. The Bible takes on a reality to them based not so much on a priori assumptions as on empirically rooted experiences. Ironically, in their appeal to experience, new paradigm Christians may be aligned more closely with a truly empirical scientific worldview than are those theologians who anchor their theories in armchair reflection.

As "postmodern primitivists"—if such an oxymoron may be used—new paradigm Christians are involved in a project of resacralizing their world, breaking down the barriers between the sacred and the profane that Enlightenment scholars have imposed.[20] For those caught in a critical, "modern" consciousness, God and the supernatural are part of one realm, with humans in another and the two seldom interpenetrating. In contrast, new paradigm Christians are decidedly postmodern in refusing to absolutize the last 200 years of science-dominated thinking. For them, the sacred is active in everyday reality. Indeed, it is liberals who sound defensive when talking about the sacred, constantly relegating God to the realm of the inexplicable. New paradigm Christians are quite comfortable with an epistemology that breaks with critical thought and interjects God into everyday experience, denying the sacred-profane split.

New Paradigm Pastors vs. Presbyterian Clergy

In our survey of pastors, we asked an open-ended question regarding what descriptive terms, if any, they use to identify their theological position.[21] A common response was that they do not identify with traditional Protestant theological terms such as *Calvinist* or *Arminian,* which distinguish whether Christ died only for the elect or for all persons. "No labels please," one pastor wrote. "I don't fit into any one camp. I'm a follower of Jesus," declared another. "Unfortunately," still another explained, "systematic theology is sometimes at odds with biblical theology."

When pastors did use the terms *Calvinist* and *Arminian,* they often hyphenated the two words, saying that both views are present in the narrative of the Bible, but neither is to be held as dogma. One pastor explained: "I think the two truths of the sovereignty of God and the free will of man need to be held together in tension." Another pastor said he was Calvinist *and* Arminian, declaring that "God is able to exist in paradoxes." In analyzing nearly 400 responses by pastors to this question, I was compelled to conclude that their theology is always subservient to the biblical narratives of God's activity in the world, and these stories do not conform neatly to the theological doctrines that organize many denominations.

In contrast, on fixed-choice answers to standardized questions about the truth of Christianity, new paradigm pastors responded in very conservative ways. All of the Calvary and Vineyard pastors we surveyed disagreed with the statement that "all the great religions of the world are equally good and true." With a similarly worded statement—"All the different religions are equally good ways of helping a person find ultimate truth"—98 percent of both groups of pastors disagreed. Nearly equally strong sentiment was expressed in agreement to naming Jesus Christ the "absolute truth" or the only way that people can be "saved." The certitude of new paradigm pastors is consistently stronger than, for example, that of Presbyterian clergy—a good reflection of the attitudes of mainline pastors—on the same questions.[22] Specifically, while half of the Presbyterian clergy disagreed with the statement that "only the followers of Jesus Christ and members of his church can be saved," virtually no new paradigm pastors disagreed. On a similarly worded statement that "the only absolute truth for humankind is Jesus Christ," well over 90 percent of new paradigm clergy strongly agreed, while substantially under half of the Presbyterian clergy shared this degree of certitude.

On questions related to the importance of the institutional church, new paradigm pastors were much more likely to emphasize the personal quest for truth than the mediation of institutional religion. For example, nearly 70 percent of the Presbyterian clergy disagreed or strongly disagreed with the statement that "the individual can find religious truth without any help from a church," in contrast to 37 percent of the Vineyard pastors and 20 percent of the Calvary pastors. The irony of this statistic is that the fastest-growing movement, namely Calvary Chapel, was the least inclined to stress the role of the institutional church.

Even though new paradigm pastors emphasize the individual experience of truth unmediated by the church, they do not believe that all proclamations of the truth by churches are equal. Ninety percent of Calvary clergy and half of the Vineyard pastors strongly agreed with the statement that "not all the churches have God's truth; many are in serious error," while only 16 percent of the Presbyterian clergy felt as strongly.

The conviction that only certain churches have the truth, teamed with a conviction that Christ will soon return, is undoubtedly linked to the sense of urgency that new paradigm pastors have about evangelism. Forty percent of the Vineyard pastors believe that Christ will return within the decade or their lifetime, and about 70 percent of the Calvary pastors hold this view. Furthermore, over 90 percent of both Vineyard and Calvary pastors, in contrast to only 19 percent of Presbyterian clergy, strongly believe that those who have not accepted Christ will be punished. In general, Presbyterian clergy are decidedly more this-worldly in their focus than new paradigm clergy, with over 70 percent of the Presbyterian clergy disagreeing with the statement that "the primary purpose of men and women in this life is to prepare for the next life" (in contrast to 27 percent of Vineyard pastors and 14 percent of Calvary pastors who disagree).

Over two-thirds of the Vineyard and Calvary pastors believe that if they do not preach Christ to people who have never heard about him, these individuals will be damned forever. In contrast, only 15 percent of Presbyterian clergy share this view. In general, Presbyterian pastors are much more likely than new paradigm clergy to say that one should respect other religions rather than impose Christianity on people who do not believe.

Presbyterian clergy—and I assume many other pastors of mainline churches—reveal an ambivalence about the truth of their message, in contrast to the conviction of new paradigm pastors. It thus seems ironic that Presbyterian clergy tend to put more emphasis on the role of the church as interpreter and mediator of the truth than do new paradigm pastors. Yet, despite their declining congregations, Presbyterian clergy express less evangelism than the leaders of the fast-growing new paradigm churches.

As indicated, new paradigm pastors tend to act from internal convictions about the imminent return of Christ, believing that nonbelievers will be eternally damned and that the only way to truth is through Jesus Christ. They possess a strong, experientially based belief structure that contrasts sharply with secular culture. In contrast, Presbyterian clergy have accommodated their views to a pluralistic culture and its competing truth claims. While it is not my intention in this chapter to argue which position is correct, one conclusion might be that religious ambivalence does not market very well, nor does it motivate people to sell their "product."

Purity of Heart over Doctrine

Although new paradigm churches are insistent on the belief in Christ, they disavow dogma. As indicated, in all three movements we studied, the emphasis is on the individual's relationship with God rather than on holding the correct theological doctrine. One Calvary Chapel associate pastor said, "There are a lot of people who have their theology down but are not in love with Jesus." A Vineyard Fellowship pastor echoed this sentiment, saying that purity of heart is more

important than purity of doctrine. Another Vineyard pastor cogently
stated this view: "The apostles didn't know theology. They just knew
Jesus." And a Hope Chapel pastor claimed to welcome different theological views, in marked contrast to many of his colleagues in other
churches who, he says, follow the "party line" in an effort to produce
"theological clones."

In commenting on Chuck Smith's teaching, a Calvary Chapel pastor
said that he was amazed while listening to various taped Bible studies at
how Smith avoids talking about divisive doctrinal issues such as election,
predestination, and various views of the return of Christ and the end of
the world. "The average student listening to Chuck will never even be
faced with that stuff." Reflecting on the experience of sitting in Calvary
Bible studies, he emphasized: "You may not come out a theologian, but
you'll be excited about God's love, you'll be excited about the reality,
the possibility of a relationship with God, and you'll want to serve the
Lord." In other words, new paradigm Christianity is not primarily a
matter of cognitive assent; it is an attitude and a relationship between
the individual and God.

In this regard, new paradigm churches differ from older-style fundamentalism, in which doctrinal orthodoxy was the hallmark of who was
"saved" and who was "lost." Using the metaphor of a circle, Chuck
Smith told us that fundamentalists know exactly who is inside and who
is outside the circle. In contrast, he said, you are in the Calvary circle if
you are present and "fellowshipping" (in relationship with others in the
movement). "We don't have the distinct lines of definition that they
draw," he stressed, implying that new paradigm churches are not sectarian, that they do not create doctrinal boundaries distinguishing one
group from another.

Many new paradigm Christians indicate that it is a sign of Christian
maturity to be tolerant of denominational pluralism. After admitting, "I
used to do a lot of denominational bashing," one pastor explained that
he now sees denominational differences as being primarily a matter of
temperament: "Some people really like a high Episcopal type thing, and
other people like to swing from chandeliers and leap out of windows."
Chuck Smith reflected the same view: "I see the place of denominations.
I don't think that everyone should worship in a free way like we do, nor
should everyone worship in a liturgical way. I see the place for liturgy. I
see people who need liturgy. I see people who need the extreme emotionalism that they find within the Pentecostal church. And so I am not
opposed to that emotionalism." He sees himself as offering a middle

course, what he calls a "casual" approach to worship. "If you want to be emotional," he says, "go down to the Assemblies [of God]. If you want to be liturgical, then go on down to the Presbyterian church. God uses them and God blesses them and they have their place in the Body of Christ as I have my place."

In a somewhat more colloquial fashion, a member of the Vineyard echoed this spirit of openness toward other Christian traditions. "It's not like the Vineyard is the only place on a Sunday where the Lord is saying, 'Hey, this is nice. Thank you.' Or, 'I appreciate this . . . I like this.' I in no way think that the Vineyard has the market on the church. I think that it's just one stream that the Lord is using. Although he is certainly using it in my life, I don't think that everyone should go there. In fact, a lot of people I've invited haven't felt the same way we've felt about it. So, I think it's a real cultural thing—[with] sociological factors involved—which I appreciate. They don't have to like it. They should go to a place where they feel comfortable."

Exemplifying this attitude, John Wimber, the current head of the Vineyard, has attempted to be inclusive in his renewal ministries, and may be better known among Anglicans in Europe than among evangelicals in the United States. He willingly speaks to Catholic groups, gatherings of Quakers, and Pentecostal meetings. He is interested in points of agreement rather than what divides denominations.

Over and over, new paradigm Christians express their emphasis on personal conviction over doctrine. A representative from a Calvary ministry that was ecumenical in its outreach to youth offered this formula for participation in the program: "If you love Jesus Christ, if he's your personal Lord and Savior, and you love kids, then you're in." A Vineyard pastor we interviewed said, "I think we need to find out what we need to do in our dad's house [i.e., for God's kingdom] and be tolerant of others. Unless there is a clear theological wrongdoing, or biblical wrongdoing of some kind, I think we should be tolerant and give people some room. I don't want to go to heaven being 'Mr. Right.' Do you want to go to heaven as the 'Scripture Answer Man'? Is that what it is? God help us!"

Reading the Bible

Although assent to doctrine is deemphasized in new paradigm churches, reading and study of the Bible are deemed to be extremely important. In our survey of over 3,500 new paradigm Christians, two-thirds said that they read the Bible at least daily, including nearly one-fifth who indicated that they read the Bible more than once a day. Another quarter of those we surveyed said that they read the Bible two to three times a week. New paradigm Christians are thus well versed in biblical narratives, and in the absence of doctrinal principles, they seek guidance for daily living in biblical analogies to their own experience.

In asking new paradigm Christians how they view the Bible, we found that they take a fairly literal view. Thirty-two percent said that the Bible is the actual word of God and is to be taken literally, word for word. A strong majority (65 percent) favored a somewhat less fundamentalist response, agreeing with the statement that "the Bible is the inspired word of God"; that "it contains no errors, but some verses are to be taken symbolically rather than literally." It was this second option that most new paradigm pastors agreed with, although Calvary pastors proved to be somewhat more conservative than Vineyard pastors on this question. Presbyterian clergy, probably predictably, were more liberal than either Vineyard or Calvary pastors.

In spite of their relatively conservative reading, however, new paradigm Christians do not see the Bible as a legalistic "rule book" so much as an instrument through which the Holy Spirit speaks to them. For new paradigm Christians the Bible is God's way of communicating to humans, and it is in meditating on scripture that individuals receive guidance and instruction for their lives. When they read the Bible, they claim, the Holy Spirit speaks to them regarding things they should change in their behavior, people they should nurture and care for, and new directions they should take in their career or service to God. New paradigm members have a dynamic relationship to the Bible, and this spirit-filled interaction with the text underlies their ability to cite chapter and verse as a proof-text for why a particular behavior is right or wrong.

New paradigm Christians believe that they are continually being humbled and transformed and that it is through daily interaction with God's word (the Bible) that they are given direction. An individual who had been heavily into drugs explained: "When I first got born again, there were some struggles that I had. But as I began to read the Word of God, a lot of those things began to fade away, and I started experiencing the power of God through his Word and how the Word of God renews a mind and changes a life. I don't mean that in a rational thinking way that it [the Bible] changes you, but it makes things clear."

Far from interpreting it as a fundamentalist book of rules, new paradigm Christians depict the Bible as something that encourages and instructs. Individuals often claim that a particular verse has special meaning for them, and they see it as being paradigmatic for their lives. For example, a young Calvary Chapel pastor told me how, before he entered the ministry, he felt led by the Holy Spirit to quit his job and finish school. As he had just married and had virtually no savings, he thought that perhaps he had made a foolish mistake. While experiencing this conflict, he encountered a passage written by one of the Hebrew minor prophets: "This was the passage the Lord gave me. It's Habakkuk 3:17–18: 'Though the fig tree do not blossom, nor fruit be on the vines, the produce of the olive fail and the fields yield no food, the flock be cut off from the fold and there be no herd in the stalls, yet I will rejoice in the Lord, I will joy in the God of my salvation.' What I did was type it up. I stuck it on our refrigerator door. I said, 'Lord, if I ever open this door and it's empty, I'm going to rejoice in you. I'm going to jump up like a deer.' And you know what, the next four years God supplied every one of our needs."

What typically gives stridency to biblical literalism is its use in the service of doctrinal dogmatism, as the justification for an attack on other beliefs. However, the deemphasis of doctrine by new paradigm Christians puts a different spin on the way scripture is utilized. Although they view the Bible as authoritative, there seems to be a certain modesty in terms of the conclusions that one should draw. Referring to his first encounter with a Calvary Chapel pastor, one interviewee said: "I asked him some basic questions on eternal security, on positions on gifts, and he was the first pastor that I had talked to who flat out just gave biblical lists of what the Bible says, stating: 'On that, I am not really sure, but this is what the Bible seems to be saying,' and it wasn't a church doctrinal position."

To clarify how one figures out the Bible's application to one's personal experience, one pastor used the analogy of a ship entering a harbor in the fog and attempting to line up three different navigational lights. In his view, the scripture is one guidepost, but it should be confirmed by circumstances indicating that the particular direction is appropriate, as well as a profound sense of peace about the decision, which he believes is provided by the Holy Spirit. "If there is a peace in my spirit," he stressed, "no matter if everybody else is freaking out, as long as I've got a peace about it and it's in the Word and the circumstances are going that way, I'll go."

New paradigm Christians may be biblical literalists, but it is often biblicism with an "unorthodox" twist. When a Vineyard pastor reflected on his conversion experience, he recounted: "I read the Bible and, to me, it meant what it said. When it said, 'Love your enemies,' it meant 'Love your enemies.' When it said, 'Give to him without asking for anything in return,' that's exactly what it meant. I didn't have the filters, or the lenses that the church puts on you over the years to filter all of that simplicity out." Another Vineyard pastor said that he is a "Western rationalist" and has great difficulty with the plausibility of miracles. However, he could find no biblical warrant for not praying for the sick (believing they would be healed) or casting out demons. So he does both because the Bible says one should, and to his surprise he sees people healed and demons cast out. He stated: "While it's sometimes real hard to believe it [referring to the supernatural], I see results. And over this period of time, as I see them happen, I become more and more of a believer. The thing that amazes me is that when my faith level is the lowest, I see the most healing."

Concluding Reflections

The faith of new paradigm Christians is empirically based. The Bible seems to assume authority for these individuals as they practice what it says and have prayers answered, see people healed, watch people being transformed morally, and experience the "leading" of the Holy Spirit in their own lives. Reason plays a secondary confirming role as these Christians attempt to interpret what God is doing in the world. Few of them claim to be able to prove God's existence through abstract arguments. It is one's "relationship" with God, they believe, that brings certitude. If there is an assumption, it is that the Bible contains the narratives for understanding how God relates to humans. Yet even this assumption is verified empirically, as the Bible becomes validated in everyday life.

One question to ask is why this particular expression of "postmodern primitivism" is selling. The answer is complex, and cannot be divorced from the organizational issues discussed in the next chapter, but there seems to be something very attractive about primitivism to many people today, including those outside new paradigm churches. We see an appeal to "primitive" methods, for example, in many of the "alternative healing" groups and strategies with which middle-class people are experimenting. New Age religions often draw on ancient religious symbols and techniques. And various women's spirituality groups are rediscovering the female voice in ancient rituals and a mythic past.

Each of these examples illustrates a certain exhaustion with reason. Furthermore, their leapfrogging over recent tradition to the ancient past reveals a distrust of encrusted religious bureaucracies as repositories of truth: people seek a return to primal experiences of the sacred. They are tired of bland universals—including ethical calls to a generic justice—which reflect the modern worldview. The ills of contemporary existence, they suggest, require a much stronger medicine.

CHAPTER 6

Giving the Ministry to the People

The Postmodern Organization

It was a warm summer night and about 7 P.M., with some anxiety, I rang the doorbell of a typical tract home in a sprawling southern California suburb. For some months I had been visiting the Sunday worship services of various Calvary, Hope, and Vineyard churches, but this was my first venture into the intimate setting of a home Bible study. In the larger group meetings, no one had minded if I scribbled notes, sang when I wanted, got out of my seat to observe healings, and otherwise played the role of an urban anthropologist involved in field research. But tonight I knew the ground rules would change. I could no longer be anonymous.

Earlier, speaking by telephone with the host for tonight's meeting, I had ascertained that only a dozen or so people would be present. They would be here to study the Bible and pray together. I knew that I would have to introduce myself, and I struggled with my identity as a liberal Episcopalian who feels more comfortable *reading* prayers addressed to the deity than reaching out extemporaneously to God. I also feared the awkwardness of being an observer of people's private lives and felt acutely the boundary between participant and observer.

I was relieved to be greeted by Jim, who ushered me into the living room and jokingly told his friends that the sociologist from the University of Southern California had arrived. "Don is here to check us out," he said, and the lack of defensiveness that I had noted in all of my encounters with new paradigm clergy seemed to be mirrored in these lay members. I was offered a glass of iced tea and chided by a UCLA fan for the failures of the Trojans, USC's football team, last year. So far so good! Feeling this could be any cocktail party, I relaxed and put down my sociological guard.

At about 7:20 P.M. I heard someone tuning a guitar, which seemed to be the cue for people to gather in the living room. I sat on a recliner in one corner of the room, where it was easy to observe, and after the sofa and a few other easy chairs were filled, the remaining people found a comfortable place on the carpeted floor. Mary played a few chords on her guitar and then quietly said, "Jesus, we enter into your presence with thanksgiving and praise. Please give us a heart for your service, and direct our sharing with one another. And thank you for Don. Please guide his research. In Jesus' name, Amen." I opened my eyes and counted thirteen people: four couples and five single individuals. About half the people were wearing shorts, befitting the hot weather. The mean age was early to mid-thirties, although several of the single people may have been in their mid-twenties, and our hosts, Jim and his wife, were probably about forty.

Everyone knew the choruses that we sang. The melodic, repetitious phrases were similar to the songs that I had heard in the regular church services. I noticed one person on the carpet kneeling for a while in prayer as we sang, and several people spontaneously lifted their hands in the air when the songs praised God. These physical acts seemed very natural to the participants, and I felt increasingly relaxed myself, jotting a few notes as well as occasionally joining in singing some of the refrains.

About 7:45 P.M. Mary quietly concluded, "Thank you Jesus. Thank you for your greatness. We praise you." After a few moments of silence, Jim, our host, welcomed us. I was again introduced, and then Jim asked if anyone had something to share. One of the single women asked the group to pray for her. She was supporting two small children on a modest salary, and said that she needed patience with her children and wanted to find better child care for them. A man in his mid-thirties said that he was concerned about a coworker. He had invited his friend to join the church softball team, which he thought would be a good place to meet men who love Jesus. A young woman stood, smiled, and said that this week was her one-year anniversary of "being clean"—off drugs. Everyone applauded. Several prayer requests were made: for an elderly mother who was entering the hospital, for a teenage daughter who several days last week had not returned home until the early morning hours, and for a former member of their group who was now a missionary in Ukraine.

Jim then opened his Bible to chapter 5 of the book of Acts, and a forty-minute discussion ensued. It was obvious that everyone had read the text during the week. Jim made a few opening comments, but his role was one of facilitator rather than teacher. Group members made applications to their own lives and pointed to the parallels between the early Christian church and their rapidly growing congregation. The unspoken assumption was that the practices of these first-century Christians were to be emulated in their fellowship. Paul's teachings were taken as authoritative regarding church governance and daily living.

I began noting who spoke and very shortly realized that women were equal participants with men, even though I heard references to different roles being appropriate to men and women within the church as well as the family. By the time the Bible study portion of the meeting ended, it appeared that only one person had not spoken. I also noted the noncompetitive character of the social interaction in the group; people seemed to be searching for answers to practical problems of everyday life; there was no posturing, preaching, or arrogance in the discussion.

Jim then turned to me and explained that they always end their meetings by dividing into small prayer groups, and that I was welcome to join one if I wished. Somewhat awkwardly, I stated that this time I would rather observe, if no one minded—and felt relieved that no one objected. Groups quickly congregated and dispersed throughout the house. Watching a group at the kitchen table and another trio who had pulled their chairs together in the living room, I noted that for a few minutes people talked quietly, then began to pray very conversationally. At one point I saw that the single mother was quietly weeping, and both of her prayer partners reached out to touch her, one putting an arm around her shoulder and the other placing his hand on her knee.

By now it was nearly 10 P.M., and people began to congregate in the kitchen. I smelled coffee brewing and decided that it was time to quit hiding behind my professional role. The UCLA fan spotted me, and we quickly engaged in a discussion of ratings for the upcoming season. Jim interrupted our jocular exchange to invite me back next week, or to drop in whenever I wanted. In several weeks they would be holding their meeting at a local beach. Their children were coming, and I was welcome to bring my family if I wanted.

The Family I Never Had

At the core of new paradigm churches are small, weekly meeting groups, like the one at Jim's house. Depending on the church, these groups go by different names, variously called Kinships, MiniChurches, Home Fellowships, and Care Groups. In commenting on the importance of this weekly gathering, a Hope Chapel member said, "MiniChurch is the family that I never had." It is a gathering where she feels loved unconditionally. At MiniChurch she shares her worries and concerns the same way that one might do around the dinner table in a normal, functional family. Like a family, MiniChurch offers her emotional support and, in a pinch, even financial help. In our society of broken families, a deeply ingrained ethic of self-sufficiency, and high-stress jobs, it is not surprising that individuals often view these church-based cell groups as more central to their personal and spiritual lives than large group worship.

To me, one of the startling things about visiting a home fellowship was to observe the degree of physical interaction among all the members. The warmth of human contact that characterized extended family relations of yesteryear is being rediscovered in the mutual care experienced in home fellowships. Men hug each other and prayer partners touch those who are in pain. Unlike group therapy, which may be intimate but also a short-term experience, members of fellowship groups support each other, week after week. These individuals do what extended families have done for centuries: they share each other's burdens, comfort one another, rejoice with each other's victories, and acknowledge their dependency by reaching out to grasp one another, dissolving the separation on which autonomous, self-sufficient modern urbanites so pride themselves. They also hold each other accountable to shared standards of behavior.

Home fellowships have considerable independence from the larger congregation, but there is a well-honed system of oversight by lay leaders. Home fellowship hosts gather periodically in a group meeting with a member of the pastoral staff, but direct oversight is from a lay "shepherd," who is responsible for a half dozen or so of these groups. His function is not to check up on the leaders, but to offer them support and to visit their groups on a regular basis, sitting in as a member of the group. In the ever-expanding system of home fellowships growing and splitting, the goal is to continually "disciple" new lay leaders. This training is done through mentoring relationships between home fellowship overseers, leaders, and understudies, with the goal being moral and spiritual maturity rather than growth simply in cognitive knowledge of the faith.

From an organizational standpoint, the existence of home fellowships allows for a considerable shifting of responsibility from clergy to lay leaders. The mega-churches would need an enormous paid staff of pastoral counselors if lay leaders and home fellowship groups did not assume these responsibilities. More than an economic measure, however, the extensive network of home fellowships in new paradigm churches is part of a strategy to deprofessionalize religious functions, returning the priesthood to the people. A sign of a routinized religion is that functions previously performed by ordinary members are delegated to specially certified professionals. New paradigm Christians are reclaiming these roles in the home fellowship.

Empowering Lay Members

Home fellowship groups are one element of a highly decentralized social structure that characterizes new paradigm groups. Even in the mega-churches, the organizational chart is extremely flat and bureaucratically lean. The senior pastor sets the vision and defines the spiritual culture of the institution, but he typically gives substantial autonomy to individual staff members in overseeing specific programs. There is a strong sentiment that the real work of ministry should be done by the people, so the clergy see their task as nurturing and training lay leaders rather than initiating programs and running them.

Not only home fellowships but also dozens of other types of ministries emerge through individual congregants' efforts. The method for starting a new group is this: A person who feels a responsibility toward homeless families in the neighborhood, or someone who sees the need for a program for people recovering from divorce, expresses this concern to the senior pastor or a member of the staff. Typically, full encouragement is given to the individual to pioneer a new ministry. The role of the pastor or staff member is to support this individual in his or her ministry, rather than to micro-manage the program. The general philosophy is that "the people" are much closer to the needs of the congregation and the community than is the pastoral staff.

In many instances, lay commitment to a particular ministry grows out of an individual's personal experience. As we have seen in previous examples, a woman who gave up a child for adoption as a teenager initiates a project matching unwed mothers with prospective adoption parents; an individual who served time in jail, and knows the loneliness and isolation of this experience, establishes a program of prisoner visitation; a frustrated athlete sees the potential of sports to reach out to individuals who are not part of the church community. Many of these needs might never occur to a pastor because they are not part of his personal experience. By creating an institutional culture that emphasizes lay ministry and lay initiation of programs, new paradigm churches have heightened the likelihood of meeting the complex needs of a diverse group.

Such an emphasis on lay ministry does not strip the pastor of leadership, because many of these pastors are very strong visionaries. Furthermore, they maintain veto power over programs. But their primary role is to inspire, lend confidence, and work on the spiritual development of the individual. In a growing new paradigm church, there are dozens and sometimes hundreds of people who feel passionately about different ministries. The pastor and even a large paid staff could never duplicate the intensity of commitment to such a variety of programs.

What is remarkable in new paradigm churches is not only the variety of different groups and programs, but also the rapidity with which they are started. In large part, this is due to the flat structure of the organization. In interviews with clergy and laity alike, I heard numerous derisive jokes and comments about committees—that they guarantee that nothing will get done, or that if a committee does finally agree on a program, the need will have changed and the program will be outmoded. Instead of forming committees, new paradigm churches try to honor lay initiative, take risks with people who have a vision, and offer these individuals clergy support as needed, without overregulating and thereby denting enthusiasm for a project.

As the founder of Calvary Chapel, Chuck Smith displays the prototypical style of leadership for new paradigm churches. Even though the Costa Mesa church he pastors has at least 15,000 people who attend, Smith has only two staff meetings a year, and even then, a staff member at the church told me, he typically forgets about these meetings and has to be reminded the day before. He gives nearly full autonomy to staff members and generally offers only a "yea" or "nay" to plans that are passed by his desk. The ministry, in his view, is between staff members and the Holy Spirit, not between the staff and Chuck Smith. Yet Smith keeps his door open, to meet with dozens, if not hundreds, of people who seek his counsel each week. Communication is informal rather than memo- and policy-driven.

Occasionally a pastor exercises his veto power, and problems inevitably occur, but these awkward moments become the occasion for people to mature in their faith and leadership skills. Not taking risks and not honoring lay initiative may avoid potential embarrassments but would also result in a much less creative, less cutting-edge ministry, in my opinion. Often, in a more traditional organizational structure, new policies are issued to deal with mishaps of one sort or another; in contrast, new paradigm pastors prefer to deal relationally with problems. They see establishing an impersonal policy to deal with conflict or incompetence as a denial of a "spirit-led" style of ministry.

One stimulus to a decentralized ministry is the availability of computers, desktop publishing, and communications networks. In the past, denominations needed headquarters to produce uniform material, in part because of the economies of scale of typesetting and reproduction, and tended to produce "generic" publications intended to serve many different constituencies. Today, each ministry can produce its own tailor-made material. This leads to niche marketing and first-order communication, without intermediate production staff, one or more steps removed from the program.

Decentralization does not, however, mean disorganization in individual projects. First-rate planning is evident whenever one walks through a new paradigm Sunday school filled with hundreds of volunteers, or when one attends an evangelistic crusade attracting tens of thousands of people. The paradox of these churches is that their leaders create a "corporate" culture in which excellence is expected, and yet they give relative autonomy to their staff and members in implementing the vision they so skillfully articulate. From inside the organization, things may appear a little messy—because people are grabbing hold of the vision at many different levels—but hierarchical boundaries are not important so long as the job is getting done.

A Decentralized Movement

The decentralization model applies not only within the local church, but also at the movement or denominational level. Most mainline denominations have uniform curriculum offerings for Sunday schools; they have commissions and committees that make decisions about new hymnals; they go through elaborate hearings and study reports on new mission initiatives; and they have procedures and policies for starting new churches. None of this regulation exists in successful new paradigm movements. Local churches are writing their own teaching aids and programs (what works for kids in a beach community in southern California, for example, may not be appropriate for youth living in upstate New York). Similarly, why have a standardized hymnal? The worship leader in most new paradigm churches is writing his own music and adapting the best that he hears from other churches and movements, as well as taking advantage of the songwriters in his own congregation. The social ministries are also homegrown efforts, varying from community to community. They do not need denominational approval, nor do they rely on centralized denominational funding.

The same principle applies to starting a new church. If your home fellowship has been continually splitting and multiplying due to new members joining, and if you believe that God has spoken to you about planting a new church, then why not just do it? What is the point, ask potential new paradigm pastors, of going through multiple levels of bureaucracy—of first attending seminary, then being approved for ordination, then apprenticing for several years in various assistant pastor roles, and eventually working through a denominational job placement service for employment as a senior pastor? By this time one is middle-aged, one's vision has become tarnished—if it still survives—and fellow clergy have become one's dominant peer group. The pattern in new paradigm movements is to honor the calling for ministry, release an individual to expand his home fellowship group into a church, and, in some cases, even to give him some of the best leaders to augment this nascent congregation.

With new churches, pragmatism substitutes for bureaucratic and procedural oversight. According to a frequently cited axiom of Calvary Chapel founder Chuck Smith, "God does not call the qualified, but, instead, he qualifies the called." In other words, if someone is truly called to ministry, then the home fellowship will grow, and the lay leader's pastoring skills will improve. At some point he will have to quit his secular job because of the demands of the position, but by then, the congregation will be large enough to support him. On the other hand, if the home fellowship does *not* grow, then its leader does not have the gift of pioneering a church; he may instead find his "calling" as an active lay volunteer in a local church. The same is true for starting new programs within an existing church. If a lay leader does not attract fellow volunteers to the new program, then God may not be behind it, according to the new paradigm perspective.

The organizational philosophy practiced in many of the new paradigm churches is similar to that in fast-growing businesses. With a decentralized leadership, more ideas can surface. Not all of these will have merit, but a decentralized organizational structure unleashes people's creative potential—as well as their willingness to assume leadership. The price of "sure" successes is a decrease in the likelihood of product innovation. The goal of management, say new paradigm pastors, is to avoid clogging the arteries of the church "body." Things that typically slow responsiveness to the community's needs are policies that inhibit creative lay initiative, committees that are difficult to schedule and require a long time to work to consensus, and micro-management by paid clergy.

The organizational genius of the founders of new paradigm movements is that they are willing to risk failure by giving autonomy to creative upstart leaders. In the Calvary Chapel movement, for example, Chuck Smith has exerted extremely strong theological leadership, but he has given almost complete organizational autonomy to the hundreds of young pastors who have established churches. He requires no reports and avoids creating codependent relations with his many "sons" who have founded mega-size churches. Instead, a type of satellite system has evolved in which accountability of individual pastors is relational and flows back to the senior pastor of the church *from which they emerged,* rather than to the mother church that Chuck Smith pastors.

The usual tendency of a movement that has over 600 churches, as does Calvary Chapel, is to establish a seminary to train new pastors and to otherwise centralize leadership. Instead, Chuck Smith has encouraged the large churches to establish their own pastor training programs, utilizing the creative energies of members and staff in writing curricula and setting requirements for graduation. This approach results in programs that are sensitive to local market needs and conditions. It also avoids creating a stratum of professional theologians and seminary professors who are removed from local congregations. The leaders of training programs in different churches may be in contact, creatively cross-fertilizing each other's ideas and materials, but there is no attempt to create a uniform curriculum.

This same decentralization is observed in materials available to congregational members. Most of these churches have bookstores, and a major section of the store contains cassette tapes of the pastor's sermons from that particular church—not the sermons of Chuck Smith. The organizational and market logic of this approach makes sense: pastors tend to attract people who resemble themselves (in terms of social background, education, and race and ethnicity). Why have a homogenized product when technology makes it possible to individualize tapes, books, and instructional materials for the particular constituency that one is serving?

Centralized bureaucracies value uniformity. They also build, almost by definition, a hierarchical organizational structure with layers of managers and supervisors in between the constituency and the leader at the top. Managing this structure requires uniform policies and a regular flow of memorandums. Advancement in the organization often depends on seniority or accumulation of credentials, and leaders with new ideas are typically held in check because of the threat they pose to the prevailing organizational structure. By decentralizing authority, new paradigm churches and movements circumvent this movement toward routinization. Governance is based on trust and personalized relationships rather than policies and procedures. And training occurs through mentored relationships rather than through formalized and centralized educational institutions.

Attitudes toward Money

Nowhere is this nonbureaucratic approach to ministry more evident than in the way money is raised and administered in new paradigm churches. Repeatedly, Calvary Chapel pastors quoted Chuck Smith's axiom that "where God guides, he provides," and consequently they put almost no effort into fund-raising. Their view is that if God wants a ministry, then he will lead individuals to pay for it. Receiving money through pledge programs or high-pressure appeals from the pulpit contradict this deep conviction.

Deemphasizing money in new paradigm churches is not a marketing technique, as it is for some pastors in "seeker-sensitive" churches, who base their low-key approach to fund-raising on the calculation that people are "turned off" from religion because of the focus on money. Rather, new paradigm pastors genuinely believe that God is the provider and they are merely the stewards. Somewhere in the meeting space they provide a box for anonymous offerings, but the size of the gift is between the giver and God; it is not a result of social pressure to contribute or a function of future accolades from the pastor.

Many new paradigm pastors told us that they never know who contributes or the amount of individual members' gifts. To do so might lead to preferential treatment. One person I interviewed said, "Really, as pastors, we basically stay out of the tithes and offerings because, you know, when pastors get involved in the personal finances of the people, human nature being what it is, there's a tendency to view people differently when you know what's going on behind the scenes financially."

Accurate records are kept (often on computer), but the pastoral staff leaves it to the bookkeeper to supply records to the Internal Revenue Service when requested and does not try to find out who tithes and who gives the most. No plaques commemorate large capital contributions, nor are "pledge account statements" billed to members. Accountability is between individual members and God. If a person is going to receive a reward, the church teaches, it will be in heaven. One Calvary member explained, "You either tithe to the church because you want to and do it unto the Lord, or you keep your money. God doesn't want it. God's not poor. God owns a cattle on a thousand hills, so if you can't give your money *hilariously*, put it back in your pocket."

Pastors, especially in their early years of ministry, learn to "live by faith." Without salaries, they develop a spirit of dependence on God as well as an attitude of humility, recognizing that they are not creating the church by themselves. Referring to the first years of his church, one pastor said, "If it were not for people putting groceries at our doorstep, or people knocking on our door saying, 'The Lord told us to bring this to you,' we never would have survived."

As churches grow and develop, of course, salaries are established and regular paychecks are issued. This is the inevitable process of routinization. However, in some new paradigm churches, salaries are not based on skill level or rank, but on a pastor's need. In one mega-church, I was told, staff members fill out a form indicating their basic expenses, whether they are single, how many children they have, whether their spouses are working or not, and so on. And several pastors of large new paradigm churches receive no salary. Instead, they live off royalties from songs they have written, the sale of tapes and music CDs, and conference speaking fees.

If there is financial corruption in these institutions, I did not detect it in my several years of research. In part, I think this is because there is a strong institutional ethos that money is not the measure of personal success. A typical comment came from a young pastor who indicated that his father had been a highly paid executive and there was considerable wealth in his family. "I was very driven in that direction," he said, "but that's something the Lord has just taken out of me. Wealth, for wealth's sake, means absolutely nothing to me."

Certainly, some of the large churches do have substantial budgets, and tens of thousands of dollars worth of transactions occur weekly for building maintenance, mortgage costs, utilities, staff salaries, outreach to the community, missionary support, day schools, radio programs, and so on. New paradigm churches are not afraid of money; they are not seeking a return to some premonetary society. Indeed, they frequently have very up-to-date sound equipment, computer networks, and in-house printing capacities. They also have attractive bookstores, teeming with culturally current product lines, as well as Bibles and commentaries and, as mentioned, tapes of the pastor's sermons.

Sophisticated accounting methods are required to track all of this activity, and cynics might view this as the "selling of God."[1] Admittedly, the commercial character of the hawking of Jesus T-shirts, sweatshirts, hats, bumper stickers, and music might tempt one to reflect on the story of Jesus and the money changers in the temple. However, new paradigm leaders see this paraphernalia as a way of communicating a message to people outside the Christian fold. Also, as a side benefit, wearing this clothing or displaying a bumper sticker reinforces believers' sense of belonging to a community of Christians.

I should also note that the attitude toward money is often not as pure as the ideal presented in the first few paragraphs of this section. While there are still some new paradigm churches with only a box in the back, most do pass an offering basket, although quite inconspicuously, and sometimes guests are specifically instructed not to put in any money. Also, the more routinized of the new paradigm churches sometimes ask for pledges when they start building programs. Nevertheless, there is still a much different attitude toward giving and tithing within these churches than I have experienced in a broad range of mainline congregations.

The Role of the Holy Spirit

While one might think that new paradigm pastors are students of recent business management research, it is more accurate to draw on Max Weber's idea of "elective affinity" and connect their organizational structure with some of their first-century notions about the Holy Spirit.[2] The Jesus in whom these pastors believe is the carpenter who was an itinerant preacher. And the church they affirm is one that had not yet become institutionalized.

The truth to which new paradigm Christians commit their lives is based on the original gospel, rather than emphasizing twenty centuries of interpretation and rationalization. For them, the appeal of the simple worship of the first-century church is that it was not conditioned by professional clergy, by specialists in managing access to the sacred. Those early Christian radicals worshiped in house churches, where very little doctrine had evolved and a complex liturgy, artfully constructed by professional priests, had not yet been born. New paradigm pastors identify with these first-century Jesus followers, who were seeking a more direct relationship with God.

People who join new paradigm churches are often as critical of the Christian "religion" as the first-century Jesus followers were of the Jewish "religion." Religion to them is a human construction made to serve the interests of the priestly class and to insulate the people from the source of true power. Given their opposition to institutions, it is not surprising that the early Jesus people—whether of the first century or late twentieth century—met for worship in homes and distanced themselves from established religion. It is also not surprising that the leaders of new paradigm churches rediscovered the power of the Holy Spirit and described its influence in much the same way as the early Christians. Experiences inspired by the Holy Spirit inevitably give the lie to human institutions and conventions, and consequently relativize all "religion."

Several factors conspired serendipitously to produce new paradigm pastors who understand the power of decentralized, lay-oriented churches. Because of their immersion in the sixties counterculture, these new-converts-turned-pastors intuitively comprehended the artificial and often self-serving nature of social institutions. Correspondingly, their cultural orientation turned them away from the historic denominational churches, whether Catholic, Protestant, or Orthodox. They formed their own churches, which grew rapidly because of the direct access they gave people to the sacred and because their worldview coincided with a flexible management style, allowing them to modify the delivery system for their message. In short, new paradigm clergy have refused to absolutize the "religious" trappings of the gospel they preach. Worship style, medium of expression, and physical structures are not sacred; they are but the husk surrounding the kernel of the spirit-filled union people seek.

Whether in religion or business, organizations losing market share are typically slow to respond to the needs of customers because of organizational structures that isolate the leadership from consumer desires. In the history of religion, rapid growth has often been preceded by a reform of organizational structure that removes hierarchical strata and simplifies ritual access to the sacred. According to sociological theory, routinization and bureaucratization are inevitable in religious as well as other organizations, but as this increases the rate of membership growth typically slows; eventually, if strategic restructuring does not occur, the organization dies.

In relation to the rapid growth of new paradigm churches, it would appear that there has been a happy coincidence between the leaders' cultural suspicion of bureaucratized institutions, including religion, and their theological conviction that access to God is through the Holy Spirit rather than through man-made institutions. Specifically, new paradigm Christians believe that direction for daily living comes from the Holy Spirit, especially as one studies the Bible, meditates on its meaning, and seeks in moments of solitude to hear the will of God for one's life. All other claims to divine revelation are secondary, including the dictates of clergy.

It is precisely this view of the Holy Spirit that legitimates a decentralized, laity-empowered church. It directly challenges the legitimacy of a hierarchical structure, as it forcefully raises the question of why another human being should supersede the authority of the relationship between God and the individual. In this view, the Holy Spirit leads laypeople to establish programs and to engage in acts of service. New paradigm church members believe there is no reason why these instructions should percolate down from the top of the organizational hierarchy (although the Holy Spirit speaks to pastors, also). In this regard, the theology of new paradigm groups appears relatively egalitarian, involving laypersons in ministry, and it invites organizational innovation from the bottom up.

The measure of when a new paradigm religion starts to become an "old paradigm" religion is when it begins to substitute procedures for guidance by the Holy Spirit, and when it relinquishes the job of ministry to professional clergy rather than claiming this for the entire congregation. The slide toward routinization is always gradual, but it can be measured by a desire to centralize authority, standardize training, ritualize worship, and install mediators between God and the people. A good indicator of routinization is to observe the response of the younger generation to new paradigm churches. Inevitably one will see more gray heads as the members of these baby boomer churches age, but the true test of their routinization will be whether a young generation of leadership is evident (or if they are starting a new movement of Generation X churches). If not, it means that institutional structures have been created that are retarding the process of meeting current needs in culturally appropriate ways.

In addition to organizational change, a sign of a healthy new paradigm church is a constant turnover of personnel (excluding the senior pastor from this generalization). New converts come into the church seeking community and, for some, leadership roles. As they are trained and mentored, they assume increasing responsibilities within these churches. Older staff then leave their positions to start new churches, creating opportunities for new members to fill these vacated positions.

Paying high salaries and other benefits to the staff of new paradigm churches may be a deterrent to turnover, because money has a way of making people comfortable and entrenched. The problem is that without regular turnover, there is little chance for people to move within the organization, so mentalities and practices get frozen in place. More important, there is no opportunity for people who are new to the organization to assume leadership roles, which is a key component to retention within voluntary associations. Organizations benefit from having younger people, as well as new converts, in leadership positions, because they are inevitably closer to secular culture and therefore more able to alter the organization to respond to cultural changes.

Lead by the Holy Spirit

Max Weber distinguished between three types of authority: charismatic, traditional, and legal-rational.[3] In a curious way, new paradigm pastors appeal to both the charismatic and traditional forms of authority: charismatic authority in the sense that God communicates directly with them through the Holy Spirit, and traditional authority in the sense that the biblical tradition is referred to as normative for contemporary life and practice. What is not present in new paradigm churches is any appeal to legal-rational authority, such as church law.

The charismatic leadership of new paradigm pastors is a very unique form of charisma, but on reflection it is probably the only type of charisma that could appeal to a broad spectrum of middle-class people. Unlike the exaggerated theatrics of some televangelists, new paradigm pastors connect with their audiences on the basis of a spirit of humility and repentance, serving as vessels of God's communication. They approach their leadership with what is frequently referred to by members as a "servant's heart," and their egos seem to have been pruned through encounters with a God who knows no equals. The charisma of these leaders lies in their transparency, their lack of pretense. In my conversations with them, I found a genuine humility rather than the claim to self-authenticity so often manifest in people wedded to the ethic of individualism.

Consistent with the definition of charismatic leadership, new paradigm pastors tend to be authoritative and even autocratic. Thus, in spite of espousing a decentralized form of social organization, the pastor holds ultimate veto power over individual programs, and he sets the vision that defines the institutional culture of the church. This power could erupt in a hundred destructive ways—and occasionally it does—but it is moderated by the pastors' firm belief in accountability, not only for the laity but also for themselves.

A senior pastor typically views himself as accountable to his spiritual mentor, who is often the pastor in whose church he received his principal spiritual formation. In addition, the senior pastor surrounds himself with a counsel of spiritually mature and wise individuals.[4] Typically this advisory group includes some laypersons from his own congregation, as well as several staff members, but it may also include individuals from outside the local church.[5] Some of these individuals often have special skills, such as business or construction experience, since managing money and property are inevitable concerns for a growing congregation. This body of counselors meets periodically and usually comes to a consensus on issues, rather than governing by majority rule. It is a self-perpetuating body, with the senior pastor playing a strong role in deciding who should join as members rotate. These churches are not run democratically, by popular vote of the congregation.[6] Someone agrees to serve on the governing board because he or she wants to contribute to the vision announced by the senior pastor.[7]

The purpose of such boards is to insure integrity in major decisions—especially regarding building projects and other financial matters. But it is also the board's function to encourage the senior pastor to spend enough time with his family and take care of his health, and to offer him support if he is experiencing personal problems. In meetings, the guidance of the Holy Spirit is sought for decisions. This spiritual quality of decision making is intended as a check on personal ambitions triumphing over the welfare of the congregants.

For the individual lay member, a similar system of accountability exists. Typically there is a mentor to whom one can turn for spiritual guidance. Within new paradigm groups there is frequent reference to "discipling" someone who is younger in the faith. This process is very informal and may involve having breakfast with this individual every week or two, meeting occasionally for Bible study and prayer, and otherwise serving as a resource to someone who is seeking to make his or her way in the faith. At the beginning of these relationships, the interaction may be relatively frequent, but even in the later seasons of a person's spiritual journey it is common for these connections between fellow Christians to remain strong, although the conversations may become somewhat episodic.

For lay members, the equivalent of the pastor's board of counselors is the home fellowship group. Within this group individuals share their problems and their joys, but an informal accountability also develops. Group members may inquire about whether an individual is regularly setting aside time for prayer and Bible study, and if the group perceives marital problems or a lack of personal discipline, it may gently confront the individual with his or her shortcomings. Accountability in this setting is not authoritarian, but it is often quite direct. People discuss what constitutes a "Christ-like" life in everyday terms, and guidance is offered not only by citing biblical examples but also through personal accounts of how individual group members have confronted similar problems or temptations. In reproving members, a balance is maintained between biblical standards and a God who is loving and forgives those who fail. Every member is perceived to be on a journey to greater Christian maturity, but perfection is never achievable; hence, new paradigm pastors and leaders affirm the necessity of God's grace triumphing over judgment.

An example of accountability and Christian nurturing was offered by one of the new paradigm leaders we interviewed. He mentioned a young pastor who had been unfaithful to his wife, and whose affair was threatening to rip the church and the marriage apart. A bureaucratic way of dealing with the problem would have been to place the pastor on probation, hire an interim replacement, and hope the church could weather the storm. Instead, this movement leader and his wife telephoned the errant pastor and his wife and asked if they could come and spend some time with them. The offer was accepted, and for several weeks the two couples lived together in the same household. The movement leader assumed responsibility for pastoring the church during this period, and in the off hours the two couples talked about the marital problems that had led to the infidelity. The outcome was that the marriage was renewed, the pastor asked forgiveness from the congregation for his betrayal of their trust, and he sought secular employment for a time before returning to the ministry.

Authority was clearly exercised in this situation, but it was relational rather than bureaucratic. There was no formal hearing into the allegations, no official censure, and a minimum of scandal. The issue was dealt with directly, at a personal level, the marriage was saved, and the church members learned the meaning of public repentance and restitution. The pastor was held accountable for his behavior, but in a spirit of caring about both his marriage and the ministry. The problem was resolved in the way a mature family might deal with a wayward member.

In all issues related to accountability, new paradigm churches represent the antithesis of the prevailing pop psychology culture, in which self-actualization and self-fulfillment are the highest values. According to this therapeutic ethic, the individual, not the community, is the center of value: accountability is to oneself; one is the master of one's life; and giving oneself up to meet the demands of society represents inauthentic living. It is precisely this ethic that new paradigm Christians have found impoverished. In new paradigm groups, worship of self is replaced with worship of God, and meaning and purpose are rediscovered in communal bonds tempered by spirit-directed living.

New paradigm pastors are hostile to traditional forms of psychotherapy and counseling. To me, this antipathy is understandable, since therapy often involves the language of self and release from guilt—the guilt of not living up to the demands of the other. In contrast, I see new paradigm Christians as affirming responsibility to one's neighbors and community, and as accepting guilt as an appropriate response to sin that hurts members of the community. For new paradigm Christians, personal meaning is achieved in living rightly ordered relationships as revealed in scripture; therein lies freedom, not in self-driven pursuits of individual happiness.[8]

Serving the Whole Person

While home fellowships are central to the life of new paradigm Christians, there is a dizzying array of other programs, especially in the large congregations. People today have many needs and many interests, and if the church is to achieve its role as the mediator of meaning, then it is important that church-based programming reflect this diversity. New paradigm churches clearly seek to serve the multiple needs of their membership, to service the "whole" person rather than simply his or her "spiritual" needs. In this regard, new paradigm churches reject the segmentation of modern society, which parcels out different specialized tasks to a diverse range of public and private institutions. Instead, new paradigm churches seek to reunite the various selves of the fractured individual by providing a full menu of services at one location. These churches are recapturing some of the roles that religious institutions lost in the process of modernization and secularization. To some degree this reunification of services is being assisted by the devolution of the welfare state, which may, ideologically, account in part for the predilection of new paradigm members to conservative politics.

A casual overview of bulletins from the mega-church congregations reveals an incredible array of issues being dealt with in classes and meetings: debt reduction, drug and alcohol recovery, divorce, single parenting, eating disorders, sexual abuse, adoption, coping with teenagers, and the specific needs of younger age groups, ranging from preschool through college. There are also sports and entertainment programs, as well as the social ministries and missions. Some of these groups have a small nucleus of members; others have hundreds of participants.

With this extensive array of programming, the new paradigm church is asserting itself as a comprehensive community. Some churches even have well-developed primary and secondary schools. For new paradigm Christians, the church is the center of their lives. In addition to attending both morning and evening Sunday services, a congregation member may be involved in a Wednesday home fellowship and a Saturday church sports league, attend church-sponsored movies Friday night, go on weekend retreats with church-organized groups, participate in seminars on family finances, spend time in a foreign country working in a church-sponsored orphanage, and so on. However, unlike many sectarian communities, new paradigm churches encourage groups with permeable boundaries, inviting nonbelievers and new converts into many of the programs. There is a decided bias against segregating these programs from "the world." In fact, quite the opposite philosophy is at work: these programs are a means of attracting nonbelievers into the Christian fold, and for this goal to be met these programs have to be culturally relevant.

In competing with equivalent alternatives in secular culture, marketing would dictate that new paradigm churches must have a distinctive edge to their programming, and indeed they do. The movies shown on Friday night lack the violence and sex that permeate their secular counterparts. The sporting events are competitive, but end at someone's home for ice cream rather than in the local bar. The seminar on family finances demonstrates how to reduce debt and at the same time give a responsible tithe to the church. The men's retreats highlight family values, and marital counseling emphasizes the need to forgive and reconcile. At the center of this diverse programming is a consciousness that one exists for a purpose other than self-gratification. Not everything is permissible; truth is not a matter of opinion. It is this message, wrapped in culturally current programming, that is attracting people to new paradigm churches.

A Postmodern Sect

In some ways, new paradigm churches resemble what sociologists call sects.[9] As a type of religious community, sects are typically demanding of their members, are relatively exclusive in terms of who is admitted to membership, and usually require that their members separate themselves from the world to avoid moral corruption. In addition, sects tend to flourish among the impoverished and dispossessed of society, in part because their members are seeking a rationale for why they should not participate in worldly pleasures—since they cannot afford such indulgences.

However, a number of studies have shown that by the second or third generation of a movement—with the sons and daughters of the founders and their grandchildren—the religious intensity of the group wanes, and, correspondingly, the growth rate slows. The typical scenario is that the sect evolves into a denomination and in the process accommodates to the morals and mores of the dominant culture, eventually resolving the tension between their religious worldview and the political values of the state. Part of this transformation is a function of sect members growing more affluent due to their strict religious ethic (and with wealth, the motivation for separation from worldly pleasures diminishes).[10]

The sect-denomination framework is useful in understanding new paradigm churches for several reasons. First, as these churches age, one would predict that they will become more denominational in form and content. Specifically, one might predict a move to be more "reasonable" in their moral demands and more "rational" in their theological position. Furthermore, one would predict increased organizational complexity, in which they will live by rule more than by spirit-led inspiration. In addition, one would expect worship to be less intimate and more performance oriented. (Some of these changes will be addressed in the next chapter.)

Second, the sect-denomination typology is useful as a way of explaining how new paradigm churches differ from historic patterns of religious evolution. While new paradigm churches have some sectarian qualities, such as intensity of religious experience, they are not cultural separatists in the way scholars normally think about religious sects. Rather than calling their members away from cultural engagement, they actually appropriate many aspects of contemporary culture, transforming these aspects for their own purposes. In addition, these churches do not ask members to disassociate themselves from culture, but to see these associations as the vehicle for inviting a secular friend to radically change his or her life. And while new paradigm churches may be less organizationally complex than most denominational churches, they do not view this as first-generational simplicity so much as an acknowledgment—shared by many of their fellow baby boomers—that institutionalization and bureaucratization are to be avoided in all spheres of life, whether political or religious.

Because of this curious blending of cultural currency and high moral and spiritual commitment, I believe one might label new paradigm churches "postmodern sects." As we saw in the last chapter, theologically they do not fit many of the norms of the modern worldview. And the same is true organizationally. Modern organizations are involved in mass production, whereas new paradigm churches seek to serve the niche-related needs of people.

This move from uniformity to specialized services is a hallmark of postmodern business practice, as is the broader trend of moving from global mass marketing to focusing on the consumer needs of local constituencies. More generally, new paradigm churches fit a number of the postmodern trends emphasizing decentralization, flexibility, and networking, rather than centralized management.[11]

What makes new paradigm Christians sectlike is their insistence that there is one truth, not many, and that authority is a meaningful category, not simply a social construction rooted in material self-interest. Yet, although they impose high moral standards on their members, new paradigm Christians are anything but sober and life-denying in their demeanor; quite the contrary, they celebrate as joyously and boisterously as anyone in secular culture. While they have a definite image of what it means to lead a Christ-like life, they do not prize conformity in dress and appearance. I see them as representing a new style of Christianity that utilizes the moral and spiritual energy associated with sectarian religion, and yet embraces many—although certainly not all—of the aspects of postmodern culture.

Concluding Reflections

Peter Drucker, one of the twentieth century's most influential business theorists, argues in his recent book *Post-Capitalist Society* that "every organization of today has to build into its very structure *the management of change*."[12] He applies this principle not only to the corporate world, but also to government, education, and the nonprofit voluntary sector, which would include the church. Drucker states emphatically that the successful organization "has to build in organized abandonment of everything it does. It has to learn to ask every few years of every process, every product, every procedure, every policy: 'If we did not do this already, would we go into it now, knowing what we now know?'"[13] He says that, increasingly, organizations will have to *plan* for abandonment rather than try to prolong the life of successful policies, practices, or products.

New paradigm churches are experimenting with organizational change. They have latched onto the model of first-century Christianity, and it has provided a powerful point of reference for critiquing the institution of the contemporary Christian church. But new paradigm Christians have not only been critics, they have also accepted Drucker's challenge to innovate. In my opinion they have created a form of human community that addresses many of the crises of our late-twentieth-century postmodern culture, and they have also established a perspective that endorses change in their organizational structure. Drawing on their vision of the role of the Holy Spirit, they have transferred authority from the socially constructed institution of the church to a divine presence, who can take them in unpredictable directions. What saves them from the potential chaos, the unpredictability, of a "spirit-led life" is their belief in the Bible as an immutable reference point and their conviction that all impulses and ideas should be tested in one's ongoing relationship to a worshiping community.

For new paradigm Christians, little is sacred except God. They are living out the "Protestant principle," which relativizes all human claims to absoluteness, thus allowing for bold and entrepreneurial experimentation. They have also grabbed hold of another Protestant notion, the "priesthood of all believers," and this idea has provided the human staffing to address many different issues and problems, creating a smorgasbord of specialized offerings to meet individual needs.

What is clearly not functional as we enter the next century is a religious organizational form that is pyramidal in structure, deriving authority from the top and delivering answers and policies to those at the bottom. This structure may have worked in feudal society, when the serfs were both impoverished and unempowered, but it is highly dysfunctional in the information age. What is called for is a much more democratized structure, giving people access to power at many different levels. One reason for the growth of new paradigm groups is that their organizational form enables people to experience the sacred more directly than is possible through the more pyramidal and reified forms of the mainline churches. But their future growth will depend on their ability to follow Drucker's advice of managing for change.

In Drucker's scenario, "post-capitalist society has to be *decentralized*. Its organizations must be able to make fast decisions, based on closeness to performance, closeness to the market, closeness to technology, closeness to the changes in society, environment, and demographics, all of which must be seen and utilized as opportunities for innovation."[14] If Drucker is correct, then it seems to me that new paradigm churches have an organizational jump-start on the future.

CHAPTER 7

Franchising New Groups

Church Planting and Growth

Albuquerque, New Mexico, might seem a strange place for Skip Heitzig to start a church. He had grown up surfing on the beaches of southern California, and when he first arrived in Albuquerque, he thought he was entering another country. It was March, there was snow on the ground, and everything looked brown. Furthermore, he had been told by people that this was not fertile soil to start a Calvary Chapel. The population was largely Catholic, and it was a military town, filled with transients. He had been warned not to expect a repetition of what had occurred in Costa Mesa. But it was the very challenge that attracted him. He wanted to plant a church in virgin soil, and he wanted to do something on his own, independent from what he viewed as the "Christian Disneyland" atmosphere of Orange County, which seemed to have a Bible study in every other apartment complex.[1]

After arriving in Albuquerque during the summer of 1981, Skip immediately got a job as a radiology technician, and shortly thereafter he started a Bible study in the club room of the Lakes Apartments. In addition to Skip and his wife, Lenya, five people showed up that first Thursday night, including a good friend who had moved there to start a Christian radio station and several people Skip never saw again. But within a few weeks there were twenty people, then forty, fifty, sixty. He told the people attending, "This is not a church. You have a church; stay plugged into your church. All we want to do is provide a Bible study for you to supplement your growth." In his mind, the people in the group would have to decide when it was appropriate to formalize this gathering of Christians as a church. He did not want to be accused of "stealing sheep." But gradually the group members began to tell him that they wanted more than just a Bible study, and so one Thursday evening he asked, "What do you think about starting a Sunday morning service, and even moving toward incorporating as a church body?" The response was unanimous.

The decision to start a church was not, however, without moments of discouragement. After six months of living in New Mexico, Skip missed the temperate weather of southern California. In fact, over Christmas he and Lenya returned home, and Skip announced that he wanted to stay. But in our interview, Skip said the Holy Spirit spoke to his heart, saying, "You owe me six more months"—since he had made a commitment to God of one year. So reluctantly he and Lenya returned to Albuquerque and shortly thereafter started searching for a meeting place for their nascent church.

One day he was in a strip mall and saw a sign that said, "Rent this theater." The next day he walked in and asked for the manager, who indicated that the only time the theater was available was Sunday before 1 P.M. Although there were two auditoriums, only the larger one, which seated 260, was available. The price was right, so Skip reluctantly took it. To his amazement, 175 people showed up the first week, and within two months the place was filled with 275 adults. Meanwhile, the kids were meeting for Sunday school in a nursery school a mile up the road.

In February 1982 Skip and his congregation incorporated as a church, filing the papers themselves at a total cost of thirteen dollars. By summer they had outgrown the theater and found a storefront in another mall, where they stayed a year. They ended up knocking out walls to enlarge it, then went to two services, rented space across the street for the children, and by the end of 1983 were averaging nearly 1,000 people a Sunday. Skip told me, "Where they came from, I don't know. It must have been word of mouth. We didn't announce it; it just filled up." So they moved down the street to a shopping center with a vacant store, and in the next three years the congregation grew to several thousand people. When the owner of the building saw the number of people attending, he tried to raise the rent substantially, which provoked Skip and the board to begin looking for a facility to purchase.

One day a church member told Skip he had found a building. When Skip looked at it, he was overwhelmed by its size. It was a sports facility that was losing money, but was complete with racquetball courts, a full-size indoor soccer field with Astroturf, and other amenities. Immediately Skip imagined turning the soccer field into a sanctuary and converting the handball courts into Sunday school classrooms, but his board thought the asking price of $2.2 million was beyond their means. Skip, however, continued to hold out the vision of how this building could serve their needs. Finally, he said, "We bought this building on a real estate contract instead of going through the banks because at that point we were the biggest risk in town. And they took it. They negotiated, we negotiated, and we got it for $1.75 million."

When I visited the church in the early 1990s, it had grown to nearly 7,000 adults. The church held triple services on Sunday morning and was contemplating adding a Saturday night service. Approximately 500 high school and junior high students attended, and a first-class hard-rock band played for the youth worship. In addition, there was a full-service bookstore, which mailed out or sold about 3,000 audiotapes a month of Skip's Bible studies. Several good-size churches had been started in neighboring cities, including one with about 500 members in nearby Santa Fe. In addition, the congregation had started a church in Ukraine and had missionaries in Uganda, Mexico, and several other places. They had also recently opened a School of Evangelism to train people interested in pioneering new churches.

In visiting with Skip and Lenya, I asked them both how they managed to keep pace with the growth of the church. Their answers were very similar. Lenya said that it seemed like the church grew in spite of them, exclaiming, "I was overwhelmed. I kept saying, 'God, stop! It's too much, too fast, we can't handle it.'" Skip was similarly modest, drawing an analogy to a baseball game: "I felt like a spectator, or someone in the dugout watching this great event. You're cheering God on, and he's making all the bases and you're catching all the foul balls. It seemed to be nonstop, and still our heads are spinning, playing catch-up."

The Market

In understanding how new paradigm groups are "franchised" in cities such as Albuquerque, it is important to understand the market for such an undertaking. As I indicated earlier, by introducing market vocabulary, I am not implying that new paradigm groups think of religion as a business in which they are selling a product. Quite the contrary. They believe they are responding to the "calling" of the Holy Spirit, and their efforts at starting new churches are part of the "Great Commission" to share the message of salvation. Personal meaning, not money, seems to be their motive. Furthermore, the most successful efforts at evangelism, such as those by Calvary Chapel, are self-consciously hostile to church growth techniques, demographic studies, and various "how to" manuals.[2] They see their growth as the work of the Holy Spirit. Nevertheless, as an outside analyst, I believe it is informative to look at the market dynamics affecting the growth of new paradigm churches.

The statements of Calvary and Vineyard senior pastors in our survey suggest that members of new paradigm churches are predominantly middle class, with a strong representation of people from blue-collar backgrounds. Senior pastors say that only a very small percentage of their congregants can be viewed as upper class. These estimates fit the profile of the new paradigm church members we surveyed, although 15 percent of our sample had annual incomes above $80,000.

Descriptions of educational level, from both the pastors and congregants, also fit a middle-class profile. A strong majority of congregants are high school graduates or have some college education, about a quarter are college graduates, and a tenth hold postgraduate degrees.

Pastors said that males and females attend in nearly equal proportions, and this observation was validated by our congregational surveys, to which slightly more males responded. According to our surveys, conducted in 1993–94, most of the adult congregation is between twenty-five and forty-five, with people thirty-one to thirty-five being the most strongly represented group. Most new paradigm church members are married couples with at least one child, but approximately a quarter are single and slightly more than one in ten is divorced or separated. A strong majority of the members are white. Depending on the church location, there may be a number of Hispanics; for example, the California Calvary Chapel we surveyed had 28 percent Hispanics, reflecting the ethnic composition of its neighborhood. Relatively few blacks or Asian Americans belong to new paradigm churches, although there are exceptions. For example, in the Hope Chapel in Hawaii that we surveyed, 32 percent identified themselves as Asian, 12 percent as Polynesian, and 5 percent as Filipino.

In summary, then, the typical member of a new paradigm church is middle-income and white, with some college education and at least one child. It is also important to identify who is *not* represented and, by implication, not likely to join a new paradigm church: highly educated, upper-income people, those over fifty, members of ethnic minority groups, and low-income individuals (other than students).

Means of Growth

Theoretically, there are three ways that new paradigm churches can gain members: (1) they can be born to parents who are members, (2) they can switch from another denomination or church to a new paradigm congregation, and (3) they can join as a result of conversion. Which of these is most responsible for the growth of congregations is a matter of debate. One argument holds that growth in evangelical churches is due simply to the fact that the birthrate is higher than in mainline liberal denominational churches. Another line of argument states that very few new converts are joining these conservative churches, but instead there is a "circulation of the saints" from one evangelical church to another.[3] Still another argument is that conservative churches are better at retaining children when they become adults.[4] Fortunately, our congregational survey findings can help some of these theoretical quandaries.[5]

The growth of new paradigm churches cannot be explained by high birthrates; these churches are too young and their growth too rapid. But it is valuable to note the religious background of new paradigm affiliates. Forty-seven percent were Protestants, which is perhaps not surprising, but 28 percent were Roman Catholics, 13 percent had no affiliation, and 12 percent fit the classification "other." In other words, not only were former Catholics significantly represented in the ranks of new paradigm churches, but also more than one in ten members grew up in a home without religious affiliation. Furthermore, if one counts as "unchurched" those who attended religious services once a month or less during their childhood, then slightly more than a quarter of new paradigm members fit this profile. In short, new paradigm churches seem to be attracting people who one might not expect to be attending a Protestant church as adults.

From a marketing perspective, it is important to know what members were doing immediately prior to joining a new paradigm church, because it is possible that someone else is doing the recruiting and these churches are simply "stealing sheep." In our survey we asked what affiliation people had the year prior to attending a new paradigm church. Nearly 30 percent stated that they were unaffiliated (in contrast to 13 percent during childhood). It seems highly possible that these individuals might have completely dropped out of organized religion had they not encountered an expression of it that they found palatable.

With regard to individuals who had switched from another church, we were interested in whether they came exclusively from other conservative Protestant churches or if liberal Protestants and Catholics were also represented. About two-thirds came from either independent churches or conservative denominational churches. But 17 percent had been members of liberal Protestant churches, and 15 percent had been practicing Catholics. Thus, while there is some "circulation of the saints" from within the evangelical fold, new paradigm churches are also drawing from markets one might not predict.

Furthermore, it appears that many of these recruits, from whatever background, are finding a more intense experience of religion within new paradigm churches. In our surveys, 48 percent of Calvary respondents, 39 percent of Hope respondents, and 18 percent of Vineyard respondents reported a "born-again" experience while attending their current new paradigm church. I suspect that, had they not had these conversion experiences, many would have continued to be "seekers" rather than making a commitment to a specific church.

The Product

What is the "product" that is attracting people to new paradigm churches? A necessary, but not sufficient, explanation is that they deal in a profound way with the need for transcendent meaning. People are drawn to these groups because they desire something more than what secular culture is offering them. As one youth minister told me, kids today are depressed, many have low self-esteem, feel unloved by their parents, and consequently are angry. It is not surprising that they desire something, "someone," they can trust, who will give them a sense of significance and purpose, define right and wrong, comfort them, and give them a vision for the future. Many adults are in no better shape. They come to new paradigm churches in search of healing, feeling broken by drugs, divorce, children who are disappointing them, and financial difficulties.

One of the staff members at Skip Heitzig's church said that people are like sponges, soaking up the teaching that is provided week after week. I saw them for myself. To my amazement, Skip sat on a stool with his Bible on his lap before several thousand people and—without any theatrics—simply shared his insights into the particular biblical passage under discussion. People had their Bibles open, underlining verses, making marginal notes, and writing in notebooks. It appears that those attending new paradigm churches want to anchor their understanding of themselves and their world in an authoritative framework of meaning—and seemingly the Bible provides them the narratives for doing this.

The product is not merely cognitive, however. Many people teach the Bible in mainline churches, but they have no more than a few dozen present who want to listen. So something more is happening in new paradigm churches, and much of that has to do with *how* the message is communicated. When Skip Heitzig is not managing church affairs or spending time with his family, he is riding his Harley-Davidson motorcycle or skiing in the local mountains. He is not the typical mainline, seminary-trained pastor. His personal charisma helps communicate his message as he sits on a bar stool in jeans and a sweater, teaching the Bible—but charisma is not a sufficient explanation. It is the content of the message he is teaching that appears to captivate people rather than merely its stylistic accompaniment, although that should not be overlooked.

People in the late twentieth century crave a sense of significance in their lives. Perhaps this has always been the case, and that is why the famous French sociologist Emile Durkheim seized on the term *collective effervescence* to explain what he saw in the rituals of aboriginal people.[6] In this regard, I believe the "product" that new paradigm churches offer has the character of self-transcendence, not only in the sense that the message is something other than one's own voice, but in a more profound personal sense of encountering in worship a presence that connects one with the infinite and other people in very powerful and transformative ways.

But if people need a sense of significance in their lives, they also need a sense of worth within a community. One way to gain this is through serving others, and the Albuquerque church provides multiple opportunities for individuals to play a role in the community life.[7] In Albuquerque congregants participate in teaching the 2,500 children who come to Sunday school. They lead Bible studies in their homes, work in the benevolence program, and much more. In these activities they see themselves as participating in a "vision" to make this a better world. In helping others they appear to be healing themselves as well as gaining a sense of significance in a world that blocks many of them from achieving more than modest economic success.

How Are New Franchises Created?

The process of starting a new paradigm church is quite different from the pattern in founding a mainline church. The main differences mirror the differences in organizational structure pointed out in the preceding chapter. In the next few pages I want to systematize some of the ideas from earlier examples.

BEING CALLED

The typical Calvary, Hope, or Vineyard pastor is someone who had a strong religious awakening or conversion experience sometime in his early adulthood years. This experience thrust him into a sustained period of Bible study, often followed by nonsalaried leadership roles within his church. At some point, usually after several years of service, this individual began to feel that God was "calling" him to more full-time work in the service of the church. On occasion, this calling was accompanied by a vision or dream; other times it was simply a growing conviction that this was where the Holy Spirit was "leading" him.

Typically the individual sought out his pastor for counseling, explaining what he thought "God was doing" in his life. Depending on the leadership and behavior this individual had thus far demonstrated while serving in his church, the senior pastor might encourage or discourage him from thinking further about a clerical vocation. At times, a senior pastor might actually initiate the calling, speaking to an individual about seeing the "gifting" of the ministry on him—in, for example, his leadership of home fellowship groups or other programs—and suggesting that he consider full-time ministry. In a further variant of the call, an individual is asked to join the church staff, perhaps to lead the youth program, and is then invited to assume an official role in the church even though he has had no professional training in the ministry.

The ordination of individuals who are called to a religious vocation is typically understated and nonritualized. God is viewed as the one who calls people to full-time ministry, and thus all a senior pastor can do is acknowledge what God has done. As one person at Calvary Chapel Costa Mesa indicated, one's ordination papers may suddenly show up in one's mailbox at the church. A staff member of Greg Laurie's church explained that Greg simply called him into his office, handed him a piece of paper, and said, "Here is your ordination certificate." Someone on Skip Heitzig's staff recalled that one day after he had been leading the high school program for a while, Skip spontaneously gathered a few elders and members of the pastoral staff together, they prayed for him, and Skip proceeded to sign his papers. This process of ordination, with new paradigm leaders simply acknowledging a step they believe God has already taken, obviously contrasts with the formalized rituals and procedures of most mainline churches.

MINISTRY SCHOOL

While considering their call to the ministry, some individuals enter formal educational programs, variously called schools of evangelism, pastor factories, and ministry schools. The courses are typically a year or two in length. They usually meet from seven in the morning until an hour or two before lunch, so that individuals can still hold down a job in the afternoon and/or evening. None of the movements has a central seminary; instead, these are local training programs, allowing students to be mentored in responsibilities at the local church while attending classes. Much of the learning occurs hands-on, through watching a pastor perform his role and then following that example.

While formal seminary training is not prohibited, it is not seen as a prerequisite to pastoring a church. In fact, many of the pastors of mega-size congregations have neither been to seminary nor attended a school of ministry training program. All of their learning took place in mentored relationships and through trial and error. Illustrating this hands-on approach, the person in charge of the internship program at

Horizon Christian Fellowship said that he disappears for the interns' first week because he believes new interns should "turn to Jesus" for support rather than run to him for solutions to problems. Chuck Smith casts a jaded eye on seminaries, even though he attended a Bible college himself. With reference to several pastors of expanding mega-churches who were pursuing doctorate of ministry degrees, one of Smith's staff members quoted him as saying, "If they get enough education, maybe they'll bring their congregations down to a manageable size."

The chief objection to seminary as the avenue to ministry is that fellow seminarians become the person's peer group, rather than the congregation, and this creates a distance that is difficult to bridge. Furthermore, several individuals told me that attending seminary, thinking that one will then receive a call to ministry, is to put the cart before the horse. God must first call one to be a pastor; only then might it make sense to get a professional degree. One Hope Chapel member who was attending a well-known evangelical seminary even told me that his seminary classes had led him to greater skepticism than faith, because now he wondered about issues that had never occurred to him before, such as the multiple authorship of the first five books of the Old Testament.

For pastors who attend neither seminary nor a ministry training school, the principal form of tutelage is personal study and exposure to congregational teaching. A number of Calvary pastors have listened at least once to all of Chuck Smith's hundreds of Bible teaching tapes. Through these tapes, they have been significantly influenced by Smith, even without direct mentorship.

STARTING A CHURCH

One way to start a new church is the way Skip Heitzig did. He felt himself called to Albuquerque and started a Bible study; it began to flourish, and from it a church emerged. But Skip's story makes it sound easy. In actuality, most pastors go through a considerable period of trial and error, and many fail. As already mentioned, the Calvary practice is to give new pastors only a minimum amount of financial support and assistance, in the belief that the strong leaders—those who really have a calling—will endure and those who fail *should* fail. In other words, to prop a pastor up with a guaranteed salary, housing allowance, car, and so on, is to provide artificial assistance. A pastor who is truly "gifted" for ministry will succeed; he will be forced to give up his secular job to meet the demands of his congregants, who, in turn, will gladly provide his financial support.

Mentors play an important role for these young pastors, giving them emotional support and offering sage advice. Chuck Smith, for example, reports that many of the pastors of the current mega-size congregations called him after six months or a year and told him that they were coming "home," back to Costa Mesa. Smith's advice was for them to endure for a while longer, that they had spent the first year "plowing" and "planting," and must now wait patiently for the seed to sprout. Indeed, numerous pastors told us how painful their early years were. They met with little success at first, sometimes moving from one area of the city to another before suddenly their church began to grow.

Another path to starting a church is found in many urban areas where there is a mega-church. People are commuting from some distance to this church, and at some point the senior pastor, a staff member, or sometimes a commuting layperson suggests that a branch of the main church should be planted in an outlying community or city. Someone is identified to pastor this new church, and the senior pastor then announces to the congregation that people commuting from that area are invited to join the new fellowship. Subsequently, fifty or a hundred people may separate from the mother church, giving the new fellowship a jump-start. I have also heard of instances where a number of couples from a church volunteered to move physically with a pastor to a new location so that the new congregation would start with a nucleus of members.

What is remarkable about this second model is that a senior pastor would willingly part with fifty or a hundred congregants and, simultaneously, release one of his most gifted staff members or lay leaders to pastor them. Most ministers of mainline churches would be too protective of their size and strength to encourage such an act. Yet new paradigm pastors seem to have a different vision, one that resembles the perspective of high-tech firms that are constantly spinning out subsidiaries, rather than attempting to keep everything under one roof. They recognize that new leadership will develop in the vacuum created by those who depart.

The organizational structure of these three new paradigm movements reveals multiple hub sites with spokes going out to spin-off churches in the same region and an occasional outlier in another part of the United States or a foreign country. As we have seen, for a movement such as Calvary Chapel, the traditional, pyramid-type organizational chart simply makes no sense. A better image is of a wagon supported by a number of spoked wheels, with each wheel (or network of daughter churches) connected to the basic frame of the wagon (the movement). Accountability of the various daughter churches is to the pastor of the church out of which they were born, rather than to a central office of the movement. To extend the analogy further, each of these wheels remains with the Calvary movement so long as it stays connected to the wagon. But, on occasion, a wheel may detach itself from the wagon, as the Vineyard movement did, and launch out on its own, taking its daughter churches with it.

MEETING PLACES

When he moved from one location to another to accommodate his growing congregation, Skip Heitzig chose typical meeting places. New paradigm churches prefer commercial spaces to traditional "churchy" buildings as a way of distancing themselves from the look of formal religion. But there are other advantages of commercial space. For one thing, it is typically less expensive than new construction. New paradigm churches often take advantage of warehouses, grocery stores, storefronts, and other commercial buildings whose occupants have gone bankrupt or have moved. Also, if a new paradigm church outgrows a leased space and decides to vacate it, or if the church fails, the building can be returned to commercial use—a consideration that appeals to the church's creditors. Sacred-looking spaces tend to be limited to a single use as a church.

In the early years of the new paradigm church movement, there was a decided bias against purchasing a meeting place. The argument was that this limited the church's flexibility and that, with a large mortgage, the church would be investing more in buildings than in staff to serve the congregation. Many large new paradigm churches still uphold this philosophy. They rent school auditoriums or theaters, or engage in short-term leases that allow them to customize some of the space into classrooms and offices. Some of these groups may be accumulating money in a building fund. A number of new paradigm leaders feel debt is bad, and they stress that one should not become too tied emotionally to a physical structure—that God dwells not in the building but the lives of his people.

The mega-size congregations that we studied reported that every time they moved to larger quarters, they quickly filled to capacity. Had these churches purchased space, they would have been reluctant to move, and building onto the existing facility might have been too expensive. Thus, a building can be a serious constraint to a growing church, limiting their growth and perhaps limiting their vision. On the other hand, once Skip Heitzig had a huge facility, the very challenge of all that space seemed to increase his vision for his ministry.

While Chuck Smith has a cautious attitude toward money and has decided not to build a 10,000-seat auditorium in Costa Mesa, he has been very helpful to other rapidly expanding Calvary Chapels that need short-term loans or loan guarantees. His philosophy, however, has been to assist these congregations only after they are bursting at the seams, and then to provide short-term funding. Long-term support would create dependency that he does not want. Furthermore, as he points out, there is no indication that a beautiful building makes for a large church; programming and the right kind of leadership are the essence of successful growth.

LEADERSHIP

Our profile of new paradigm pastors reveals that they are generally in their late thirties to mid-forties; they have a high school education and some college; they are married; and many, although certainly not all, have some musical talent. Their religious backgrounds resemble their congregants. Of the Calvary pastors surveyed, a quarter were raised as Roman Catholics, approximately a fifth had no religious affiliation as children, and fully a quarter said that they seldom went to church. A third of the Calvary pastors had no religious affiliation the year before they started attending Calvary Chapel. In contrast, Vineyard pastors were more likely to come from evangelical backgrounds and to have gone to church as children.

More important than their demographic characteristics, however, is their profile as leaders, and here I am forced to rely on my subjective observations as well as on what these pastors say about each other. One pastor of a mega-church characterized the pastors of similar churches as "restless," "iconoclastic," and "independent." These adjectives fit my perception of the most successful pastors. They have an enormous amount of drive; many are extremely creative; and they are risk takers. My impression is that they have surrounded themselves with staff members who have the same characteristics, so that when these individuals start their own churches, they, too, are likely to succeed.

Perhaps this list of characteristics should not be surprising. Anyone who has built an organization of 5,000 to 10,000 people probably shares many of these leadership characteristics. But why are the main-line denominations not creating leaders with the same qualities? One possibility is that their selection and acculturation process weeds out people with innate leadership ability. Successive levels of higher education may domesticate leadership, rewarding those who think and write well but are not risk takers and entrepreneurial innovators. Conversely, it is possible that the young leaders of new paradigm churches—in part because of their lack of education—do not realize the odds against them in building a mega-church. Still another possibility is that the leaders of the mega-churches simply happened to be in the right place at the right time and rose to the occasion.

One individual I interviewed, a record producer who is quite sympathetic to the movement, said that "any pig can fly in a hurricane." His assessment is that something was happening culturally in the seventies and early eighties that invited an alternative expression of Christianity, and these young pastors simply got caught up in this cultural whirlwind. In this sense, when Skip Heitzig says that he feels like a bystander to what God is doing, he may be right. Something, whether God or the culture—and perhaps these two are not mutually exclusive—created a condition in which his style of simple Bible teaching had considerable cultural resonance.

There are other possible explanations for the emergence of these leaders. For example, I suspect that most of the leaders of the mega-churches have high IQs. On the other hand, they are relatively uneducated, and most did not grow up in homes that gave them models of corporate leadership. So perhaps they instinctively directed their talents into an arena where lack of education and social status were not barriers to success. In no way do I mean this explanation to sound cynical or demeaning. Rather, I see these individuals' "calling" as an extremely constructive engagement of their gifts, for the current reinvention of Protestantism would not be happening without them.

To label these new paradigm pastors entrepreneurs is a compliment to the role that they are playing in the history of Christianity. Entrepreneurs break new ground, shunning traditional ways of doing things, and they are risk takers with a high tolerance for criticism and failure. On the negative side, entrepreneurs are associated with taking advantage of others and using tactics of manipulation and exploitation. In this regard, I have looked for abuses of power by new paradigm clergy, and occasionally I have seen them, but the more consistent theme that I have found is that these are leaders marked by integrity and commitment, dedicated to loving people into wholeness.

The Ethic of Evangelism

New business firms are franchised because of the profit motive. But among new paradigm pastors, one has to look for a different motive. First, both the pastors and their congregants want to convert others because they have found Christianity to meet their personal hunger for ultimate meaning. Many new paradigm Christians offer persuasive testimonies: their lives were not working—they were depressed and despairing, their marriages were falling apart, they could not relate to their children, they were abusing their spouses and others, they were addicted to drugs—and something about their commitment to Jesus has changed all of that. They are proselytizing out of thankfulness, assuming that what happened to them has the potential to transform others.

Second, evangelism is part of their ideology. They believe in the Great Commission to spread the "good news," so that is what they do. This explanation may sound simplistic, but it fits in with the way they take the Bible seriously in so many other areas. Consider, for example, the stated mission of the Horizon Christian Fellowship: "Win, disciple, send." This slogan reflects their commitment to "win" people to Jesus, to "disciple" them in the Christian lifestyle, and to "send" them to missionize others.

Third, having pulled their own lives together, new paradigm pastors are in a position to commit themselves to a broader agenda. Just as liberal Christians are seeking to transform the world through social justice programs, these new paradigm pastors are working out their own civic agenda. The difference lies in their analysis of what is wrong. Rather than focusing on changing social structures through political initiatives, their diagnosis is that the human heart is sinful and corrupt, and that long-lasting change will occur only when enough individuals are transformed. From this perspective, their evangelism can be seen, not as a defensive gesture, but as a reflection of their vision for building a better world.

The missionizing activity of new paradigm Christians is extensive. Official counts indicate that annually 3,000 teenagers go forward on Monday nights at Costa Mesa to be "born again." Greg Laurie's staff estimates that 16,000 conversions occurred at Harvest Christian

Fellowship in the five-year period from 1986 to 1991. Admittedly, perhaps only 10 percent of these decisions result in long-term changes in personal behavior, but even with these attrition rates a substantial number of people have been affected.

New paradigm churches have been highly innovative in their evangelism strategies. From the early history of these movements, many new and potential converts were picked up at concerts. Currently, however, many people in these movements feel that the concert era has passed, and some critics blame their ineffectiveness on the fact that "domesticated Christians" are no longer playing cutting-edge music. Still, new methods seem to be emerging, such as the crusades described in chapter 3 or the use of sports ministries and similar recreational activities to connect with nonbelievers.

Radio, Tapes, and Music

Although word-of-mouth advertising from satisfied customers is the principal way in which new paradigm churches grow, various media play a secondary role. For example, a Calvary-sponsored FM station blankets southern California with contemporary Christian music and the Bible teaching of Chuck Smith, Raul Reis, Mike McIntosh, Greg Laurie, Skip Heitzig, and other Calvary Chapel pastors. People already affiliated with a Calvary Chapel may spend an hour or more a day "in church" as they commute to and from work or listen to their portable radios during leisure hours. In addition, a surprising number of people learn for the first time about this alternative form of Christianity by flicking the radio dial, encountering music that is contemporary and yet Christian, as well as teaching that is biblical and yet not preachy. In some areas, such as southern California, new paradigm churches actually own their own radio stations, but in other regions they buy radio time for relatively nominal amounts, and at the end of a Bible study broadcast may include a "tag-on," giving the location of a new church that is forming in the area. A number of people told us that they first heard about a new paradigm congregation in their area through this means.

Radio has also been a very effective marketing device outside the United States, especially where the airwaves are not highly regulated. I was told, for example, about a missionary who took a complete FM radio station to Ukraine in his carry-on luggage.[8] He then established himself in a high-rise apartment building and dropped a wire out of the window, blanketing the entire city with Christian radio programming. In the United States and overseas, anecdotal evidence indicates that thousands of people connect with new paradigm Christianity through radio broadcasts. Some individuals apparently have conversion experiences "over the radio" and then go in search of a community of people with whom to worship.

Another marketing tool is the distribution of teaching tapes by new paradigm pastors. Although many of these are purchased by congregation members, thousands of tapes are also mailed to people who have requested them, including individuals who do not have a new paradigm church in their area. Then, if a new paradigm church does start in their city, they are predisposed to seek it out.

The music emanating from new paradigm churches, however, is probably the most pervasive and yet subtle marketing mechanism. Stores featuring Christian music and books exist in cities across the United States, and within these stores there is a good representation of worship tapes and music by artists nurtured in various new paradigm movements. The sales of these tapes and CDs amount to many millions of dollars annually, and thousands of people attending traditional denominational churches listen to this music during the week, even though they continue to sing the standard hymns on Sunday. If these individuals discover that this music is sung regularly at a church in their neighborhood, they may be tempted to check it out and may then join the church.

Alternative Mainline Worship Services

The impact of new paradigm Christianity is most startlingly expressed in the number of mainline churches, including Catholic churches, experimenting with "alternative" worship services. Typically these services occur on Saturday night and seem to be imitations of new paradigm worship. Dress is informal; worship music is contemporary; and there is a decided focus on appealing to young people, families, and those outside the church. Many churches that have launched these experiments have seen their alternative service rapidly grow to equal the size of Sunday morning worship. Furthermore, these services do not attract only people under forty; something about the "fresh" quality of worship also seems to appeal to members of an older generation who wish to break out of the standard routine.

The alternative services that evidence rapid growth typically involve youth bands playing music they have written, or which fits into their popular culture, and a minister who is a youth leader close to the experience of the audience. In this regard, alternative worship services are most successful when they emerge out of a strong high school youth program, typically led by a charismatic staff member who has had a significant religious turning point and understands the ethos of the culture he or she is appropriating.

A relatively recent phenomenon is not alternative religion but alternative-style churches within mainline denominations. The flourishing Saddleback Community Church in Orange County, California, is officially part of the Southern Baptist denomination. However, this affiliation is not apparent in their name or how they advertise themselves. Their worship is extremely contemporary, and the sermon addresses the felt needs of the audience without any "religious" overtones, although biblical themes are taught. When I visited this church, they were still meeting in a large open-air tent. I counted fourteen high-amp speakers encircling the "stage," and there must have been fifty temporary Sunday school classrooms in trailers. Much like new paradigm churches, they had dozens of small groups meeting during the week, including numerous programs addressing specific needs ranging from money management to divorce recovery. The "ripple" effect of new paradigm churches, then, is beginning to reach far beyond the actual members of Calvary, Vineyard, or Hope. The music of new paradigm churches is starting to infiltrate mainline Christianity, and various experiments in worship style, however imitative, are transforming the way people conceive of the worship experience.

Adoptions

A few churches not only imitate the worship style and organizational form of new paradigm churches, but they have chosen to join with one of the three movements we studied. According to our survey of senior pastors, 12 percent of the Calvary Chapels and 35 percent of the Vineyard Fellowships are "adoptions" of one sort or another. Typically these were independent churches that at some point decided to affiliate with Calvary or the Vineyard, but there have also been some Calvary Chapels that decided to become Vineyards and vice versa. The decision to affiliate with the Vineyard usually represented a desire on the part of the senior pastor to emphasize the gifts of the Holy Spirit in more visible ways. Correspondingly, churches that decided to break with the Vineyard and join the Calvary fold often felt that the Vineyard puts too much emphasis on tongues, healings, and spiritual manifestations. Additionally, some pastors felt that the Vineyard's recent decision to become a denomination violated the original mission of the Vineyard, and they turned to the Calvary movement because it seems less inclined toward routinization.

One reason that the Vineyard has a larger percentage of adoptions than Calvary is John Wimber's "renewal" ministry. For a number of years his conferences have been attended by thousands of pastors from different denominations. During these conferences pastors have often experienced manifestations of the Holy Spirit, which have radically altered their perceptions of Christianity and their own ministries. When these pastors take the new vision back to their own congregations, sometimes the church members reject it, but in many instances they embrace it. Wimber's stated intention has never been to recruit churches through his renewal ministry, but if a church persistently expresses a desire for affiliation, then it may be adopted into the Vineyard fold.

Conclusion

It is important here to place decision making about religion within a cultural framework. It should not be surprising that enormous shifts are occurring in the American religious economy. In many spheres of life, individuals feel less constrained by tradition and freer to express individual choice than ever before. Critics of this transformation of consciousness have labeled this individualism "pathological," especially as people pursue their personal, and sometimes narcissistic, paths to self-fulfillment. A more generous appraisal is that this "new voluntarism," as it has been called, is liberating to the human spirit, leading to greater freedom of expression, creativity, and self-determination.

For religion, the implication of this change is that religious "switching" may increase. Many baby boomers and their offspring will ask why someone should stay with the church of one's birth simply for the sake of tradition. Shopping for a religion may sound commercial, but the upshot of this expression of individuality is that churches that are not meeting people's needs will fail and new upstart churches that are filling a need will prosper. It is not surprising to me that the mainline churches are falling on hard times. Many of these churches are culturally out of step, having failed to modernize the medium for their message.

CHAPTER 8

Can the Mainline Church Survive?

Some Lessons from History

The growth of new paradigm churches in the last third of the twentieth century fits a pattern of renewal and religious change found throughout the history of Christianity and well illustrated in various periods of religious revival in the United States, particularly the Second Great Awakening (1800–30). Nathan Hatch's prize-winning book, *The Democratization of American Christianity,* offers an interpretation of religion in the early nineteenth century with many parallels to the pattern of religious renewal seen in the three new paradigm movements examined in this book.

Hatch offers a number of insights into why the Second Great Awakening had such widespread appeal, energizing the religious passions of so many Americans. A central argument is that this was a populist movement in which the common people were reclaiming religion from the more educated elites. The establishment religion of the Episcopalians and Congregationalists had become domesticated. The clergy gave learned sermons filled with literary allusions and finely tuned philosophical arguments, but they did not connect to the everyday experience of the common person. Furthermore, religious authority had become captive to the religious hierarchy, and the people's access to God was mediated by salaried clergy. Not only was doctrinal interpretation the province of the clergy, but church programming was under the jurisdiction of paid professionals—rather than something the people initiated and organized. This top-down organizational style rewarded people with education and bureaucratic skills, but it retarded innovation and suffocated the commitment that stems from direct lay involvement in institutional decision making and program implementation.

In contrast, the reformist revival movements have typically been led by people who were self-conscious outsiders. Often they were not highly educated and in this regard spoke the common people's language. They were typically hostile to the refinements of sophisticated theology, procedural decision making, and ritualized forms of worship. Instead, preaching from the heart rather than from notes or prepared sermons, they passionately communicated a vision of God's ability to change people's lives. They recognized the legitimacy of direct religious experience and were not afraid of people being seized by the spirit, expressing themselves bodily as well as orally. Moreover, they boldly embraced opportunities to spread their gospel, ignoring territorial boundaries of the more established religious institutions.[1]

This style of religious leadership fit ordinary people's search for direct religious experience and their resentment of educated clergy's attempts to control access to the sacred. Referring to the rapid growth of the Baptists, Methodists, and Disciples of Christ during the early part of the nineteenth century, Nathan Hatch asserts: "Increasingly assertive common people wanted their leaders unpretentious, their doctrines self-evident and down to earth, their music lively and singable, and their churches in local hands."[2] By democratizing access to the sacred, by denying the distinction that established clergy as a separate order of human beings, ordinary people were energized in their religious commitments. They experienced a sense of self-esteem and personal power as they seized the opportunity to address God directly, interpret scriptures for themselves, and act in response to personal visions of God's calling.

In tent meetings and outdoor revival meetings during the Second Great Awakening, preachers often engaged in criticism of institutional religion, pointing out that religious virtue did not depend on educational degrees, but on the attitude of one's heart. Their counsel to abandon standardized religious forms often opened the floodgates to fits of religious ecstasy, which were interpreted as visitations by the Holy Spirit. People cried, wailed, and wept uncontrollably as they repented; but they also shouted for joy, "jerked" in response to the infilling of the spirit, and reached ecstasy of the highest mystical sort as they opened themselves to experiences paralleling what saints of ancient times have described. From the perspective of traditional religious decorum, all of this seemed a bit messy. Women, children, free blacks, and slaves were all testifying and being "slain" (knocked to the floor) by the spirit. Traditional social boundaries collapsed in this experience of democratized religion. In this regard, it is no wonder that city officials and the educated elite sometimes felt threatened, seeking to discredit such eruptions of the spirit. The evangelists who initiated the revivalist movements were encouraging the people to take control.[3]

To the educated and sophisticated classes, these revival meetings appeared to unleash a crude supernaturalism, one they felt they had outgrown. People were claiming divine guidance from dreams and visions, as well as witnessing "signs and wonders" that seemed right out of the first century. Miracles and bodily manifestations of the spirit may have happened during Christianity's founding period, but these experiences did not make sense from the Enlightenment worldview of the educated elite. To their dismay, putting the Bible in the hands of the people encouraged untempered religious exuberance and a kind of independence, because there is ample testimony in the Bible of people having their own lively encounters with God. In short, people learned to trust their own religious impulses, and that resulted in a newfound collective self-confidence, which was threatening to the established classes.[4]

Many interpreters of revivalist movements have seen these expressions of religious primitivism as serving the need for emotional catharsis but as holding few implications for political reform.[5] Hatch suggests a different reading of these movements. Biblical literalism, he contends, empowers common people in that they do not have to rely on learned theologians to interpret the Bible for them. He thinks that many of these revivalist movements, including Mormonism, Pentecostalism, the Holiness movement, and the Jehovah's Witnesses, are part of a more general populist impulse that contributes to democracy.[6] Putting the Bible in the hands of the people empowers them to engage in their own interpretations, rather than rely on others for information and instruction. This religious spirit, according to Hatch, is easily transferred to the political arena, where common people claim authority for interpreting events for themselves rather than depending on the tutored interpretation of experts.

Hatch is charitable toward fundamentalists, arguing that their literal reading of the Bible is not an attempt to return to the dark ages of religious sensibility.[7] He thinks that the strength of fundamentalism in the latter part of the twentieth century is as an expression of a populist crusade, "a revolt of people who feel they are being disfranchised from the core institutions of American culture."[8] In his view, the fundamentalist assertion of "no creed but the Bible" is an extreme statement of individualism as well as populism. While progressivist prophets may attack the structures that permit poverty, Hatch is impressed that in the early twentieth century groups such as the Pentecostals, Nazarenes, and fundamentalists were founding churches among the dirt farmers of Oklahoma, the automobile workers of Detroit, and the mill hands of North Carolina, *which were empowering to them,* giving members a sense of meaning in this world and salvation for the next.[9]

The Third Great Awakening

The parallels between the Second Great Awakening and the advent of new paradigm churches are remarkable. In both instances, establishment religion is rejected. New paradigm pastors see the mainline denominations as confusing true spirituality with religion and seek to restore the priesthood of all believers. Church buildings and religious symbols are unimportant, along with all of the codified doctrines, church rules, and procedures. The goal is unmediated communication between an individual and God. The Bible is viewed as the instrument of God's revelation, and individuals are invited to read it themselves, rather than relying on sermons and clerical interpretation. The people attracted to new paradigm churches in turn desire something concrete to believe in, rather than rarefied theology or culturally rationalized teachings. For them, primal religious experience (a daily encounter with Jesus) is the heart of religion.

Within the American religious economy there will always be room for mainline Christianity, just as there was during the Second Great Awakening. Not everyone is going to be attracted to primal religion. While new paradigm churches draw some highly educated people, the largest percentage of their membership has a high school education with some college. These are principally middle-class and blue-collar people who want their religion "straight-up," ministering to direct needs. The preferred idiom for worship is music that speaks to the heart, not just the mind. In contrast, mainline religion is always more modulated: the music is more traditional, the worship form more sedate, and the sermons more qualified.

Drawing on the theories of the German sociologist Max Weber, we can say that religion becomes progressively routinized over time. The founding prophet's teachings are rationalized by followers to harmonize with the prevailing worldview, and over time simple acts of religious expression take on more abstract levels of symbolization. Priestly roles are identified, sacred texts are canonized, rules and procedures for mediating access to the sacred evolve, and in this process the people become more and more distanced from the transforming source of the sacred. Taken to an extreme, religious institutions become encrusted bureaucracies that survive with low levels of commitment, primarily through habit and because they are integrated with other aspects of institutional life.

It is from this religious context that reformist movements emerge, often stimulated by social-political events that send large numbers of people in quest of a more adequate meaning system. Religious "primitivism" has a long history of appeal, with individuals abandoning the encrusted form of religion and searching for its earliest expression, before it was encased in doctrine and ritual. Religious life that appropriates the primitive forms typically has very little distance between the leaders and the people. Believers achieve direct access to the realm of the supernatural, which more domesticated forms of religion, over time, have found increasingly unseemly and magical.

Applying this model to new paradigm religion explains, among other things, why clergy dress like ordinary members, why they insist on biblical literalism (i.e., as a way of undercutting more authoritarian claimants to power), and why they emphasize lay ministry. The model also helps us understand the inevitable evolution of new paradigm groups toward denominationalism. In time, they will start centralizing authority, insisting on uniform practices, and creating bureaucratic layers of approval for acts that previously were spontaneous and spirit-led. Indeed, many of the current debates within new paradigm groups are over whether to resist routinization or to embrace it.

The more routinized a movement becomes, the less room there is for charismatic leadership. People are not "called" to service so much as "appointed" to well-defined offices. Professions of purity of heart and absoluteness of devotion give way to less demanding expressions of adherence to a creed and observance of particular moral norms. Enthusiasm for proselytizing also wanes because religion is not the center of one's life, but just one group membership among others.

Revivals like the Second Great Awakening play a powerful role in religious history as renewal movements. They attract people outside the religious fold, and they intensify the faith of those who are members by promoting encounters with the sacred that go far beyond ordinary religious experience. Drawn by the emphasis on vision rather than institutional maintenance, new converts accept the religious call to transform their world. They engage in superhuman acts of commitment to the cause and in turn energize the movement. (A striking example is the heroic commitment of Methodist "circuit riders" during the mid-nineteenth century, half of whom reportedly died before thirty years of age because of the rigors of life on horseback.)[10]

Why Are New Paradigm Churches Growing?

The 1960s were a watershed era in American culture with important ramifications for people's current religious choices. Whatever one may think of the political events of this period, many individuals developed a deep cynicism toward public institutions as well as an inclination to make autonomous decisions irrespective of tradition and conventional mores. With this revolution in consciousness, individuals no longer felt compelled to follow the religious tradition of their parents, and churchgoing was no longer a matter of social obligation. Conventional religious practices (such as confession for Catholics) were viewed as optional, as were many of the moral dictates of religion. A deep layer of distrust surrounded all forms of institutional religion.

Research on the religious attitudes of baby boomers reveals that many people make a distinction between "religion" and "spirituality."[11] Religion is seen as institutional and man-made; thus defined, it is of marginal interest to many people. Spirituality represents individual attempts to connect with the larger mysteries of the universe. While many critics have argued that the sixties led to narcissistic expressions of individualism, this is only one result. New paradigm churches are another, embodying numerous values of the 1960s while rejecting many of the social pathologies that the counterculture spawned. Indeed, many people who joined new paradigm churches did so because of their dissatisfaction with aspects of countercultural values, although their aesthetic tastes and understanding of institutional life were products of the sixties.

It is not surprising that baby boomers opted to attend churches that did not look religious, to worship in a home, a civic center, a converted warehouse, or a storefront. Since spirituality was the goal, not public conformity, little virtue was associated with "dressing up" to go to church. Because authority was distrusted, pastors were viewed with suspicion if they dressed differently from the congregation. Furthermore, pastors were expected to share reflections from their meditation on scripture rather than to preach from some authoritative position.

Given this cultural shift in values, the worship of new paradigm churches evolved in very different ways. In place of the rituals of what was viewed as man-made religion, relatively simple services emerged. Hymns of the past were replaced with contemporary melodies. People were free to raise their hands, kneel, or prostrate themselves as they were moved by their encounters with God, rather than at prescribed, ritualized moments. The sacraments were released from their formalized structure and engaged in much more spontaneously. A love feast, for example, might reenact the Last Supper, rather than reducing "communion" to a sip of wine and a wafer. Baptisms, held in natural settings, were not much different from the dunkings people received in the River Jordan, in contrast to the established church's symbolic sprinkle of water on the head.

Organizationally, the people took back their roles as initiators, organizers, and facilitators of programs. While efficiency dictated hiring some staff, the people were viewed as the "ministers" and the pastors were the administrators, with the senior pastor also having a special gift for teaching. If they were going to institutionalize religion, baby boomers nevertheless wanted their church to be bureaucratically lean and empowered by laypeople. Special degrees and theological certification were not required to do the work of ministry. They were the inventions of the established churches to professionalize the ministry, but they did not give these professionals a purer heart or clearer vision of the sacred than dedicated lay members.

To summarize: new paradigm churches eliminated many of the inefficiencies of bureaucratized religion by an appeal to the first-century model of Christianity; this "purged" form of religion corresponded to the countercultural worldview of baby boomers, who rejected institutionalized religion; with their bureaucratically lean, lay-oriented organizational structure, new paradigm churches developed programs sensitive to the needs of their constituency; new paradigm churches offered a style of worship that was attractive to people alienated from establishment religion because it was in their own idiom; this worship and the corresponding message provided direct access to an experience of the sacred, which had the potential of transforming people's lives by addressing their deepest personal needs.

A key point is that new paradigm churches appropriated elements of contemporary culture without accommodating all its values. This is a powerful combination and the opposite of what establishment religion often does, accommodating cultural values yet lagging behind the culture in its musical and organizational innovation. Even when establishment religion is culturally avant-garde, it typically regurgitates dominant societal values and therefore fails to engender commitment. In contrast, new paradigm churches make demands on their members, morally and spiritually. These churches provide a definite alternative to mainstream culture that constitutes much of their attraction.

New Paradigm Religions and Contemporary American Culture

To what human need are new paradigm churches responding? This is an extraordinarily important question because even if religion is contemporary in form, culturally avant-garde, even entertaining, if it is not addressing deeply felt needs it will not sustain the commitment of potential members. I would suggest that new paradigm churches are addressing at least four needs faced by people in urban America.

First, human community is in short supply in American society. Many people come from families fractured by divorce; they do not have access to extended family networks. The church is a place where they can experience a sense of community. New paradigm churches are places where human touch is welcomed, as demonstrated by the warm embraces that characterize small group meetings and worship. They are places where people can share their needs and know that someone will care for them, week after week. Such warmth is rare in American society.

Second, many people perceive America as a frightening place to live and raise children, and it is not surprising that they turn to the church as a safe haven for taking care of their social as well as spiritual needs. When one looks at the range of recreational programs of a large new paradigm church, one might be tempted to say that this is just another health club. But that would be a serious mistake. People are bringing their children to the church, and participating in church-related activities because of the type of environment it represents and the shared values of those with whom one is associating.

Third, many people seek support for specific needs: they are recently divorced with several small children to raise, they have an addiction problem, they are facing failure at work, they are having problems with their children, their marriage is in trouble. The list of personal troubles is extensive, and there are also people who are fundamentally unhappy, searching for something deeper and more meaningful than what our consumer society has to offer. People with big problems need strong forms of religion, which new paradigm churches represent with their biblical literalism, supernaturalism, and demanding structure.

Fourth, for many people in this country there is a "hope deficit," to which new paradigm churches are responding. People need not only healing of specific problems but also a sense of destiny, a conviction that their lives have purpose and meaning. New paradigm churches are particularly effective at projecting hope (sometimes in rather millennial terms) and joy. In content this may be the "old-time religion," but in spirit it addresses the fundamental need for ecstasy, which consumerism does not supply. Indeed, one of the draws of new paradigm religion is that it is fun! This may seem like an embarrassingly simple observation, but it parallels a similar observation about camp meetings during the Second Great Awakening: namely, that as many souls were conceived (through procreation) as were saved at these meetings.[12]

Within the free market of religious alternatives, new paradigm churches are competing with other groups in offering community, safety, life transformation, and hope, the four needs I believe are most pressing in American society. Many self-help and community groups attempt to address some of these needs: one can join an Alcoholics Anonymous group or be part of a Neighborhood Watch program. But new paradigm churches are unique in offering a full menu of programs, projects, and groups to address all these needs. In this regard they re-create some of the characteristics of small town life, not in the sense of removing people from their urban environment, but as an enclave within mass society where many fundamental needs can be addressed comprehensively.

Implications for Mainline Denominations

Although the strength of the mainline denominations is eroding, I do not expect them to disappear in the near term. In fact, I am a member of a liberal Episcopal church that has been growing

remarkably in the last decade. In some ways, it is the ideological antithesis of many new paradigm theological views. As a church, we have
strongly affirmed the rights of gays and lesbians to be part of the Christian community, and we have also taken a strong pro-choice stand on
abortion. Furthermore, the rector states every Sunday that all are welcome to participate in the Eucharist, regardless of where they are on the
journey of faith. In short, the church is inclusive rather than exclusive
in its message, and members are encouraged to think about their faith
as well as experience it.

In spite of the apparent differences between the church that I
attend—All Saints Episcopal Church in Pasadena, California—and new
paradigm churches such as Calvary, Vineyard, and Hope, there are some
structural parallels, which perhaps explain their similar growth. For example, the clergy at All Saints Church are as dogmatic about the truth
of their message as are new paradigm clergy, only "truth" is defined as
one's responsibility as a Christian to pursue issues of justice and peace.
The clergy at All Saints preach with authority as they attack the evils of
a society that ignores its poor, undereducates its children, denies economic opportunity to women and minorities, and blames a victim for
his or her sins.

Worship is culturally current and powerful at All Saints, even though
the sound is quite different from what one hears in a new paradigm
church. The members of All Saints are typically upper middle class,
many have classical musical tastes, and they would prefer a pipe organ
and orchestral instruments to an electric guitar and drums, although
these instruments may make their way into occasional Black gospel
masses and Cinco de Mayo worship celebrations. While people don't
raise their hands during worship, it is not at all unusual to see people
wiping tears from their eyes during the liturgy. Religious experience is
by no means absent at All Saints, even though its members would recoil
at the "born-again" rhetoric of new paradigm Christians. For example,
the rector, Ed Bacon, spends at least a week each year in silent retreat,
as well as one full day a month in contemplative reflection; and, in spite
of a heavy schedule, he spends at least an hour in prayer each morning.

In a survey I did at All Saints a few years ago, I was surprised at how
many members came from non-Episcopal backgrounds: they were former Catholics (who rejected their church's teaching on divorce and sexuality), former evangelicals and fundamentalists (who no longer believed that there was only "One Way" to God), gays and lesbians (whose
churches had condemned them), and so on. They were people who

were seeking a more pluralistic ideology, and yet they were drawn to All Saints by the high level of commitment expected of people who were going to be peacemakers and advocates of social justice in their city and world. They were drawn by the grandeur and richness of worship. And, yes, they also were "wounded" people who were seeking wholeness and healing in the mystery and mysticism of the liturgy.

I cite the example of All Saints as a growing church—in spite of its mainline identification and liberal bias—in part to stress the fact that within the American religious economy one group is not necessarily growing at the expense of another. For example, it is highly unlikely that people going to All Saints would be attracted to Calvary Chapel—and the converse is equally true. Rather, All Saints and Calvary Chapel draw from different customer bases in the religious marketplace.

Nevertheless, I worry about All Saints and the mainline churches. In spite of the apparent health of this one Episcopal church, no new churches have grown from it in recent decades. For a church its size, it has very few high school or college students. Rather, it seems dependent on other religious groups to socialize people into the Christian faith before they make the transition into a more liberal religious community. This does not seem to me to be a successful formula for religious leadership in the twenty-first century, especially when compared with the aggressive evangelism that characterizes so many of the more conservative churches. Still, All Saints fills an important niche, for it is because of churches like All Saints that some of us remain within the Christian fold.

Unfortunately, however, I see most liberal churches missing the mark: their message is ambiguous, lacking authority, and their worship is anemic. Furthermore, they are mired in organizational structures that deaden vision as people gather endlessly in committee meetings. While tradition is an important anchor in any community, it, along with church law, has the potential to stunt innovation. Given the level of creativity and innovative leadership among new paradigm Christians, I do not see how mainline churches can compete with new paradigm churches unless they radically reinvent themselves.

If the mainline churches are going to regain their leadership, they must do two things that the new paradigm churches already have mastered: first, they must give the ministry back to the people, which implies creating a much flatter organizational structure; and, second, they must become vehicles for people to access the sacred in profound and life-changing ways.[13] This is not the place for announcing a detailed prescription for renewing mainline Protestantism, but I do think some lessons can be drawn from new paradigm churches, so long as one recognizes that the theological content may differ substantially.

In terms of organizational restructuring, let me suggest a few ideas, some rather tame, some deliberately provocative. To me, the current downsizing of denominational offices—forced by financial exigency—seems a very good step. The centers of energy and creativity in this decade lie at the local, not the national, level, and that will probably hold true in the twenty-first century. The really innovative ideas for reshaping the church will come from people working in the trenches, addressing the needs of people in their churches and communities, not from denominational officials. Therefore, I believe that denominations would be well served by radically decentralizing their organizational structures—abandoning central offices and locating themselves in local churches, especially those flagship churches that are demonstrating leadership.

I also think that seminaries need to be radically restructured, allowing more theological education to be done in the local churches. Let clergy who want a graduate education go to a major university and study philosophy, church history, or theology. Seminaries, in contrast, should be professional schools where people are mentored and taught while they serve within a local congregation. Learning disconnected from day-to-day practice may be appropriate for those pursuing a Ph.D. and doing graduate-level research, but I am not certain that it is appropriate for those responding to a pastoral calling. Indeed, I would favor downsizing the physical plant of most seminaries and instead creating "lay institutes" on the campuses of the larger mainline churches.

The current method of clergy recruitment is not conducive to attracting people with exceptional leadership skills; seminaries may even dull the vision and passion of those who might lead the church in the twenty-first century. Specifically, the radical decentralization of clergy training within new paradigm churches should be examined as a possible model for mainline churches. When it is time to hire a new staff member, for example, perhaps someone should be selected from the ranks of the laity. Why? Because that person has proven his or her leadership abilities and fully understands the vision and culture of the institution. Restructuring the clerical vocation in such a radical way would be deeply threatening to many ministers who have been trained more traditionally, but simply tinkering with the organizational structure of mainline Christianity will serve little purpose.

In local churches, I believe clergy should abolish at least 80 percent of the committee meetings that currently occur, thereby freeing up people to join small group home fellowships. The fastest-growing and largest churches in the world are cell based, with all of the church ministry flowing out of small groupings of people who meet weekly, worshiping together, studying together, praying together, and often engaging in highly imaginative service to people in their neighborhoods. Pastoral care, evangelism, and cross-generational interaction all occur within these groups, which are led and organized by laypeople. The current form of community for Christians in many mainline churches is the committee meeting, a very poor structure for the type of nurture and care that many are seeking.

The second issue that liberal mainline church leaders need to radically rethink is how to engender experience of the sacred. Some of the Jesus rhetoric of the new paradigm churches may not be appropriate, but there is a definite need for the mainline churches to explore whatever it is that is implied by the Holy Spirit in the Christian tradition. There is an emerging movement within the Protestant mainline to rediscover the value of the ancient tradition of various spiritual disciplines, including silent retreats, spiritual direction, fasting, and spiritual exercises associated with the traditions of Saint Ignatius, Saint Benedict, and other pioneers of probing soul and psyche.[14] I celebrated my own fiftieth birthday by spending a week at a Jesuit Retreat Center and had some physiological and spiritual experiences that were not too different from what members of the Vineyard might describe, although they were nurtured from within a completely different interpretive context. Hence, I am convinced that charismatics do not have a "corner" on the marketplace of religious experience.

I also believe that mainline churches should begin breaking down the dichotomy between mind and body in worship. For this to occur, some radical restructuring of liturgy may be needed. People must have time to enter into the deep recesses of the human spirit, assisted by the right type of music and a liturgy that is not interrupted by announcements and greetings. I have been enormously impressed during my visits to Taizé, a spiritual pilgrimage site in France to which hundreds of thousands of young people come annually. The worship at Taizé is very simple and yet incredibly beautiful, utilizing chant and song to trigger access to the sacred in ways that much mainline worship does not begin to accomplish.

Finally, mainline churches need to begin to experiment with worship styles and music that communicate to a new generation of young people. Initially, these may be Saturday or Sunday night alternative services that are culturally current in form and utilize the musical talents of teenagers and the twenty-something generation. These services need to be led by young men and women whose lives have been transformed by their experience of the sacred. The future of the mainline churches depends on raising up leaders from the next generation.

Indeed, if the mainline church is going to survive, it will need to spawn new churches led by a new generation of young people, and these youth (even as adults) may choose to meet in entirely different types of worship spaces and may organize their churches in radically different ways from those of their parents and grandparents. Church architecture is a direct reflection of cultural and technological revolutions, and the "digital age" church may not work in the Gothic and "churchly" structures that characterize the mainline denominations. Therefore, mainline church leaders should be open to radical experimentation by their Generation X youth.

Finally, a new generation of theology needs to be written that speaks to the experience of liberal mainline churchgoers. This theology cannot be derivative, but must emerge out of mainline members' own encounters with the sacred. However reified mainline theology may be currently, Aquinas, Calvin, and Wesley wrote out of the wellsprings of their direct encounters with the holy. Religious experience, not social criticism or the latest philosophical school of thought, is the basis for all genuine theology. Liberal theology of the twenty-first century must have three benchmarks: reason, tradition, and religious experience. If the last element is missing, the first two—reason and tradition—are extremely poor sources for a theology that is going to enliven the human spirit.

Can the mainline church survive the twenty-first century? I believe it can if it is willing to reinvent itself, taking seriously the need for organizational reform and the importance of fostering life-changing encounters with the sacred.

Geographical Distribution of Churches

Table 1 *Churches in the United States, Spring 1996*

State	Vineyard	Calvary
AK	1	2
AL	5	2
AR	11	26
AZ	0	0
CA	100	255
CO	18	15
CT	4	5
DE	0	0
FL	21	26
GA	11	6
HI	0	14
IA	4	1
ID	4	13
IL	20	9
IN	11	12
KS	6	8
KY	4	6
LA	11	0
MA	10	3
MD	2	1
ME	3	3
MI	9	6

Table 1 *(continued)*

State	Vineyard	Calvary
MN	8	2
MO	9	8
MS	3	0
MT	5	7
NC	9	10
ND	0	0
NE	1	1
NH	1	1
NJ	2	11
NM	3	12
NV	6	7
NY	9	18
OH	17	9
OK	3	5
OR	14	25
PA	3	7
RI	1	1
SC	2	4
SD	1	0
TN	3	5
TX	18	10
UT	2	4
VA	10	9
VT	1	2
WA	17	35
WI	1	5
WV	2	0
WY	0	3

	Total	
50	406	614

Table 2 *Churches Outside the United
States, Spring 1996*

Country	Vineyard	Calvary
Australia	13	7
Austria	2	2
Belarus	0	1
Canada	49	3
Chile	4	1
Columbia	1	1
Costa Rica	2	1
Croatia	0	1
England	24	5
France	0	1
Germany	3	3
Ghana	0	1
Guam	0	1
Hong Kong	0	1
Hungary	0	5
India	0	4
Indonesia	0	1
Ireland	1	1
Japan	4	6
Kenya	1	0
Lebanon	3	0
Macau	0	1
Macedonia	1	0
Malawi	2	0
Mexico	7	7
Namibia	2	0
Netherlands	1	1
New Zealand	13	0
Norway	1	0
Peru	0	1
Philippines	2	11
Romania	0	1
Russia	5	13
Scotland	1	1
Serbia	0	2
South Africa	18	0
Spain	1	0
Sweden	6	0
Switzerland	2	2

Table 2 *(continued)*

Country	Vineyard	Calvary
Taiwan	0	1
Tonga	0	1
Transkei	1	0
Trinidad	0	1
Uganda	0	1
Ukraine	0	5
Zambia	2	0
Zimbabwe	1	0
Other African	0	2
	Total	
48	173	97

Congregational Surveys

	All Three Churches	Calvary	Vineyard	Hope*
Your sex?				
Female	48	61	44	43
Male	52	39	56	58
Your race?				
White	75	64	88	67
Black	2	2	1	3
Hispanic	13	29	6	6
Asian	7	2	4	15
Other	3	2	1	6
Your age?				
Under 20	4	3	4	5
21–25	7	6	7	8
26–30	16	14	13	20
31–35	19	19	19	20
36–40	18	18	17	18
41–45	12	12	13	11

*Unless otherwise indicated, figures represent percentage of respondents. Because the figures are rounded off, some totals may not equal 100 percent.

	All Three Churches	Calvary	Vineyard	Hope*
46–50	8	7	10	6
51–55	6	5	7	4
56–60	5	6	5	4
61–65	3	3	2	3
Over 66	4	6	3	2

Your marital status?

Never married	24	18	23	31
Married, never divorced	46	47	47	42
Married and previously divorced	15	18	14	14
Divorced	12	13	11	10
Separated	2	2	2	1
Widowed	2	3	2	2

Does your family household include a stepparent or a stepchild?

Yes	13	15	12	12
No	87	85	88	88

What is the highest level of formal education you have completed?

Less than high school graduate	6	10	4	6
High school graduate	14	24	9	11
Some college, trade, or vocational school	42	46	42	37
College degree	23	15	22	31
Postgraduate work	6	2	9	7
Postgraduate degree	9	3	15	9

What is your present employment status?

Working full time	61	56	63	64
Working part time	13	13	11	15
Unemployed, laid off, looking for work	5	7	5	4
Not working because of temporary illness, vacation, or strike	2	3	2	2
Retired	6	7	4	3

	All Three Churches	Calvary	Vineyard	Hope*
In school	3	3	3	4
Keeping house	11	12	12	8

In which of these groups did your *total* family income from all sources fall before taxes in 1992?

Less than $20,000	16	18	17	14
$20,000–$39,999	30	35	29	27
$40,000–$59,999	25	26	24	27
$60,000–$79,999	14	13	14	15
$80,000–$99,999	6	5	6	7
Over $100,000	9	4	11	9

How many years have you lived in southern California [or Hawaii for some Hope respondents]?

Less than 1 year	1	1	2	1
1–2 years	2	0	2	4
3–4 years	4	1	4	6
5–9 years	9	4	10	11
10–19 years	14	10	17	16
20 or more years	70	85	65	62

How likely is it that you might move out of southern California (Hawaii) within the next 5 years?

Definitely will move	6	4	5	9
Probably will move	9	8	8	12
Might move	28	26	28	31
Unlikely to move	57	62	59	48

Which of the categories comes closest to the type of place you were living at age 16?

Small town (under 50,000)	26	20	28	30
Medium city (50,000–250,000)	42	51	43	35
Large city (over 250,000)	26	25	24	29
Open country but not on farm	4	3	3	4
Farm	2	2	2	2

	All Three Churches	Calvary	Vineyard	Hope*

How long does it usually take you to travel from home to Calvary/Vineyard/Hope?

	All Three Churches	Calvary	Vineyard	Hope*
Under 15 minutes	45	55	33	51
15–29 minutes	38	41	36	36
30–44 minutes	13	3	22	11
45–59 minutes	3	1	7	2
60 minutes or more	1	0	2	1

Would you say that you have been born again or have had a born-again experience—that is, a turning point in your life where you committed yourself to Jesus Christ?

	All Three Churches	Calvary	Vineyard	Hope*
Yes, I'm sure I have	93	92	95	91
Yes, I think I have	5	6	4	6
No, I don't think I have	1	2	1	2
No, I'm sure I have not	1	1	0	1

At what age did you have your born-again experience?

	All Three Churches	Calvary	Vineyard	Hope*
Under 5 years of age	2	1	4	1
5–9 years	8	5	11	7
10–14 years	13	10	15	12
15–19 years	19	17	22	18
20–24 years	16	17	15	18
25–29 years	13	15	10	15
30–34 years	10	12	9	10
35–39 years	8	9	6	9
Over 40 years	11	15	9	11

How would you describe the religious affiliation of your upbringing?

	All Three Churches	Calvary	Vineyard	Hope*
Fundamentalist Protestant	21	16	25	20
Evangelical Protestant	15	12	20	12
Liberal Protestant	11	5	11	15
Roman Catholic	28	38	23	27
No affiliation	13	16	12	12
Other	12	13	10	16

In a typical month [during your upbringing], how frequently did you attend church?

	All Three Churches	Calvary	Vineyard	Hope*
Less than once per month	13	17	9	13

	All Three Churches	Calvary	Vineyard	Hope*
Once a month	8	7	5	11
Twice a month	7	5	7	10
Three times a month	8	7	8	10
Four times a month	37	35	42	31
More than four times	28	29	29	25

How would you describe your religious affiliation during the year before you came to Calvary/Vineyard/Hope?

	All Three Churches	Calvary	Vineyard	Hope*
Fundamentalist Protestant	14	11	15	15
Evangelical Protestant	27	14	41	23
Liberal Protestant	5	5	4	5
Roman Catholic	11	19	6	9
No affiliation	29	38	18	34
Other	15	14	17	13

In a typical month [during the previous year], how frequently did you attend church?

	All Three Churches	Calvary	Vineyard	Hope*
Less than once a month	22	34	13	24
Once a month	6	9	3	6
Twice a month	5	5	4	7
Three times a month	5	4	5	7
Four times a month	34	26	35	40
More than four times	28	22	41	17

As a child, how frequently did you attend church?

	All Three Churches	Calvary	Vineyard	Hope*
Less than once a month	24	24	21	27
About once a month	5	6	4	4
2–3 times a month	17	19	16	18
Every week	54	51	60	51

How long have you been attending Calvary/Vineyard/Hope?

	All Three Churches	Calvary	Vineyard	Hope*
Less than 1 year	13	14	14	11
1 year	11	12	9	13
2 years	9	10	7	11
3 years	10	10	9	12
4 years	8	7	8	8
5 years	9	7	10	9

	All Three Churches	Calvary	Vineyard	Hope*
6–7 years	14	9	17	14
8–9 years	10	8	10	11
10–14 years	14	19	16	8
15 or more years	4	6	1	4

How often do you attend Calvary/Vineyard/Hope Sunday morning worship services?

Less than once a month	8	6	12	5
About once a month	2	2	3	2
2–3 times a month	15	14	16	14
Every week	75	78	69	80

How often do you attend Calvary/Vineyard/Hope *evening* worship services?

Less than once a month	49	61	22	72
About once a month	10	9	12	8
2–3 times a month	16	13	25	9
Every week	25	17	42	11

Do you regularly attend one or more churches in addition to Calvary/ Vineyard/Hope?

Yes, almost every week	7	4	10	5
Yes, once or twice a month	6	5	7	7
No, Calvary/Vineyard/Hope is the only church I regularly attend	87	90	84	88

If you're married, how frequently does your spouse attend Calvary/Vineyard/ Hope?

Less than once a month	12	16	9	12
About once a month	2	3	2	2
2–3 times a month	14	12	15	14
Every week	72	68	75	71

Approximately how much did your family household contribute to Calvary/ Vineyard/Hope during the 1992 tax year?

Under $500	30	42	25	25
$500–$999	14	18	13	12

	All Three Churches	Calvary	Vineyard	Hope*
$1,000–$1,999	14	16	12	15
$2,000–$2,999	12	11	14	12
$3,000–$3,999	8	6	9	9
$4,000–$4,999	6	3	7	7
$5,000–$5,999	5	3	5	7
$6,000–$6,999	3	1	4	4
$7,000–$7,999	3	1	4	3
Over $8,000	6	1	8	8

Overall, how satisfied are you with Calvary/Vineyard/Hope?

	All Three Churches	Calvary	Vineyard	Hope*
Very satisfied	70	71	65	74
Satisfied	28	26	32	24
Dissatisfied	2	2	2	1
Very dissatisfied	1	2	1	1

How often do you read the Bible?

	All Three Churches	Calvary	Vineyard	Hope*
More than once a day	11	12	12	8
Daily	40	39	41	40
2–3 times a week	34	33	34	35
2–3 times a month	10	11	9	10
Once a month	2	2	2	2
Less than once a month	3	4	2	3
Never	1	1	0	1

Which of these statements comes closest to describing your feelings about the Bible?

	All Three Churches	Calvary	Vineyard	Hope*
The Bible is the actual word of God and is to be taken literally, word for word.	32	44	24	29
The Bible is the inspired word of God. It contains no errors, but some verses are to be taken symbolically rather than literally.	65	54	71	68
The Bible is the inspired word of God, but it may contain historical and scientific errors.	3	2	4	3

	All Three Churches	Calvary	Vineyard	Hope*
The Bible was not inspired by God, but it represents humankind's best understanding of God's nature.	0	0	0	1
The Bible is an ancient book of human fables, legends, history, and moral precepts recorded by men.	0	0	0	0

Of your three closest friends, how many regularly attend Calvary/Vineyard/Hope?

	All Three Churches	Calvary	Vineyard	Hope*
None	25	28	24	23
One	20	21	19	21
Two	23	21	21	26
All three	32	29	36	30

Of these three friends, how many would you consider to be committed Christians?

	All Three Churches	Calvary	Vineyard	Hope*
None	9	14	5	9
One	16	21	10	19
Two	23	25	19	25
All three	53	41	66	47

Of people I know at Calvary/Vineyard/Hope, I almost always feel free to touch and/or hug:

	All Three Churches	Calvary	Vineyard	Hope*
Most of the people	60	57	60	64
About half of the people	14	11	15	16
Only a few of the people	21	25	22	17
None of the people	5	7	4	3

Here are a few statements about religious experiences. For each one, please indicate if you have had the experience and, if so, how often.

A. *A vision from the Lord:*

	All Three Churches	Calvary	Vineyard	Hope*
Often	8	4	15	4
A few times	29	20	38	26

	All Three Churches	Calvary	Vineyard	Hope*
Once	13	13	11	13
Never	50	63	35	57

B. *Speaking in tongues:*

Often	41	15	72	27
A few times	13	13	11	14
Once	4	6	3	4
Never	42	66	15	55

C. *A word of knowledge:*

Often	25	21	32	20
A few times	43	41	46	40
Once	6	6	5	8
Never	26	32	17	33

D. *Been prayed for by people at Calvary/Vineyard/Hope who have laid hands on you:*

Often	31	9	56	19
A few times	39	41	33	47
Once	11	17	5	13
Never	19	34	6	22

E. *Have prayed for other people at Calvary/Vineyard/Hope by laying hands on them:*

Often	38	14	59	33
A few times	38	43	28	47
Once	6	9	3	6
Never	18	34	9	15

F. *Been miraculously healed:*

Often	7	4	11	6
A few times	18	12	24	14
Once	19	19	20	17
Never	57	65	45	64

I have experienced God's healing of my emotions in a way other than through psychological counseling.

This is very true for me	65	65	67	63
This is somewhat true for me	25	23	24	27
This is not true for me	10	12	9	10

	All Three Churches	Calvary	Vineyard	Hope*

Please circle one number corresponding to each of the contrasting statements below.

A. 1 My faith is completely free
   of doubts.

1 My faith is completely free of doubts.	44	59	36	40
2	39	29	44	43
3	5	4	5	6
4	9	7	11	9
5 My faith is mixed with doubts.	3	2	3	3

B.
1 I always feel close to God.	25	39	17	22
2	61	51	67	63
3	10	7	11	12
4	3	2	4	2
5 I never feel close to God.	1	1	0	1

C.
1 I feel satisfied with the level of pastoring I receive at Calvary/Vineyard/Hope.	51	71	33	57
2	29	19	36	29
3	10	5	14	8
4	7	3	12	4
5 I feel unsatisfied with the level of pastoring I receive at Calvary/Vineyard/Hope.	3	2	6	1

D.
1 I experience God more at Calvary/Vineyard/Hope than I do at any other church.	59	61	62	54
2	21	16	22	22
3	10	12	7	10
4	6	5	5	7
5 My experience of God at other churches is the same as at Calvary/Vineyard/Hope.	5	6	3	6

E.
1 Compared to other churchgoers, people at Calvary/Vineyard/Hope seem willing to sacrifice everything for Christ.	20	26	16	18

	All Three Churches	Calvary	Vineyard	Hope*
2	43	37	45	46
3	31	32	32	30
4	5	4	5	5
5 Compared to other church-goers, people at Calvary/Vineyard/Hope seem reluctant to sacrifice everything for Christ.	1	1	1	1
F. 1 Compared to other church-goers, people at Calvary/Vineyard/Hope seem driven by the desire to win others to Christ.	28	45	14	29
2	42	36	45	49
3	24	17	34	18
4	4	1	7	3
5 Compared to other churchgoers, people at Calvary/Vineyard/Hope seem reluctant to share their beliefs with non-Christians.	1	1	1	0
G. 1 There should be no differences between the roles of men and women in Calvary/Vineyard/Hope ministries.	20	18	18	23
2	23	15	30	22
3	18	15	19	19
4	22	20	23	23
5 Calvary/Vineyard/Hope ministries should involve distinctly different roles for men and women.	17	31	10	14
Did your parents divorce?				
Yes	30	33	27	30
No	70	67	73	70

	All Three Churches	Calvary	Vineyard	Hope*

Did one or both of your parents abuse alcohol or drugs?

Yes	37	44	36	33
No	63	56	64	67

How often have you had the following experiences in your past?

A. *Smoked marijuana and/or used illegal drugs:*

Often	27	31	21	30
A few times	21	21	18	25
Once	10	10	11	9
Never	42	37	50	37

B. *Abused alcohol:*

Often	26	30	23	27
A few times	31	30	29	33
Once	5	5	6	5
Never	38	35	41	35

C. *Engaged in homosexual activity:*

Often	1	1	2	1
A few times	4	3	5	4
Once	4	2	4	5
Never	91	93	90	90

D. *Engaged in premarital sex:*

Often	37	39	31	43
A few times	31	32	31	30
Once	6	7	7	6
Never	26	22	32	21

E. *Engaged in extramarital sex:*

Often	4	5	4	3
A few times	10	12	9	11
Once	8	10	7	8
Never	78	73	80	79

F. *Was physically and/or sexually abused:*

Often	9	8	11	8
A few times	16	14	19	12

	All Three Churches	Calvary	Vineyard	Hope*
Once	9	9	9	9
Never	66	67	61	71

G. *Received professional therapy:*

Often	11	7	15	9
A few times	23	19	25	23
Once	11	10	11	11
Never	56	63	49	58

Please indicate your level of agreement with each of the following statements.

A. *Prayer is an important part of my daily life.*

Strongly agree	87	89	87	83
Somewhat agree	12	10	12	14
Somewhat disagree	1	1	1	1
Strongly disagree	0	0	0	0
Not sure/Don't know	1	0	0	1

B. *I am very interested in politics and national affairs.*

Strongly agree	28	29	24	33
Somewhat agree	48	45	50	47
Somewhat disagree	15	15	17	12
Strongly disagree	5	6	5	4
Not sure/Don't know	4	6	4	4

C. *The public elementary schools in this area should teach sex education in grades four through eight.*

Strongly agree	9	7	8	12
Somewhat agree	18	15	18	21
Somewhat disagree	19	16	21	18
Strongly disagree	45	52	43	40
Not sure/Don't know	10	9	10	10

D. *I would object if a member of my family wanted to bring a friend of a different race home to dinner.*

Strongly agree	2	3	2	2
Somewhat agree	2	3	1	1
Somewhat disagree	3	4	3	2
Strongly disagree	92	87	94	94
Not sure/Don't know	1	2	1	2

	All Three Churches	Calvary	Vineyard	Hope*

E. *Minority races should not push themselves where they're not wanted.*

Strongly agree	3	4	2	2
Somewhat agree	8	11	7	8
Somewhat disagree	17	17	18	16
Strongly disagree	63	59	64	64
Not sure/Don't know	9	9	9	10

F. *There should be laws against marriages between minority races and whites.*

Strongly agree	1	2	1	0
Somewhat agree	1	3	1	1
Somewhat disagree	4	6	5	3
Strongly disagree	90	85	91	94
Not sure/Don't know	3	4	3	2

G. *Women should take care of running their homes and leave running the country up to men.*

Strongly agree	7	14	4	3
Somewhat agree	16	22	13	14
Somewhat disagree	24	24	25	22
Strongly disagree	51	37	57	59
Not sure/Don't know	2	4	2	2

H. *I approve of a married woman earning money in business or industry if she has a husband capable of supporting her.*

Strongly agree	38	26	40	46
Somewhat agree	30	31	31	29
Somewhat disagree	12	17	12	9
Strongly disagree	13	19	11	10
Not sure/Don't know	7	7	7	7

I. *Most men are better suited emotionally for politics than most women.*

Strongly agree	12	18	8	9
Somewhat agree	28	30	30	25
Somewhat disagree	22	18	25	22
Strongly disagree	27	22	26	33
Not sure/Don't know	12	13	11	11

J. *It should be possible for a pregnant woman to obtain a legal abortion if she is married and does not want any more children.*

Strongly agree	3	4	2	4

	All Three Churches	Calvary	Vineyard	Hope*
Somewhat agree	3	3	2	5
Somewhat disagree	4	5	3	5
Strongly disagree	87	84	91	84
Not sure/Don't know	3	4	1	4

K. *It should be possible for a woman to obtain a legal abortion if she wants it for any reason.*

	All Three Churches	Calvary	Vineyard	Hope*
Strongly agree	3	4	2	4
Somewhat agree	3	4	2	5
Somewhat disagree	4	6	3	4
Strongly disagree	87	84	91	84
Not sure/Don't know	3	3	1	4

What is your political party affiliation?

	All Three Churches	Calvary	Vineyard	Hope*
Republican	62	53	70	60
Independent	5	6	4	6
Democrat	16	24	11	13
No affiliation	18	17	15	21

How often during elections do you try to show people why they should vote for one of the parties' candidates?

	All Three Churches	Calvary	Vineyard	Hope*
Often	16	20	10	19
Sometimes	33	34	27	38
Rarely	28	24	34	25
Never	23	21	29	19

In terms of politics, do you consider yourself:

	All Three Churches	Calvary	Vineyard	Hope*
Extremely liberal	0	0	0	0
Liberal	2	3	2	2
Slightly liberal	4	3	4	4
Moderate, middle of the road	10	11	10	9
I don't care about politics	7	10	7	5
Slightly conservative	16	13	19	14
Conservative	43	39	45	42
Extremely conservative	9	9	6	13
I don't know	10	12	7	10

	All Three Churches	Calvary	Vineyard	Hope*

In the 1992 presidential election I voted for:

George Bush	70	64	75	68
Bill Clinton	8	10	5	9
Another candidate	5	11	2	3
I didn't vote in this election	18	15	18	20

Should someone who is against all churches and religion:

A. Be allowed to make a speech in your city?

Yes	67	53	73	73
No	19	29	15	15
I don't know	14	17	12	12

B. Be allowed to teach in a college or university?

Yes	57	43	63	63
No	27	38	22	23
I don't know	16	19	15	15

If some people in your community suggested that a book written against churches and religion be taken out of our public library, would you favor removing this book or not?

Favor	32	42	29	27
Not favor	50	41	54	54
I don't know	18	17	18	20

Suppose there is a community-wide vote on the general housing issue. Of these two possible laws, which would you vote for?

A law saying that a home-owner can decide for himself/herself whom to sell his/her house to, even if he/she prefers not to sell to minority races	24	20	27	24
A law saying that a home-owner cannot refuse to sell to someone because of his/her race or color	68	71	64	68
I don't know	8	9	8	8

	All Three Churches	Calvary	Vineyard	Hope*

What is your opinion about a married person having sexual relations with someone other than the marriage partner?

	All Three Churches	Calvary	Vineyard	Hope*
It is always wrong	98	98	99	97
It is almost always wrong	1	1	1	2
I don't know	0	0	0	1
It is wrong only sometimes	0	0	0	0
It is not wrong at all	0	0	0	0

What is your opinion about sexual relations between two adults of the same sex?

	All Three Churches	Calvary	Vineyard	Hope*
It is always wrong	97	97	98	95
It is almost always wrong	1	0	1	1
I don't know	2	2	1	3
It is wrong only sometimes	0	0	0	0
It is not wrong at all	1	1	1	1

Growing up, how frequently did you attend rock concerts?

	All Three Churches	Calvary	Vineyard	Hope*
Often	16	17	14	17
A few times	36	30	34	44
Once	9	9	9	8
Never	40	45	43	30

How important do you believe the following involvements are for a Christian?

A. *Success in one's job or profession:*

	All Three Churches	Calvary	Vineyard	Hope*
Unimportant	8	9	9	6
Important but not essential	67	67	71	64
Important and essential	24	24	20	30

B. *Telling neighbors and work colleagues about Jesus:*

	All Three Churches	Calvary	Vineyard	Hope*
Unimportant	1	2	1	1
Important but not essential	18	14	20	18
Important and essential	81	84	79	81

C. *Volunteering time and/or giving money to community organizations, projects, or activities:*

	All Three Churches	Calvary	Vineyard	Hope*
Unimportant	5	6	7	3
Important but not essential	56	55	59	53
Important and essential	39	38	35	44

	All Three Churches	Calvary	Vineyard	Hope*
D. Volunteering time and/or giving money to political causes:				
Unimportant	33	37	36	26
Important but not essential	58	53	58	61
Important and essential	10	10	7	13
E. Voting in national elections:				
Unimportant	3	4	4	2
Important but not essential	23	19	29	20
Important and essential	74	77	67	78

Pastors Survey

	Calvary*	Vineyard*

Characteristics of Your Congregation and Community

How would you describe the social class composition of the neighborhood in which your congregation is based?†

Upper class	1	1
Upper middle class	6	8
Middle class—white collar	22	32
Middle class—working class	50	44
Lower middle class	19	13
Lower class	2	2

Which of the categories below most closely describes the location of the church that you pastor?†

Small town (under 50,000)	39	27
Medium city (50,000–250,000)	30	31
Large city (over 250,000)	18	23
Suburb near a medium city	3	4
Suburb near a large city	10	15

*Unless otherwise indicated, figures represent percentage of respondents. Because the figures are rounded off, some totals may not equal 100 percent.

†Median for each response category.

	Calvary*	Vineyard*

Please estimate the racial/ethnic composition of the community in which your church is located.†

Black	5	5
Asian	5	3
White	75	85
Hispanic	10	7
Other	5	1

Please indicate the racial/ethnic composition of your congregation.†

Black	2	2
Asian	2	1
White	90	95
Hispanic	8	4
Other	2	1

Please indicate the age characteristics of your congregation on a typical Sunday morning.†

Percent of children 12 years or younger	26	25
Adolescents between ages 13 and 17	8	8
Young adults between ages 18 and 22	6	5
Adults between ages 23 and 32	20	25
Adults between ages 33 and 45	28	25
Adults 46 years of age or older	9	6

Please estimate the following characteristics of adults in your congregation.†

A. *Sex:*

Percent females	52	55
Percent males	48	45

B. *Marital status:*

Percent single, never married	10	19
Percent married, never divorced	50	50
Percent married and previously divorced	20	15
Percent divorced	7	7
Percent separated	2	2
Percent widowed	2	1

C. *Education (highest levels attained):*

Percent less than high school graduates	5	5

	Calvary*	Vineyard*
Percent high school graduates	40	25
Percent some college, trade, or vocational school	25	25
Percent college graduates	20	25
Percent who have done postgraduate work or achieved graduate degrees	5	5

D. *Socioeconomic status:*

	Calvary*	Vineyard*
Percent upper-class or upper-middle-class professionals	5	5
Percent middle-class white-collar professionals	20	27
Percent middle-class blue-collar workers	40	35
Percent lower-middle-class workers	20	15
Percent lower-class workers	8	10

E. *Unemployment:*

	Calvary*	Vineyard*
Percent currently unemployed (who are seeking work)	5	5

History, Programs, and Governance of Your Church

In what year was this congregation founded?†

	Calvary*	Vineyard*
1942–64	1	2
1965–80	23	8
1981–89	53	65
1990–92	23	25

Has this church always been affiliated with Calvary/Vineyard?

	Calvary*	Vineyard*
Yes	88	65
No	12	35

Not counting yourself, how many other senior pastors of this congregation have there been since this church was started?

	Calvary*	Vineyard*
None	68	80
One	21	14
Two	6	3
Three	2	2
Four or more	2	1

	Calvary*	Vineyard*

Please indicate the typical Sunday morning attendance during each of the following calendar years.

	Calvary	Vineyard
1988	90	100
1989	97	120
1990	105	125
1991	138	150

What is the annual budget of your church?

	Calvary	Vineyard
In 1992 [median church]	$70,000	$90,000

If your church has a building fund, approximately how much money have you accumulated in this fund?

	Calvary	Vineyard
[Median]	$10,000	$5,000

In what type of facilities does your church currently meet?

	Calvary	Vineyard
Rented facilities	75	81
Own facilities	25	19

The Senior Pastor: Background and Values

Your sex?

	Calvary	Vineyard
Male	100	100
Female	0	0

Your race/ethnicity?

	Calvary	Vineyard
White	94	97
Hispanic	5	2
Asian	1	1
Black	1	0

Your age?

	Calvary	Vineyard
20–24 years	0	2
25–29 years	3	0
30–34 years	14	16
35–39 years	32	27

	Calvary*	Vineyard*
40–44 years	33	28
45–49 years	11	17
50–54 years	4	7
55 or more	3	3

Your marital status?

Never married	1	1
Married, never divorced	83	91
Married and previously divorced	16	8
Divorced	1	0
Separated	0	0
Widowed	0	0

Does your family household include a stepchild?

Yes	7	5
No	93	95

What is the highest level of (non-seminary/non-ministry-related) formal education that you have completed?

Less than high school graduate	1	0
High school graduate	15	7
Some college, trade, or vocational school	46	29
College degree	24	38
Postgraduate work	6	12
Postgraduate degree	8	14

If you are married, what is your spouse's education?

Less than high school graduate	5	1
High school graduate	25	14
Some college, trade, or vocational school	44	44
College degree	20	24
Postgraduate work	4	9
Postgraduate degree	2	8

If you are married, what is your spouse's employment status?

Working full time	11	19
Working part time	29	30

	Calvary*	Vineyard*
Unemployed, laid off, looking for work	1	1
Not working because of temporary illness, vacation, or strike	1	1
Retired	0	1
In school	0	1
Keeping house	58	48

Which of the categories comes closest to the type of place you were living at age 16?

Small town (under 50,000)	25	27
Medium city (50,000–250,000)	33	30
Large city (over 250,000)	21	24
Open country but not a farm	3	4
Farm	3	6
Suburb near a medium city	4	3
Suburb near a large city	11	6

How would you describe the religious affiliation of your upbringing?

Fundamentalist Protestant	17	12
Evangelical Protestant	15	37
Liberal Protestant	16	15
Roman Catholic	26	17
No affiliation	20	15
Other	6	4

How frequently did you attend Sunday morning services when you were growing up?

Seldom	25	14
Once a month	5	3
Twice a month	5	6
Three times a month	8	11
Four times a month	55	59
More than four times	2	7

If married, how would you describe the religious affiliation of your spouse's upbringing?

| Fundamentalist Protestant | 18 | 13 |
| Evangelical Protestant | 19 | 39 |

	Calvary*	Vineyard*
Liberal Protestant	15	20
Roman Catholic	30	16
No affiliation	13	11
Other	5	1

How frequently did your spouse attend Sunday morning services when she was growing up?

	Calvary*	Vineyard*
Seldom	15	10
Once a month	13	7
Twice a month	11	7
Three times a month	5	10
Four times a month	46	60
More than four times	10	6

How would you describe your religious affiliation during the year before you became involved with Calvary/Vineyard?

	Calvary*	Vineyard*
Fundamentalist Protestant	15	11
Evangelical Protestant	37	69
Liberal Protestant	4	1
Roman Catholic	7	2
No affiliation	31	7
Other	6	10

How frequently were you attending Sunday morning services before the year that you became involved with Calvary/Vineyard?

	Calvary*	Vineyard*
Seldom	28	1
Once a month	3	1
Twice a month	4	1
Three times a month	2	1
Four times a month	45	86
More than four	18	10

At what age did you become a born-again Christian?

	Calvary*	Vineyard*
5 or under	2	5
6–10 years	9	16
11–15 years	13	16
16–20 years	25	31
21–25 years	25	14

	Calvary*	Vineyard*
26–30 years	18	13
31–35 years	5	3
Over 35	3	2

In what Christian group or church did this born-again experience occur?

Calvary/Vineyard	27	2
Other group	73	98

Check all of the following that describe your family experience as a child:††

For some part of my childhood, I lived in a single-parent family.	55	24
My parents divorced while I was still living at home.	46	23
One or both of my parents abused alcohol or drugs.	70	41
I grew up in a loving and nurturing family environment.	124	119
One or both of my parents attended church almost weekly.	103	119
One of my parents was a pastor/minister of a church.	12	19

Please indicate your level of agreement with each of the following statements.

A. *Prayer is an important part of my daily life.*

Strongly agree	96	93
Somewhat agree	4	7
Somewhat disagree	0	0
Strongly disagree	0	0
Not sure/Don't know	0	0

B. *I am very interested in politics and national affairs.*

Strongly agree	33	25
Somewhat agree	61	62
Somewhat disagree	5	12

††Figures represent number of responses to each question, not percentage responding.

	Calvary*	Vineyard*
Strongly disagree	0	0
Not sure/Don't know	1	1

C. *The public elementary schools in this area should teach sex education in grades four through eight.*

Strongly agree	1	1
Somewhat agree	7	17
Somewhat disagree	21	27
Strongly disagree	68	49
Not sure/Don't know	3	6

D. *I would object if a member of my family wanted to bring a friend of a different race home to dinner.*

Strongly agree	1	3
Somewhat agree	1	0
Somewhat disagree	1	2
Strongly disagree	96	94
Not sure/Don't know	1	1

E. *Minority races should not push themselves where they're not wanted.*

Strongly agree	1	1
Somewhat agree	9	11
Somewhat disagree	24	29
Strongly disagree	53	53
Not sure/Don't know	13	6

F. *There should be laws against marriages between minority races and whites.*

Strongly agree	1	1
Somewhat agree	0	0
Somewhat disagree	2	5
Strongly disagree	96	94
Not sure/Don't know	1	1

G. *Women should take care of running their homes and leave running the country up to men.*

Strongly agree	10	1
Somewhat agree	23	15
Somewhat disagree	33	35
Strongly disagree	30	48
Not sure/Don't know	4	1

	Calvary*	Vineyard*

H. *I approve of a married woman earning money in business or industry if she has a husband capable of supporting her.*

	Calvary*	Vineyard*
Strongly agree	11	34
Somewhat agree	45	49
Somewhat disagree	23	9
Strongly disagree	12	4
Not sure/Don't know	9	4

I. *Most men are better suited emotionally for politics than most women.*

	Calvary*	Vineyard*
Strongly agree	15	8
Somewhat agree	37	39
Somewhat disagree	22	20
Strongly disagree	13	23
Not sure/Don't know	13	10

J. *It should be possible for a pregnant woman to obtain a legal abortion if she is married and does not want any more children.*

	Calvary*	Vineyard*
Strongly agree	1	0
Somewhat agree	0	0
Somewhat disagree	1	1
Strongly disagree	99	98
Not sure/Don't know	0	1

K. *It should be possible for a woman to obtain a legal abortion if she wants it for any reason.*

	Calvary*	Vineyard*
Strongly agree	1	0
Somewhat agree	0	0
Somewhat disagree	0	1
Strongly disagree	99	98
Not sure/Don't know	0	1

What is your political party affiliation?

	Calvary*	Vineyard*
Republican	82	72
Independent	4	7
Democrat	2	2
No affiliation	12	19

How often during elections do you try to show people why they should vote for one of the parties' candidates?

	Calvary*	Vineyard*
Often	9	3

	Calvary*	Vineyard*
Sometimes	28	23
Rarely	28	46
Never	35	28

In terms of politics, do you consider yourself:

Extremely liberal	0	0
Liberal	0	0
Slightly liberal	0	3
Moderate, middle of the road	1	7
I don't care about politics	1	1
Slightly conservative	13	24
Conservative	72	61
Extremely conservative	11	2
I don't know	2	2

In the 1992 presidential election, I voted for:

George Bush	93	87
Bill Clinton	0	1
Another candidate	1	1
I didn't vote in this election	7	11

Should someone who is against all churches and religion:

A. Be allowed to make a speech in your city?

Yes	89	91
No	9	4
I don't know	2	5

B. Be allowed to teach in a college or university?

Yes	82	84
No	14	10
I don't know	4	6

If some people in your community suggested that a book written against churches and religion be taken out of our public library, would you favor removing this book or not?

Favor	21	16
Not favor	59	70
I don't know	20	14

	Calvary*	Vineyard*

Suppose there is a community-wide vote on the general housing issue. Of these two possible laws, which would you vote for?

	Calvary*	Vineyard*
A law saying that a homeowner can decide for himself/herself whom to sell his/her house to, even if he/she prefers not to sell to minority races	33	26
A law saying that a homeowner cannot refuse to sell to someone because of his/her race or color	60	65
I don't know	7	9

What is your opinion about a married person having sexual relations with someone other than the marriage partner?

	Calvary*	Vineyard*
It is always wrong	99	99
It is almost always wrong	1	0
I don't know	0	1
It is wrong only sometimes	0	0
It is not wrong at all	0	0

What is your opinion about sexual relations between two adults of the same sex?

	Calvary*	Vineyard*
It is always wrong	100	100
It is almost always wrong	0	0
I don't know	0	0
It is wrong only sometimes	0	1
It is not wrong at all	0	0

Growing up, how frequently did you attend rock concerts?

	Calvary*	Vineyard*
Often	30	21
A few times	45	46
Once	6	4
Never	19	29

How do you rate your musical skills/aptitude compared to those of the general population?

	Calvary*	Vineyard*
Very low	17	10
Somewhat low	11	9
Average	33	34

	Calvary*	Vineyard*
Somewhat high	31	36
Very high	8	11

If you have musical skills, how frequently do you sing or play at worship services?

Never	31	32
Occasionally	29	24
Fairly frequently	8	10
Frequently	31	34

Prior to becoming a Christian, how often did you have the following experiences?

A. *Smoked marijuana and/or used illegal drugs:*

Often	44	27
A few times	26	20
Once	4	6
Never	26	47

B. *Abused alcohol:*

Often	49	38
A few times	30	32
Once	1	2
Never	20	28

C. *Engaged in homosexual activity:*

Often	0	1
A few times	3	2
Once	2	1
Never	95	96

D. *Engaged in premarital sex:*

Often	42	27
A few times	28	31
Once	6	5
Never	24	37

E. *Engaged in extramarital sex:*

Often	6	1
A few times	10	5
Once	3	2
Never	81	92

	Calvary*	Vineyard*

F. *Was physically and/or sexually abused:*

Often	1	1
A few times	8	13
Once	5	9
Never	86	77

The Senior Pastor: Leadership and Religious Views

How long have you been a pastor?

5 years or less	34	24
6–10 years	30	35
11–15 years	24	23
16–20 years	9	10
21–25 years	3	3
26 years or more	0	5

How long have you been a pastor at this church?

1 year	18	12
2 years	15	16
3 years	11	13
4 years	12	10
5 years	7	12
6 years	5	10
7 years	1	10
8 years	6	5
9 years	3	2
10 years	10	3
More than 10 years	13	7

Are you ordained?

Yes	4	11
No	96	89

Have you been a pastor at any church other than this one?

No	53	27
Yes	47	73

	Calvary*	Vineyard*

In addition to being the pastor at this church, do you also have other employment?

No	64	73
Yes	36	27

Did becoming a pastor require changing your career?

No	36	43
Yes	64	57

Please indicate the strength of your agreement or disagreement with each of the following statements:

A. *All the different religions are equally good ways of helping a person find ultimate truth.*

Strongly agree	0	2
Agree	0	0
Neither agree nor disagree	1	0
Disagree	4	10
Strongly disagree	96	88

B. *Not all the churches have God's truth; many are in serious error.*

Strongly agree	90	53
Agree	9	37
Neither agree nor disagree	1	6
Disagree	0	3
Strongly disagree	0	1

C. *The only absolute truth for humankind is Jesus Christ.*

Strongly agree	99	94
Agree	1	6
Neither agree nor disagree	0	0
Disagree	0	0
Strongly disagree	1	1

D. *All the great religions of the world are equally good and true.*

Strongly agree	0	0
Agree	0	0
Neither agree nor disagree	0	0
Disagree	1	7
Strongly disagree	99	93

	Calvary*	Vineyard*

E. *Only the followers of Jesus Christ and members of His church can be saved.*

	Calvary*	Vineyard*
Strongly agree	95	86
Agree	5	10
Neither agree nor disagree	1	2
Disagree	0	2
Strongly disagree	0	0

F. *The primary purpose of men and women in this life is to prepare for the next life.*

Strongly agree	47	23
Agree	30	34
Neither agree nor disagree	9	16
Disagree	8	16
Strongly disagree	6	11

G. *It is not as important to worry about life after death as what one can do in this life.*

Strongly agree	4	6
Agree	10	24
Neither agree nor disagree	9	14
Disagree	24	31
Strongly disagree	53	25

H. *I believe in a divine judgment after death where some shall be rewarded and others punished.*

Strongly agree	96	90
Agree	4	9
Neither agree nor disagree	0	0
Disagree	0	0
Strongly disagree	0	1

I. *Today people should think for themselves about religion and not accept the teachings of any one church.*

Strongly agree	15	9
Agree	22	26
Neither agree nor disagree	18	19
Disagree	18	29
Strongly disagree	27	17

J. *The individual can find religious truth without any help from a church.*

Strongly agree	22	7

	Calvary*	Vineyard*
Agree	49	43
Neither agree nor disagree	10	13
Disagree	13	26
Strongly disagree	7	11

K. *Religious ideas should be the result of the individual's search, without regard to any churches or church teachings.*

Strongly agree	2	1
Agree	11	7
Neither agree nor disagree	15	12
Disagree	42	52
Strongly disagree	30	28

L. *To know God's truth, it is important to follow the teachings of ministers.*

Strongly agree	6	4
Agree	17	36
Neither agree nor disagree	30	34
Disagree	31	22
Strongly disagree	16	5

M. *God's truth was given to the church, and all persons must follow the church's teachings.*

Strongly agree	8	3
Agree	13	28
Neither agree nor disagree	26	31
Disagree	34	29
Strongly disagree	19	9

Listed below are statements expressing attitudes toward people in other countries who have never heard about Christ. Please indicate the strength of your agreement with each item.

A. *I believe that if we do not preach Christ to them, they will be damned forever.*

Strongly agree	30	33
Agree	32	39
Neither agree nor disagree	15	14
Disagree	15	12
Strongly disagree	8	2

	Calvary*	Vineyard*

B. *I don't believe they will be damned, but I do have a desire to share the love of Christ with them.*

Strongly agree	16	15
Agree	9	10
Neither agree nor disagree	16	12
Disagree	33	41
Strongly disagree	26	22

C. *I believe that we shouldn't worry about them because there are so many people in this country who haven't heard about Christ.*

Strongly agree	0	1
Agree	0	1
Neither agree nor disagree	4	2
Disagree	27	34
Strongly disagree	69	62

D. *I believe we should respect their religions and stop trying to impose Christianity on them.*

Strongly agree	0	2
Agree	0	0
Neither agree nor disagree	0	1
Disagree	13	21
Strongly disagree	87	76

There are many different ways of picturing God. We'd like to know the kinds of images you are most likely to associate with God. For each set, indicate the appropriate number where you would place your image of God between the two contrasting images.

A. 1 Mother	0	0
2	0	0
3	0	0
4	3	7
5	4	13
6	8	31
7 Father	85	49
B. 1 Master	61	36
2	9	18
3	8	12
4	16	24
5	1	7

	Calvary*	Vineyard*
6	1	2
7 Spouse	4	1
C. 1 Judge	20	5
2	1	1
3	5	5
4	53	45
5	7	20
6	6	19
7 Lover	8	5
D. 1 Friend	6	2
2	1	4
3	3	5
4	65	59
5	9	18
6	4	6
7 King	12	6

Which of these statements comes closest to describing your feelings about the Bible?

	Calvary*	Vineyard*
The Bible is the actual word of God and is to be taken literally, word for word.	35	9
The Bible is the inspired word of God. It contains no errors, but some verses are to be taken symbolically rather than literally.	64	84
The Bible is the inspired word of God, but it may contain historical and scientific errors.	1	7
The Bible was not inspired by God, but it represents humankind's best under-standing of God's nature.	0	0
The Bible is an ancient book of human fables, legends, history, and moral precepts recorded by men.	0	0

What is your conviction about the return of Christ?

	Calvary*	Vineyard*
I believe that Christ will return within the next decade.	18	1
I believe that Christ will return within my lifetime.	54	39
It is not our place to speculate on the time when Christ will return.	28	60

Notes

Introduction: Winners and Losers

1. The first attempt to convene religious leaders representing this movement was the National Symposium on the Postdenominational Church, 21–23 May 1996, in Pasadena, California, called by C. Peter Wagner, Professor of Missions at Fuller Theological Seminary.

2. See C. Peter Wagner, "The New Apostolic Reformation: A Search for a Name," paper presented at the National Symposium on the Postdenominational Church, 21–23 May 1996, Pasadena, California.

3. See James Davison Hunter, *Culture Wars: The Struggle to Define America* (New York: Basic Books, 1991).

4. Roger Finke and Laurence R. Iannaccone, "Supply-Side Explanations for Religious Change," in *Religion in the Nineties,* edited by Wade Clark Roof, *Annals of American Academy of Political and Social Science* 527 (1993): 30.

5. For descriptions of American religious history that particularly inform the perspective of this book, see Nathan O. Hatch, *The Democratization of American Christianity* (New Haven: Yale University Press, 1989), and Jon Butler, *Awash in a Sea of Faith: Christianizing the American People* (Cambridge: Harvard University Press, 1990).

6. I owe an intellectual debt to theorists who are writing the "new paradigm" literature in the sociology of religion. See the important review article by R. Stephen Warner, "Work in Progress toward a New Paradigm for the Sociological Study of Religion in the United States," *American Journal of Sociology* 98 (1993): 1044–93; Roger Finke and Rodney Stark, "Religious Economies and Sacred Canopies: Religious Mobilization in American Cities," *American Sociological Review* 53 (1988): 41–49; Roger Finke and Rodney Stark, "How the Upstart Sects Won America: 1776–1850," *Journal for the Scientific Study of Religion* 28 (1989): 27–44; Roger Finke and Rodney Stark, "Evaluating the Evidence: Religious Economies and Sacred Canopies,"

American Sociological Review 54 (1989): 1054–56; and Roger Finke and Rodney Stark, *The Churching of America, 1776–1990: Winners and Losers in Our Religious Economy* (New Brunswick, N.J.: Rutgers University Press, 1992). In addition, see the important articles by Laurence R. Iannaccone, "A Formal Model of Church and Sect," *American Journal of Sociology* 94 (suppl. 1986): 241–68; Laurence R. Iannaccone, "Religious Practice: A Human Capital Approach," *Journal for the Scientific Study of Religion* 29 (1990): 297–314; Laurence R. Iannaccone, "The Consequences of Religious Market Structure," *Rationality and Society* 3 (1991): 156–77; Laurence R. Iannaccone, "Why Strict Churches Are Strong," *American Journal of Sociology* 99 (1994): 1180–1211.

7. Finke and Starke, *Churching of America,* p. 17.

8. A long list of theorists could be cited, but most important are Max Weber, Emile Durkheim, Sigmund Freud, and, of course, Karl Marx, who predated them.

9. This view of secularization continued to be echoed in many twentieth-century theorists' works, including Peter L. Berger, *The Sacred Canopy: Elements of a Sociological Theory of Religion* (Garden City, N.Y.: Doubleday, 1969) and Thomas Luckmann, *The Invisible Religion: The Problem of Religion in Modern Society* (New York: Macmillan, 1967).

10. The secularization hypothesis was challenged in an influential book by Andrew Greeley, *Unsecular Man* (New York: Schocken Books, 1972), but this was merely the beginning of an avalanche of critical commentary. See, for example, the volume edited by Phillip E. Hammond, *The Sacred in a Secular Age: Toward Revision in the Scientific Study of Religion* (Berkeley: University of California Press, 1985).

11. An assumption of this book is that religiosity is highest in countries with an open religious marketplace rather than a state-supported and regulated religious monopoly. Religious pluralism increases the likelihood that the religious needs of a broad range of people will be served, with competition between religious providers increasing the likelihood that the spiritual needs of people representing specific market niches will be addressed.

12. See the Gallup Poll data reported in *Religion in America: Will the Vitality of the Church Be the Surprise of the 21st Century?* (Princeton, N.J.: Princeton Religion Research Center, 1996).

13. See David A. Roozen and C. Kirk Hadaway, eds., *Church Growth and Denominational Growth* (Nashville: Abingdon Press, 1993), as well as the classic by Dean M. Kelley, *Why Conservative Churches Are Growing* (San Francisco: Harper and Row, 1972).

14. See Wade Clark Roof and William McKinney, *American Mainline Religion: Its Changing Shape and Future* (New Brunswick, N.J.: Rutgers University Press, 1987).

15. See the excellent overview article by David A. Roozen, "Denominations Grow as Individuals Join Congregations," in Roozen and Hadaway, *Church and Denominational Growth,* pp. 15–45.

16. The Mormon growth rate worldwide has been averaging about 30 percent per decade, according to estimates by sociologist Rodney Stark.

17. See Dean R. Hoge and David A. Roozen, *Technical Appendix to Understanding Church Growth and Decline, 1950–1978* (Hartford: Hartford Connecticut Foundation, 1979).

18. For an example of the deprivation thesis, see Robert M. Anderson, *Vision of the Disinherited: The Making of American Pentecostalism* (Peabody, Mass.: Hendrickson Publishers, 1979), pp. 235 ff.

19. See David Stoll, *Is Latin America Turning Protestant? The Politics of Evangelical Growth* (Berkeley: University of California Press, 1990), as well as Harvey Cox's excellent book *Fire from Heaven: The Rise of Pentecostal Spirituality and the Reshaping of Religion in the Twenty-first Century* (Reading, Mass.: Addison-Wesley, 1995).

20. Cox estimates that Pentecostal churches are growing at a rate of 20 million new members a year and that the current worldwide membership in Pentecostal churches is 410 million (Cox, *Fire from Heaven*, p. xv).

21. See Wade Clark Roof, *A Generation of Seekers: Baby Boomers and the Quest for a Spiritual Style* (San Francisco: HarperSanFrancisco, 1993).

22. See, for example, the excellent study by Helen Rose Fuchs Ebaugh, *Women in the Vanishing Cloister: Organizational Decline in Catholic Religious Orders in the United States* (New Brunswick, N.J.: Rutgers University Press, 1993).

23. "Special Report: Catholicism in America at the Crossroad," in *Emerging Trends,* Princeton Religion Research Center, vol. 15, no. 8, October 1993, pp. 1–5.

24. Jack Wertheimer, "Recent Trends in American Judaism," in *American Jewish Year Book, 1989,* ed. David Singer and Ruth R. Seldin (Philadelphia: Jewish Publication Society, 1990), pp. 63–84.

25. Donald E. Miller, *The Case for Liberal Christianity* (San Francisco: Harper and Row, 1981).

26. See Donald E. Miller and Lorna Touryan Miller, *Survivors: An Oral History of the Armenian Genocide* (Berkeley: University of California Press, 1993), and Barry Jay Seltser and Donald E. Miller, *Homeless Families: The Struggle for Dignity* (Urbana: University of Illinois Press, 1993).

27. Several other individuals assisted me on this project, including Mike McKenzie, David Tripp, Wendy Kohlhase, and Perry Glanzer.

28. We received 3,581 responses to the congregational surveys, 397 responses to the questionnaires mailed to senior pastors in the movements, and 888 responses to the healing testimony survey.

Chapter 1:   The New Face of American Protestantism

1. For an excellent account of the spiritual ferment of the 1960s, see Robert S. Ellwood, *The Sixties Spiritual Awakening: American Religion Moving from Modern to Postmodern* (New Brunswick, N.J.: Rutgers University Press, 1994).

2. Lyle E. Schaller estimates that there are 4,000 Protestant megachurches in the United States, and many of these churches fit the category of

new paradigm churches. See his book *The New Reformation: Tomorrow Arrived Yesterday* (Nashville: Abingdon Press, 1995), p. 13.

3. In the congregational surveys (see appendix 2), 60 percent of the respondents indicated that they felt free to touch and/or hug most of the people at their church.

4. Among the survey respondents, 51 percent said that they read the Bible at least once daily.

5. Of the survey respondents, 61 percent were married; another 14 percent were divorced or separated. Most had children. A quarter of the adults were thirty or younger, and two-thirds were forty or younger.

6. Eighty-two percent of the Calvary pastors and 73 percent of the Vineyard pastors we surveyed were under forty-five (see appendix 3).

7. Many of the pastors of these churches are musically inclined: 39 percent of the Calvary pastors and 44 percent of the Vineyard pastors indicated that they sing or play frequently at worship services.

8. The male pronoun is used in describing the activities of pastors because there are very few female senior pastors in these movements (a subject discussed in chapter 6).

9. At the Vineyard, 59 percent of the respondents stated that they "often" have prayed for other individuals by laying hands on them.

10. See Robert Wuthnow, *Sharing the Journey: Support Groups and America's New Quest for Community* (New York: Free Press, 1994).

11. In the congregational surveys, 30 percent of respondents came from homes where the parents had divorced; 37 percent said that one or both of their parents had abused alcohol or drugs.

12. Respondents to the congregational surveys strongly affirmed that they experience God more at their new paradigm church than at other churches they have attended.

13. See Robert Wuthnow, *The Restructuring of American Religion: Society and Faith Since World War II* (Princeton, N.J.: Princeton University Press, 1988).

14. A spate of books supporting this theme was published in the sixties and seventies. See, for example, Paul van Buren, *The Secular Meaning of the Gospel* (New York: Macmillan, 1963); Thomas J. J. Altizer, *The Gospel of Christian Atheism* (Philadelphia: Westminster, 1966); and Richard L. Rubenstein, *After Auschwitz: Radical Theology and Contemporary Judaism* (Indianapolis: Bobbs-Merrill, 1966).

15. These questions are the basis for Dean M. Kelley's discussion of the decline of mainline churches in *Why Conservative Churches Are Growing* (San Francisco: Harper and Row, 1972).

16. There is a voluminous literature on the attitudes and values of baby boomers. See, for example, Paul C. Light, *Baby Boomers* (New York: Norton, 1988) and Landon Y. Jones, *Great Expectations: America and the Baby Boom Generation* (New York: Ballantine Books, 1980).

17. See Dean R. Hoge, Benton Johnson, and Donald A. Luidens, *Vanishing Boundaries: The Religion of Mainline Protestant Baby Boomers* (Louisville: Westminster/Knox Press, 1994).

18. Michael E. Porter's classic book on strategy in business has direct application to an economic analysis of religious institutions. See *Competitive Strategy: Techniques for Analyzing Industries and Competitors* (New York: Free Press, 1980).

19. As previously noted, one of the first efforts to document the proliferation of these "Apostolic congregations" was the National Symposium on the Postdenominational Church, organized by C. Peter Wagner at Fuller Theological Seminary, May 21–23, 1996, Pasadena, California.

20. Willow Creek Community Church in South Barrington, Illinois, pastored by Bill Hybels, is the much-heralded exemplar of the "seeker-sensitive" church. Saddleback Community Church in Orange County, California, pastored by Rick Warren, is the West Coast equivalent. Both churches have extensive programs to promulgate their visions to other church leaders.

21. See Philip Rieff, *The Triumph of the Therapeutic: Uses of Faith after Freud* (New York: Harper and Row, 1966); Robert N. Bellah, Richard Madsen, William M. Sullivan, Ann Swidler, and Steven M. Tipton, *Habits of the Heart: Individualism and Commitment in American Life* (Berkeley: University of California Press, 1985); Christopher Lasch, *The Culture of Narcissism* (New York: Norton, 1979); Todd Gitlin, *The Sixties: Years of Hope, Years of Rage* (New York: Bantam Books, 1987); Jack Whalen and Richard Flacks, *Beyond the Barricades: The Sixties Generation Grows Up* (Philadelphia: Temple University Press, 1989).

22. Forty-five percent of the respondents to the congregational surveys indicated that they had received professional therapy at least once; 34 percent indicated they had received therapy "often" or "a few times."

23. One of the first writers to indicate a rejection of therapeutic cultural values was Daniel Yankelovich in *New Rules: Searching for Self-Fulfillment in a World Turned Upside Down* (New York: Random House, 1981).

24. See the development of this theme in Bellah et al., *Habits of the Heart*.

25. See, for example, Jean-François Lyotard, *The Postmodern Condition: A Report on Knowledge*, trans. Geoff Bennington and Brian Massumi (Minneapolis: University of Minnesota Press, 1984).

26. Sigmund Freud, *Future of an Illusion* (New York: Norton, 1961).

27. The Freudian optimism regarding rationality continued with theorists such as Erich Fromm, who in *Psychoanalysis and Religion* (New Haven: Yale University Press, 1950) distinguished between "authoritarian" religion (in which a supernatural God was the focus of worship) and "humanistic" religion (which emphasized making man's highest powers the object of religious worship).

28. William James, *The Varieties of Religious Experience: A Study in Human Nature* (New York: Collier Books, 1961).

29. The literature on Max Weber is voluminous. Beginning references include Weber's *The Sociology of Religion* (Boston: Beacon Press, 1963); *From Max Weber: Essays in Sociology*, trans. and ed. by H. H. Gerth and C. Wright Mills (New York: Oxford University Press, 1946); S. N. Eisenstadt, ed., *Max Weber on Charisma and Institution Building* (Chicago: University of Chicago Press, 1968).

30. On the appeal of the original "apostolic" age as the pure form of religion, see two books edited by Richard T. Hughes: *The Primitive Church in the Modern World* (Urbana: University of Illinois Press, 1995) and *The American Quest for the Primitive Church* (Urbana: University of Illinois Press, 1988).

Chapter 2:   Hippies, Beach Baptisms, and Healings

1. Unless otherwise noted, all quotations in this chapter are from interviews with these religious leaders. For a history of some of the larger Calvary Chapels, see Chuck Smith and Tal Brooke, *Harvest* (Old Tappen, N.J.: Choosen Books, 1987). For a popularized interpretation of Calvary Chapel Costa Mesa, see Randal Balmer, *Mine Eyes Have Seen the Glory: A Journey into the Evangelical Subculture of America* (New York: Oxford University Press, 1989), pp. 12–30, and the interesting article by Sonni Efron, "Modest Pastor Sees Costa Mesa Flock Grow from 25 to 12,000," *Los Angeles Times* 109 (12 October 1990): A34.

2. Chuck Smith, "The History of Calvary Chapel" (n.p.: The Word for Today [Calvary ministry], 1981), p. 3.

3. Ibid.

4. Our study included a few churches that did not use the Calvary Chapel name but claimed a spiritual accountability to Calvary Chapel.

5. Chuck Smith, *The Philosophy of Ministry of Calvary Chapel* (n.p.: Logos Media Group, 1992), p. 9.

6. Hayford is currently pastor of the Church on the Way, a large and highly visible Foursquare church in Van Nuys, California.

7. Ralph Moore and Dan Beach, *Let Go of the Ring: The Story of Hope Chapel* (Honolulu: Antioch Press, 1987), p. 81.

8. Ibid., p. 129.

9. On the history and sociology of the Vineyard movement, see Robin D. Perrin, "Signs and Wonders: The Growth of the Vineyard Christian Fellowship" (Ph.D. dissertation, Washington State University, 1989); also Robin D. Perrin and Armand L. Mauss, "American Religion in the Post-Aquarian Age: Values and Demographic Factors in Church Growth and Decline, *Journal for the Scientific Study of Religion* 28 (1989): 75–89; Robin D. Perrin and Armand L. Mauss, "Strictly Speaking . . . : Kelley's Quandary and the Vineyard Christian Fellowship," *Journal for the Scientific Study of Religion* 32, no. 2 (June 1993): 125–35; Nikolaus Kimla, "The Historical and Empirical: Social and Practical Theological Aspects of the Vineyard Movement" (dissertation, Evangelische Theologie, Universität Wien, 1994); Russell Chandler, "Vineyard Fellowship Finds Groundswell of Followers," *Los Angeles Times* 109 (5 October 1990): A1.

10. Clarifying why Smith had taken a more conservative view on charismatic expression, Gulliksen says: "Chuck . . . saw so much phoniness in some of the [Foursquare] churches he grew up in that he was not as open to the release of gifts in meetings because of his fear of phoniness, which is very legitimate."

11. Cynical interpreters have explained the Vineyard's recent break with the Toronto Airport Vineyard as an expression of bureaucratic control that violates the spirit of relational fellowship that characterized the movement in its early years.

Chapter 3:   Transforming Your Life

1. In this chapter I affirm the theory expressed by John Lofland and Rodney Stark that social networks play an important role in conversion. However, I also believe that neither the ideological appeal nor the state of deprivation of the convert should be ignored in the analysis. See the discussion of these three interrelated factors in Rodney Stark and William Sims Bainbridge, *The Future of Religion: Secularization, Revival and Cult Transformation* (Berkeley: University of California Press, 1985), pp. 307–24.

2. Twenty-seven percent had their conversion experience between the ages of twenty-one and thirty; 16 percent between the ages of thirty-one to forty; and 10 percent after age forty.

3. There is a large literature on conversion. See the excellent bibliography in Lewis R. Rambo, *Understanding Religious Conversion* (New Haven: Yale University Press, 1993). Other good sources include H. Newton Malony and Samuel Southard, eds., *Handbook of Religious Conversion* (Birmingham: Religious Education Press, 1992); David A. Snow, "The Sociology of Conversion," *Annual Review of Sociology* 10 (1984): 167–90; and John Lofland and Norman Skonovd, "Conversion Motifs," *Journal for the Scientific Study of Religion* 20 (1981): 373–85.

4. Peter L. Berger is especially guilty of this formulation in books such as *The Sacred Canopy: Elements of a Sociological Theory of Religion* (Garden City, N.Y.: Doubleday, 1967).

5. See Eric Hoffer, *The True Believer: Thoughts on the Nature of Mass Movements* (New York: New American Library, 1951).

6. William James, *The Varieties of Religious Experience: A Study in Human Nature* (New York: Collier Books, 1961), p. 29.

7. An assumption here is that in every society, and at all points in human history, large numbers of people experience a need to be "saved" or converted from their current way of life. These are individuals who are frustrated with their lifestyles and for whom existence is problematic. The question then becomes why some congregations experience growth through attracting converts and other groups do not.

Chapter 4:   Beyond Rationality

1. Nathan Hatch, *The Democratization of American Christianity* (New Haven: Yale University Press, 1989), p. 146.

2. Ibid., p. 150.

3. Ibid., p. 151.

4. Ibid., p. 152.

5. Hatch states: "Ordinary people crafted spiritual folk songs to assist the flock in weeping with the brokenhearted, shouting with the joyful, and proclaiming the good news of the gospel" (ibid., pp. 160–61).

6. This quotation is also attributed to John and Charles Wesley and William Booth, although the best-documented attribution is from a biography written by E. W. Broome of a nineteenth-century English preacher, the Reverend Rowland Hill: "He did not see any reason why the devil should have all the good tunes."

7. William James, *Principles of Psychology*, vol. 2 (New York: Henry, 1890), chap. 21.

8. For an elaboration of William James's theory, see Donald E. Miller, "Worship and Moral Reflection: A Phenomenological Perspective," *Anglican Theological Review*, 62 (1980): 307–20.

9. I Corinthians 12:8–11 (emphasis added). All scripture references are from the King James version of the Bible unless otherwise noted.

10. Acts 2:2–7.

11. See the discussion of these terms and the charismatic tradition in Robert Mapes Anderson, *Vision of the Disinherited: The Making of American Pentecostalism* (Peabody, Mass.: Hendrickson, 1979), pp. 10–27.

12. I Corinthians 13:1–2.

13. See, for example, Vincent Crapanzano and Vivian Garrison, eds., *Case Studies in Spirit Possession* (New York: Wiley, 1977); Clarke Garrett, *Spirit Possession and Popular Religion: From the Camisards to the Shakers* (Baltimore: Johns Hopkins University Press, 1987); I. M. Lewis, *Ecstatic Religion: A Study of Shamanism and Spirit Possession* (New York: Routledge, 1989); Felicitas D. Goodman, Jeannette H. Henney, and Esther Pressel, *Trance, Healing and Hallucination: Three Field Studies in Religious Experience* (New York: Wiley, 1974).

14. David Di Sabatino has done extensive research on the life of Lonnie Frisbee.

15. Seven percent said that they had been healed often; 18 percent claimed healing had occurred a few times; and 19 percent said once.

16. Rudolf Otto, *The Idea of the Holy: An Inquiry into the Non-rational Factor in the Idea of the Divine and Its Relation to the Rational* (New York: Oxford University Press, 1973).

17. While there may be some superficial parallels between speaking in tongues and various types of schizophrenic behavior, there are major distinctions. For example, individuals who speak in tongues appear to be able to stop this behavior at will, whereas psychotic episodes are seemingly beyond willful control.

18. People who practice various spiritual disciplines, such as prayer, meditation, and yoga exercises, report that they become more centered and, correspondingly, healthier and more productive. See Allen E. Bergin, "Religiosity and Mental Health: A Critical Reevaluation and Meta-analysis," *Professional Psychology: Research and Practice* 14 (1983): 170–84. For a broad discussion of the

issue of health and religion, see David R. Kinsley, *Health, Healing, and Religion: A Cross-Cultural Perspective* (Upper Saddle River, N.J.: Prentice-Hall, 1996).

19. See Gilbert Rouget, *Music and Trance: A Theory of the Relations between Music and Possession* (Chicago: University of Chicago Press, 1985).

20. See, for example, Michael C. Dillbeck and David W. Orme-Johnson, "Physiological Differences between Transcendental Meditation and Rest," *American Psychologist* 42, no. 9 (September 1987): 879 (3).

21. For example, in *Vision of the Disinherited,* Robert Mapes Anderson states: "Worship is characterized by overt emotional expression and a wide range of unusual phenomena like the loss of feelings in certain parts of the body, falling into catalepsy and trance, visual and auditory hallucinations, clapping, stamping, leaping, running, climbing, falling, rolling, and jerking. Strange and usual vocalizations, mysterious, ambiguous, and unintelligible speech have often been regarded as evidence of the 'Numen,' or divine presence. Such speech disorders are but one type of a general class of motor dysfunctions that includes crying, sighing and groaning, stuttering, barking and crowing, complete muteness, and sustained automatic discourse" (pp. 10–11).

22. We collected 888 forms from two healing conferences at the Anaheim Vineyard. In addition, our testimony form was distributed at two healing conferences in England, but these latter findings are not included in the statistics cited.

23. See Stephen Hunt, "The 'Toronto Blessing': A Rumor of Angels?" *Journal of Contemporary Religion* 10 (1995): 257–71. For an insider's view, see Guy Chevreau, *Catch the Fire: The Toronto Blessing, an Experience of Renewal and Revival* (London: Pickering, 1994). Numerous articles have appeared in religious periodicals and newspapers; for example, see Rae Corelli, "Going to the Mat for God: Tales of Ecstasy Draw Hundreds to a Toronto Church," *Maclean's* 108 (13 March 1996): 56 ff.; Gene Preston, "The Toronto Wave: Holy Laughter is Contagious," *Christian Century* 111 (16 November 1994): 1068 ff. Margaret Poloma (Sociology Department, University of Akron) is currently writing a book on holy laughter.

Chapter 5: Living by the Bible

1. See Robert Bellah, *Beyond Belief: Essays on Religion in a Post-traditional World* (Berkeley: University of California Press, 1991).

2. See Matthew 25:34–36.

3. Ephesians 5:22–24.

4. Ephesians 5:25, 28.

5. Judith Stacey, *Brave New Families: Stories of Domestic Upheaval in Late Twentieth Century America* (New York: Basic Books, 1990), pp. 113–46.

6. See Lynn Davidman, *Tradition in a Rootless World: Women Turn to Orthodox Judaism* (Berkeley: University of California Press, 1991).

7. Promise Keepers, a national organization headquartered in Colorado Springs, reflects many of these themes.

8. I Timothy 2:11–12.

9. Many of the women-only groups are led by the senior pastor's wife.

10. See Brenda Brasher, *Godly Women* (New Brunswick, N.J.: Rutgers University Press, forthcoming).

11. A member of Desert Stream Ministries, a Vineyard-sponsored program to "heal" the same-sex orientation of people, says that her homosexuality is rooted in the fact that she did not "bond" with her mother in the early years of her life. In her view, gays and lesbians have been "wounded" in childhood, and the only road to recovery is to forgive those who hurt you and to reestablish strong relations with people of the same sex, rather than always seeking their approval (which she sees as the basis of the sexual attraction).

12. The Calvary pastors were more likely to identify themselves as "extremely conservative" than were the Vineyard pastors.

13. See Judi Wilgoren, "Church Surveys Candidates for Voters Guide," *Los Angeles Times* 113 (29 September 1994): A3.

14. Chuck Smith travels frequently to Israel, where he meets with various government officials in addition to leading tours of Christians to the Holy Land. He has built a baptismal structure on the River Jordan.

15. George M. Marsden captures the confusions around the terms *fundamentalist* and *evangelical* in the following statement: "A fundamentalist is an evangelical who is angry about something. That seems simple and is fairly accurate. Jerry Falwell has even adopted it as a quick definition of fundamentalism that reporters are likely to quote. A more precise statement of the same point is that an American fundamentalist is an evangelical who is militant in opposition to liberal theology in the churches or to changes in cultural values or mores, such as those associated with 'secular humanism.' . . . Fundamentalists are not just religious conservatives, they are conservatives who are willing to take a stand and to fight" (*Understanding Fundamentalism and Evangelicalism* [Grand Rapids, Mich.: Eerdmans, 1991], p. 1).

16. See the excellent statement of Weber's view of the routinization of charisma in Bryan Wilson, *The Noble Savages: The Primitive Origins of Charisma and Its Contemporary Survival* (Berkeley: University of California Press, 1975).

17. On "primitivism," see Richard T. Hughes, ed., *The American Quest for the Primitive Church* (Urbana: University of Illinois Press, 1988) and *The Primitive Church in the Modern World* (Urbana: University of Illinois Press, 1995).

18. See, for example, Marcus J. Borg, *Meeting Jesus Again for the First Time: The Historical Jesus and the Heart of Contemporary Faith* (San Francisco: HarperSanFrancisco, 1994), and John Dominic Crossan, *The Historical Jesus: The Life of a Mediterranean Jewish Peasant* (San Francisco: HarperSanFrancisco, 1991).

19. See Rudolf Bultmann, *Jesus Christ and Mythology* (New York: Scribner's Sons, 1958).

20. The sacred-profane distinction is present in scholars ranging from Emile Durkheim in *The Elementary Forms of the Religious Life* (New York: Free Press, 1965) to Mircea Eliade in *The Sacred and the Profane* (San Diego: Harcourt Brace Jovanovich, 1987). One recent feminist critique of this distinction is Victoria Lee Erickson, *Where Silence Speaks: Feminism, Social Theory, and Religion* (Minneapolis: Fortress Press, 1993).

21. Our response rate from Hope Chapel pastors was too low to include them in these generalizations. Hence, all statistics on the attitudes of new paradigm pastors refer specifically to Calvary and Vineyard senior pastors.

22. All citations regarding Presbyterian clergy are from "The Presbyterian Panel: 1991–1993 Background Report" (Louisville, Ky.: Research Services, Presbyterian Church-USA).

Chapter 6:   Giving the Ministry to the People

1. See R. Laurence Moore, *Selling God: American Religion in the Marketplace* (New York: Oxford University Press, 1994). In new paradigm churches, when profits are made—at the bookstore, for example—they are used to fund missionary activity or program work.

2. See Max Weber, *The Protestant Ethic and the Spirit of Capitalism* (New York: Scribner's, 1958).

3. See S. N. Eisenstadt, *Max Weber on Charisma and Institution Building* (Chicago: University of Chicago Press, 1968).

4. I Timothy 3:1–13 is frequently cited as providing the standard for those who are in church leadership.

5. Most churches have two advisory groups: a board that makes financial decisions and elders and deacons who do the work of ministry. Integrity is frequently cited as the most important character trait for board members. Elders and deacons are typically individuals who have been involved in small group ministry and have proven their leadership skills.

6. The point was repeatedly made on the pastor's survey that the senior pastor is the final authority, not the board. On the other hand, because the senior pastor seeks the counsel of his board and because consensus and not majority rule is the norm, there is a formal check on the pastor's decision making.

7. According to the open-ended responses to a question on the pastor's survey, it appears that some boards are made up of three or four couples, rather than only men being responsible for governance.

8. See Karl Menninger, *Whatever Became of Sin?* (New York: Hawthorn Books, 1973).

9. See Laurence R. Iannaccone, "A Formal Model of Church and Sect," *American Journal of Sociology* 94 (suppl. 1986): 241–68. The classic formulation of the church-sect-mysticism typology was Ernst Troeltsch's *The Social Teaching of the Christian Churches,* 2 vols. (New York: Harper and Row, 1960). For a more contemporary analysis, see Bryan R. Wilson, *Religious Sects* (New York: McGraw-Hill, 1970), and the volume he edited, *Patterns of Sectarianism: Organization and Ideology in Social and Religious Movements* (London: Heinemann, 1967).

10. See the classic study by H. Richard Niebuhr, *The Social Sources of Denominationalism* (Cleveland: Meridian Books, 1963).

11. See the discussion of postmodern organizational structures by Nancy T. Ammerman, "SBC Moderates and the Making of a Postmodern Denomination," *Christian Century,* 22–29 September 1998, pp. 896–98.

12. Peter F. Drucker, *Post-Capitalist Society* (New York: HarperBusiness, 1993), p. 59.

13. Ibid.

14. Ibid., p. 60.

Chapter 7:   Franchising New Groups

1. I drew from three sources for this history of Calvary Chapel Albuquerque: our interviews with Skip and Lenya Heitzig, a videotape recorded in January 1992 on the history of the church, and chapter 9 ("Skip Heitzig: Calvary Chapel Enters the Southwest") in Chuck Smith and Tal Brooke's *Harvest* (Old Tappan, N.J.: Chosen Books, 1987, pp. 131–44).

2. There is an entire publishing industry devoted to church "planting" and "church growth." Also, an increasing number of consultants do demographic studies to indicate what types of churches will succeed in which areas, and what type of programming will best meet the needs of people in a particular neighborhood.

3. See Reginald W. Bibby and Merlin B. Brinkerhoff, "The Circulation of the Saints: A Study of People Who Join Conservative Churches," *Journal for the Scientific Study of Religion* 12 (1973): 273–83; and "Circulation of the Saints Revisited: A Longitudinal Look at Conservative Church Growth," *Journal for the Scientific Study of Religion* 22 (1983): 253–62.

4. See the excellent discussion by Dean R. Hoge, Benton Johnson, and Donald A. Luidens of theories explaining the decline of mainline Protestantism and the relative success of fundamentalists in maintaining their youth, in their *Vanishing Boundaries: The Religion of Mainline Protestant Baby Boomers* (Louisville, Ky.: Westminster/Knox Press, 1994), pp. 1–19, 95–102.

5. Included in the Vineyard responses are survey results from a 1987–88 study done by Robin D. Perrin, which includes responses from approximately 1,000 Vineyard Christian Fellowship members in fourteen different congregations. This information is written up in Robin Perrin, Paul Kennedy, and Donald E. Miller, "Examining the Sources of Conservative Church Growth: Where Are the New Evangelical Movements Getting Their Numbers" *Journal for the Scientific Study of Religion* (forthcoming).

6. Emile Durkheim, *The Elementary Forms of the Religious Life* (New York: Free Press, 1965).

7. A well-articulated view of the interrelated role of community service, personal meaning, and spirituality appears in Michael Lerner, *The Politics of Meaning: Restoring Hope and Possibility in an Age of Cynicism* (Reading, Mass.: Addison-Wesley, 1996).

8. Sophisticated radio equipment of this sort may be purchased for under $10,000.

Chapter 8:   Can the Mainline Church Survive?

1. See Nathan Hatch, *The Democratization of American Christianity* (New Haven: Yale University Press, 1989), pp. 4–5.

2. Ibid., p. 9.

3. Hatch elaborates this point, stating: "Those who led the meeting made overt attempts to have the power of God 'strike fire' over a mass audience; they encouraged uncensored testimonials by persons without respect to age, gender, or race; the public sharing of private ecstasy; overtly physical display and emotional release; loud and spontaneous response to preaching; and the use of folk music that would have chilled the marrow of Charles Wesley" (ibid., p. 50).

4. According to Hatch, "All of these movements challenged common people to take religious destiny into their own hands, to think for themselves, to oppose centralized authority and the elevation of the clergy as a separate order of men" (ibid., p. 58).

5. Robert M. Anderson, *Vision of the Disinherited: The Making of American Pentecostalism* (Peabody, Mass.: Hendrickson, 1991).

6. Hatch, *American Christianity,* p. 212.

7. Hatch states, "A common Fundamentalist complaint about higher criticism of the Bible was that it removed the Word of God from the common people by assuming that only scholars can preach it" (ibid., p. 215).

8. Ibid., p. 218.

9. Ibid., p. 216.

10. Ibid., p. 87.

11. See Wade Clark Roof, *A Generation of Seekers: Baby Boomers and the Quest for a Spiritual Style* (San Francisco: HarperSanFrancisco, 1993).

12. Roger Finke and Rodney Stark, *The Churching of America, 1776–1990: Winners and Losers in Our Religious Economy* (New Brunswick, N.J.: Rutgers University Press, 1992), p. 96.

13. Max Weber informs my view of organizational theory, while William James is my reference point for the emphasis on religious experience.

14. An indication of a deep cultural desire for spirituality is the success of the recent books by Thomas Moore, especially *Care of the Soul: A Guide for Cultivating Depth and Sacredness in Everyday Life* (New York: HarperCollins, 1992).

Index

Compositor: BookMasters, Inc.
Text: 10/13 Galliard
Display: Galliard
Printer and Binder: Haddon Craftsmen, Inc.